REPRINTS OF ECONOMIC CLASSICS

LABOR AND ADMINISTRATION

Reprints of Economic Classics

By John R. Commons

THE DISTRIBUTION OF WEALTH
(1893)
With an Introductory Essay
The Foundations of Commons' Economics
By Joseph Dorfman

LABOR AND ADMINISTRATION
(1913)

A SOCIOLOGICAL VIEW OF
SOVEREIGNTY
(1899-1901)
With an Introduction By Joseph Dorfman

LABOR

AND

ADMINISTRATION

BY

JOHN R. COMMONS

PROFESSOR OF POLITICAL ECONOMY, UNIVERSITY OF WISCONSIN
FORMERLY DIRECTOR OF THE MILWAUKEE BUREAU OF
ECONOMY AND EFFICIENCY AND MEMBER OF THE
INDUSTRIAL COMMISSION OF WISCONSIN

REPRINTS OF ECONOMIC CLASSICS

Augustus M. Kelley, Bookseller
New York 1964

Library of Congress Catalogue Card Number
64 - 17404

PRINTED IN THE UNITED STATES OF AMERICA
by SENTRY PRESS, NEW YORK, N. Y. 10019

INTRODUCTION

THE history of labor laws and strikes has this in common to both — laws become dead letters; the victories of strikes are nibbled away. Too much was expected even of those preparatory labor laws, universal suffrage and universal education. Amateur faith in laws and strikes weakens with experience. A law creates an abstract right — an empty ideal. A strike may be a burst of enthusiasm, then disorganization. Some philosophizers fall back on the individual's moral character. Little, they think, can be done by law or unions. There are others who inquire how to draft and enforce the laws, how to keep the winnings of strikes — in short, how to connect ideals with efficiency.

These are the awakening questions of the past decade, and the subject of this book. Attention is shifting from laws to the means of enforcing them — from strikes to the unions that safeguard the gains — from the rights of labor to the protection of its rights.

Here is a field for the student and economist — not the " friend of labor " who paints an abstract workingman, but the utilitarian idealist, who sees them all as they are ; not the curious collector of facts and statistics, but the one who measures the facts and builds them into a foundation and structure. His constructive problem is not so much the law and its abstract rights, as administration and its concrete results — not so much the struggle of a class to dominate others, as a working partnership of classes in government and industry — not so much the spectacular wage-bargaining of strikes, as the continuous organization of capital and labor for dealing justly with the millions of little wage-bargains that begin and end every day.

These chapters were written partly as a student, partly as a lecturer to university classes, and somewhat as a participant. They came out in printed form when the subject was warm, or when some suggesting editor, student, or audience asked for them. Through them run the notions of utilitarian idealism, constructive research, class partnership and administrative efficiency — a programme of progressive labor within social organization.

If Wisconsin dominates the book, it is because I can best speak of what I see and know in Wisconsin. Coming to the state in 1904, La Follette, a leader who studied his subject, was just winning a ten-year battle for the people's control of their government. Six years later, the equally forceful Victor Berger led his " class conscious " wage-earners into a partial control of Milwaukee. Here both progressivism and socialism won their first notable victories in America. Here, too, was a unique university — utilitarian, idealistic and free. Here investigation accompanied action. Here the people seem to think that democracy must be efficient if plutocracy is to stay out. Surely, ten such interesting years in Wisconsin would be expected to color the book.

For opportunity to prepare the articles I am indebted to the University of Wisconsin, the Industrial Commission of Wisconsin, the American Bureau of Industrial Research, the National Civic Federation, the Carnegie

Institution of Washington, and the Pittsburgh Survey. For permission to use them I am indebted to the *Intercollegiate Magazine, Journal of Home Economics, The Survey, Political Science Quarterly, Quarterly Journal of Economics, American Journal of Sociology, Union Labor Advocate, The Outlook, The Chautauquan, La Follette's Magazine,* American Economic Association, American Statistical Association, American Academy of Political and Social Science, American Association for Labor Legislation.

JOHN R. COMMONS.

MADISON, WISCONSIN,
  July, 1913.

TABLE OF CONTENTS

LABOR AND ADMINISTRATION

LABOR AND ADMINISTRATION

CHAPTER I

UTILITARIAN IDEALISM [1]

"MATERIALISTIC," "utilitarian," "job-getter," "does U. W. spell cow," "butter-fat university" — these are some of the epithets to which we are reconciling ourselves at Wisconsin. It may be that we have sacrificed a kind of idealism, but if so, we are part of a movement that is exalting another kind. Let us call it utilitarian idealism.

By idealism seems to be meant the yearning for perfection above and beyond the mere grind and hustle for necessities, luxuries and wealth. It is devotion to "the good, the true, the beautiful." It is esthetics — the ideal beauty of material things, unfolded to us in the fine arts of painting, sculpture, architecture, literature. It is ethics — the perfect goodness of human beings towards each other, revealed in philosophy and religion. It is pure science, with abstract mathematics and its imaginary lines and points as the ideally "true."

It is not a new idea that the idealism of art and science came into the modern world from ancient Greece, where three-fourths of the population were slaves or unfranchised merchants and artisans, and where what we know as "work" and "business" were despised. Art,

[1] *Intercollegiate Magazine*, December, 1909, pp. 267–269.

philosophy, science, were something apart from the working population. The farmer, the merchant, the laborer, were too base and ignoble to understand or appreciate them. Slavery was to the Greeks what machinery is to us. It did their work and left the citizens free to cultivate their souls and do artistic work. Our word "scholar" is merely the Greek word "leisure." One-fourth of the Greeks were idealists without utilitarianism, and three-fourths were utilitarians without idealism.

Likewise, our ethics came to us from ancient Palestine, whose people were a conquered and subject race, paying tribute to the wealthy men of Egypt, Babylon, Greece or Rome. Its admonitions of righteousness, equality, love, were directed to the service of God and not to Cæsar or men of wealth. A religious ethics, that united the slaves and masses of the Roman Empire, became corrupt or ascetic, or subservient to wealth, after it had conquered the empire. It was the idealism of hapless workers who looked to the next world for the perfection of ethics, and not that of *citizens* who demand it in this world.

But in our modern democracy all are citizens and all are workers. Even our idealists who cultivate art, philosophy and science are not above taking pay for what they now call "work" — something the Greeks would have thought disgraceful in a scholar. With idealism down on this utilitarian basis, the Greeks would have thought us quite supercilious had they seen us laugh at our utilitarians. But our utilitarians are really idealists, if we only knew where to look.

Talk with the ordinary workingman, farmer or merchant about his work. If he is not crushed down too much by poverty or overwork, if he is not a criminal or grafter, if he has had something of common education, he first of all tells you of the great importance of his work to society. From the garbage-collector or the ditch-digger, who lets you know how your comfort or health depends on him, all the way up to Rockefeller, who refers to the millions of homes now lighted where once was darkness and the thousands of workmen furnished employment, you find the instinctive idealism of service to others. What more could Socrates or Phidias boast, or Jesus and Paul admonish?

Next he tells you how particular his work is — how it requires skill, intelligence, experience, careful attention and just the knack that you didn't know about in order to do it right. Could Praxiteles with his statues, or Euripides with his dramas, appreciate the idealism of perfection more correctly than this?

Yes, our so-called utilitarianism has the elements and the aspirations of idealism in about as large proportions as the idealism of Greece. There were thousands of leisured Greeks, but only a few like Socrates or Phidias. The modern problem is how to combine idealism and utilitarianism in the same persons. The workingman or farmer usually has a third point to which he calls your attention — he is not paid enough, and his hours of labor are too long. The Greeks separated the idealists from the utilitarians, but they did it by first separating one class with all the leisure from another class with all the work. To combine idealism and utilitarianism, our modern worker asks that we combine leisure and work in the same person. This means shorter hours of work and more opportunity for education. This is the first great problem of modern democracy, — the industrial problem, — how to get a fair living by reasonable hours of work, leaving enough leisure for both childhood and manhood.

The second problem is education, — the use of leisure. Leisure is opportunity. It may be used or abused. What kind of education is called for? It is that which will develop the idealism of work — now instinctive but too often suppressed. The ethical ideal of work is service to others; the esthetic ideal is a perfect product.

He serves others who gives more than he receives. The value to society and the cost to one's self of one's work ought to be greater than the pay that one gets for it. Otherwise one is a pensioner, parasite, grafter, embezzler. The Greeks and Romans occupied much of their leisure discussing whether happiness or justice was the true object in life. The contest was fruitless, because neither the Epicureans nor Stoics had to work. Work was done through coercion and had no reference to happiness, justice or ethics. But when the worker has leisure, his work becomes ethical and should be guided by ideals. To make and sell a product of more value to society and more cost to himself than the price he gets for it becomes the ethics of utilitarian idealism.

This is perhaps a humdrum kind of ethics. It does not stir up the feelings like architecture or dramatics or oratory. But, nevertheless, it is that which the modern citizen, who has to work, shares in common with the world's idealists who did not have to work. Sophocles, Virgil, Shakespeare and the early religious teachers were never paid what their work was worth. Socrates, we would call an impecunious loafer around town, with his hand out for gifts, not pay. He and they got their living, their opportunity, and their ethical or esthetic satisfaction, as they went along — the rest of their pay they took out in applause — or in the feeling that they deserved applause.

The idealism of work craves exactly that kind of pay, — it is the business of utilitarian education to show how really satisfying it is. Wisconsin is doubtless a " job-getter,"— even idealists must get a living first of all, — and there are doubtless too many students and graduates who care for nothing more than what they can make out of a job. But, nevertheless, it would be hard to find an institution, ancient or contemporary, that has inspired a larger share of its constituency with the idealism of social and public service.

Esthetic idealism is the ideal of a perfect product. This is one object of our utilitarianism. I do not see why there is not as much idealism of its kind in breeding a perfect animal or a Wisconsin No. 7 ear of corn, or in devising an absolutely exact instrument for measuring a thousand cubic feet of gas, or for measuring exactly the amount of butter or casein in milk, as there is in chipping out a Venus de Milo or erecting a Parthenon. In fact, our agricultural education starts off at the beginning of the freshman year by requiring the student to picture in his mind the ideally perfect horse, or cow, or ear of corn, and then to cultivate his observation and judgment by showing exactly where and how far some actual cow or corn falls short of the ideal. This is the " score-card " method of instruction, which I think might well be adopted by idealists. Of course a cow is just a cow, and can never become a Winged Victory. But within her field of human endeavor she is capable of approaching an ideal. And, more than that, she is an ideal that every farmer and farmer's boy — the despised slaves and helots of Greece — can aspire to.   But, most of all, this idealism of a perfect product is the only way of rendering a perfect service to others.   The same is true of all other branches of applied science.   They are all teachers of esthetics to the common man.   And it is only as a science gets applied that its idealism gets democratic.   Utilitarianism is the democracy of idealism.

I am not so much discouraged by Wisconsin's " materialism."   Wisconsin is not an accident — it is as inevitable as democracy.   It makes a science and an art out of what to the Greeks was degrading toil.   It should make an ethics of service to others out of science, art, wealth and toil.   It has not finished its work — it is really only feeling its way in response to the demands of democracy.   It has not as yet given a conclusive answer to the idealists, nor enlisted them all in its errand.   It has only challenged them to help out. The methods of applied science, now inaugurated in agriculture, engineering and business need to be extended to sociology, law, philosophy, ethics, history and literature, where the idealists prevail.   By taking pay for their work they have themselves become grossly materialistic, from the Greek or Socratic standpoint.   For this reason they are better adapted to help in the grand mission of adding imagination to the kind of work by which others must earn their living.   This is utilitarian idealism.

CHAPTER II

CONSTRUCTIVE RESEARCH [1]

CONSTRUCTIVE research is that sort of investigation that goes along with administration and is designed to improve it. Other forms may be called academic and journalistic.

The motto of academic research is " truth for its own sake." It disregards the practical uses. But it is fundamental and first in order. In the infancy of a science, when its practical applications are unsuspected, or on the fringes of a science, where the applications are in doubt, investigation can have no other aim than the discovery of truth for its own sake. That is the period when principles are at stake; when ages of error are exposed and the world is given a new start. Galileo, experimenting with the inclined plane; Volta, with the frog's leg; Darwin on heredity; Newton on gravitation, — these and others who search for the foundations of science can have but little notion of its utility. The science is yet in its infancy, and human interests have not grown up around it nor learned to depend upon it, and demand results. The investigator is alone. He is led on by his love of truth. Academic research must always have the first place. It is pioneer — it makes epochs.

But when the principles of a science have been accepted; when its applications are being made; when the world is looking for its utility; when hundreds of in-

[1] Address before New York School of Philanthropy, September, 1907.

7

vestigators have fallen in line, research must set up a
new aim, — truth for the sake of utility. This is true
also of art. Art for art's sake is first, but great literary
artists of our day, like Tolstoi or Millet, are artists also
for the sake of social reform or revolution.

The science of political economy is now called upon
for something practical. Legislation has been left to
lawyers and politicians. The people turn to economists
and sociologists, but do not find what they need. The
regulation of public utilities, the revision of currency
and tariff laws, the relations of capital and labor, are
economic as well as legal or political questions. On
these and other subjects the science of economics remains
academic, after it has been summoned to the work of
construction.

Another form of research that has its place is that of
agitation, exposure, diagnosis, journalism. Some of it
has been called muck-raking — even by those who are
raked. Much of it has been done with ability and
conscience. We may call it one-sided, but it is often
no more so than the diagnosis of a physician who discovers your appendicitis. Agitational research is as
necessary as academic research. It awakens the public.
It carries conviction that something must be done.
Economic science has left this field to journalists. The
reasons are found in its academic precautions. The
magazine writer has been forced to pioneer without its
help, and to work out his methods and principles as he
goes along.

The service of exposure is in locating the disease.
It does not cure it or prevent it. This is the work of
constructive research. The two are related. One shows
the need of the other and leads to it. A model of con-

structive research is found in the modern trust, or syndicate, operating a number of plants that produce a similar product. Look at the organization of one of these " combines " both as a plan of administration and an instrument of investigation. It is divided into departments according to the nature of the work and the problems. In each department is a responsible head, and under him are subordinates in the different plants. Each subordinate is responsible in his own field. Every subordinate has before him the opportunity of promotion, or increase of salary. But promotion is not haphazard nor based on seniority. It is based on results, and these results are all reduced to a single economic basis, the reduction in cost of producing and selling the unit of product. The man who can show the best results, no matter how young or far down the line, is jumped over the heads of others. Those who do not get results are reduced. A stimulant is given to every man.

So it is in economic investigation. When we want hundreds of investigators to devote their energies to the same object, we must appeal to their interest or rivalry — we must make them compete with each other.

In order that individuals may be compared with one another, the trusts have devised uniform accounts and units of measurement. Every item of cost is classified according to its proper relations. When these comparative statements come into headquarters each month, and are tabulated and distributed back to the several managers, it is possible for all to know exactly at what point somebody is going ahead and somebody is falling behind. " Your labor cost has increased one cent a thousand cubic feet." " Your experiment on coal has cut down the cost two cents a thousand." Month after month these questions and results are circulating through the entire force of managers and investigators. Down to the minutest point each responsible man is put on record under a comparison with his fellows so precise that he cannot escape if deficient, nor fail if proficient.

Add to this the encouragement of individual research under the supervision of a central laboratory. Some individual may have a line of experiment which he wishes to undertake. He submits his plans to the laboratory chiefs. They authorize him to go ahead, and they furnish him the facilities for doing so. His experiment is worked out by himself, then tested by others, then adopted by all. Originality, initiative, investigation, are stimulated and are directed towards the point where they will count most.

This is constructive research. It goes along with actual administration. It carries out on a systematic and scientific basis what the common man is doing in his own way every day. Agricultural colleges used to investigate the chemistry of different kinds of food-stuffs and the physiology of the live stock. Now they weigh different kinds of food, and they weigh the hog before and after taking. They do what the hard-headed farmer would do if he had no chemistry or physiology. The agricultural experiment stations serve as central laboratories for thousands of isolated farmers. They do the same kind of experimenting that the farmers do, but they do it with instruments of exact measurement. Scientific analysis is joined to administration, and the researches are directed towards the point where they count in saving cost or increasing profits.

Experiment stations now are able to let the farmer

join in their experiments. Wisconsin has organized a thousand farmers into an association, all of them experimenting at the same time under different conditions, on corn, potatoes, fertilizers, and then sending in results to headquarters to be compared. Wisconsin has also adopted the trust method in the regulation of public utilities. Both those owned by corporations and those owned by municipalities are placed on a uniform system of bookkeeping, and when the year's accounts are made up it should be possible to compare the two systems of ownership on every item of cost. The state commission employs gas engineers, steam engineers, electric engineers, to make valuations and to supervise the comparisons. This commission, joining with the university, has recently, for the first time in the history of the gas industry, brought together the companies and standardized the meters for measuring the flow of gas. This basis of constructive research once established, both the gas industry and municipal government should become more efficient.

Standardization is essential, but not all. It is a tool. The real work of research is done by the individual investigator. Standardization measures his results. The value of his work depends on the constructive object he has in view. Take the field of historical research, frowned upon by the " practical " man. " Why do you dig up old and musty papers and records? The thing is past and gone. Take something that people are doing."

Let us see. In social sciences we cannot observe and experiment as they do in other sciences. I cannot bring into my classroom an employers' association and a trade union, put them in a glass case, bring my students around, watch them tussle, higgle, settle their differences

— the way Sir John Lubbock did when he studied his bees and ants. I must go out and find them. And I sometimes find that the most instructive ones are the dead ones. It is just as important for our guidance to know why a trade union died as it is to know what a live one is doing. The living one may seem just now to have strength, confidence and the good will of employers or the public. But it may have within it fatal microbes. These will show up later. They have already shown up in the dead ones.

Other fields and topics might be mentioned. The test by which to judge them is this : What lesson can be worked out of them to help those who are now working on similar problems? Is an experiment that fails to be wholly condemned, or can it be taken up in a different way? What is it that the law-maker wants to know in drafting his bill for legislation, and what does the judge look for in passing upon its constitutionality? Let these problems of the man responsible for results be held before the investigator, and his investigations will be constructive.

What is the value of constructive research? It reduces the coercive functions of government and increases the part played by persuasion. We speak with confidence of the power of public opinion and the value of publicity. But journalistic publicity inflames political passion, and academic publicity does not reach it. Constructive research gives exact information for the public to work upon. It analyzes the facts and reduces them to the point where the public can use them. In a democracy public opinion is more powerful than the officers of law. It makes and unmakes them. How important that the administration of law should be fully known and understood by the public exactly as it is! The people then help to enforce it by the mere unanimity of opinion.

To the constructive investigator, research is absorbing. He shares in that gradual reconstruction of society that, on occasion, arouses the orator, lawyer, preacher or politician. His science becomes progressive. His solid facts and constructive ideals are fundamental for the work of others. Theirs may be exciting; his should be equally inspiring.

CHAPTER III

STANDARDIZING THE HOME[1]

I HAD read that Glasgow was the most densely crowded of modern cities, because 14 per cent of the families lived in one room. After visiting one of the model tenements of the London County Council, I was asked by a Glasgow mechanic to look into his ancient rookery. The one room in which he and his family lived seemed to me to be larger than the three-room apartment of his fellow who enjoyed the municipal socialism of modern London. The difference was that he put up his own flimsy partitions, while paternal London got the credit of relieving congestion by merely erecting permanent partitions.

In Pittsburgh I was told by experts in housing investigations that the cost of housing there was greater than in any other city of the country, but when I compared the few houses that I saw with similar houses in Chicago, taking into account appurtenances, I could not see that the costs were different.

British workmen and employers contended that their lower wages were compensated by the lower cost of food as well as housing, compared with American wages, and I could not refer them to any authentic standards of food and prices, housing and rents, that would disprove their claims to their satisfaction.

[1] *American Statistical Association, Quarterly Publications*, Dec., 1908; *The Journal of Home Economics*, Feb., 1910, pp. 260–266.

If comparisons of this kind were a matter of profit and loss, standard units would long since have been devised. If our government were turned over to an anti-poverty syndicate on such terms that the syndicate should have a half of the increase in national wealth produced by its conservation of human resources, the syndicate would at once invent standard units for the measurement of costs and results. Uniform accounts and cost-keeping on the basis of such standard units are essential for an electric or gas or street-car or iron and steel syndicate in deciding which of its plants is most economical, which of its managers is most efficient, or which of its inventions and experiments is most promising. A gas syndicate would go bankrupt if a thousand feet of gas meant a different amount of light, heat, moisture, pressure or rate of flow in its different establishments. Every branch of engineering has its learned societies and scientific experts whose most important work is that of agreeing upon standard units to be adopted throughout the industry. Now that another kind of engineering — " social engineering " — is emerging from the speculations and theories of economics and sociology, we, too, are compelled to pause at the threshold in order, first of all, to agree upon the units by which we shall compare our costs and our results.

What is the unit that we are seeking? The electric engineer, or steam engineer, or water-power engineer, seeks a unit for measuring the output of energy — a " kilowatt " or a " horse-power." He seeks also his units of cost — the quality and cost of the coal consumed, the capacity and efficiency of boilers and engines. Our unit of output relates to the health, longevity, industrial ability, comfort and welfare of human beings.

Our units of cost are food, shelter, clothing, occupation, education. We have our statistics of health which tell us something of our output, and we are trying to do something toward minimum standards of food and housing. But our efforts are haphazard because we have no units by which we can compare costs with output. This is especially distracting, because, under our form of government, our courts forbid interference that goes beyond their ideas of what is necessary, and we have no standards by which we can enlighten them.

There is one department of sociology which eventually will make it plain that standard units of housing, food and occupation are also a matter of profit and loss. This is the health, vigor and efficiency of the working population. The trade longevity of the workman, the number of days lost through sickness, fatigue and devitalizing, the rate of mortality, are the greatest of all matters of national business, and they are largely the results of housing, food and occupation.

But, to what extent these different factors enter, it is impossible to say until standard units are devised by which to compare each factor with the resulting morbidity, mortality and fatigue.

Here the problem of the economist and that of the hygienist overlap. The economist is interested in comparative cost of living, the hygienist in comparative causes of industrial efficiency. But the cost of living is really the cost of the workman's efficiency. If so, the unit of comparison which the economist wants is the same unit that the hygienist wants. Take housing as the simplest problem. The comparative cost of housing is the comparative price paid for a unit of housing accommodation. But housing accommodation is not merely floor space or " rooms per occupant "; it is also location, air, ventilation, sunlight, structural condition, bath, laundry, running water, etc. These are also the conditions of health. The cost of housing is one of the costs of industrial vigor. If, then, we devise our standard unit with reference to the conditions of health, we shall have practically the standard needed for comparing prices of housing accommodation.

But our units are quite complex, and there is a lot of personal elements that baffle us. Is this a fatal difficulty? Only in case we attempt too much. There are margins of variation in every branch of applied science. Let us break up our problem and begin with the most essential. This is the home, and the basis of the home is the dwelling-house. When we rent or buy a home, we are paying for a bundle of house accommodations for the sake of health, comfort, education and efficiency. How much house accommodation do we get, and how much do we pay for each unit of it?

This is a complicated unit. It consists of many factors, and no two investigators attach the same weight to each of the factors. But this difficulty is exactly the one that has been met in another field, by breeders' associations and by produce exchanges, in standardizing and grading agricultural products, such as wheat, corn, butter, horses, cows and pigs. An ideal horse, for example, perfect in every particular, is represented by 100 points. The horse is mapped off and described by 36 specifications, and each specification is given a weight or value, corresponding to its importance in making up the perfect animal. Thus " general appearance " gets 29 points, composed of 5 points for " weight," 4 for " form," 6 for " quality," and so on. These standard weights, or values, are printed in a column opposite each specification, and a second or blank column is provided under the caption " Points Deficient." In using the score card, the " valuer " goes over the horse, noticing in detail all the points specified, and then marks down opposite each his judgment of the degree to which the animal before him is deficient in that particular point. The total of all points deficient is then deducted from 100, and the result is the grade of the animal scored. It is an interesting fact, illustrating the accuracy of this method of standardizing, that recently two horse valuers, using the same score card, one employed by the Wisconsin Railway Commission, and the other by the Milwaukee Street Car Company, in valuing fifty horses belonging to the company, came within one or two points of placing the same value on each horse.

In attempting to adopt this method I have drawn up the following score card for dwelling-houses. The weights, or " values," given to each of the 35 specifications are of course tentative, and can be made precise only after a large body of evidence is assembled and experts have passed upon them. But precision at this point is not important. The main object is the specifications themselves. If all investigators use the same specifications, any person afterwards can change the weights to suit his own theories or his knowledge of the facts.

The accuracy of the method consists in the fact that it limits the total margin of error by breaking it up into 30 or 40 little margins. Where measurements are possible, but little discretion need be left to the individual. This appears in the case of " window openings." Where measurements are not possible, the agents must depend on their judgment, but this judgment can be brought close to uniformity by "instructions for discrediting when depending on judgment." For convenience I have used only the weights 3 and 6 for those specifications depending on judgment, and have introduced the same kind of instructions as those given in the official score cards of breeders' associations for horses and cattle. These and other instructions will be found at the proper points on the score card.

When a house is "scored" according to this card, we shall have the "total points deficient," and the "actual score" of that house compared with a perfect or ideal house. We are then in a position to compare the rents or cost of housing by correcting the "nominal rent," *i.e.* the money rent paid by the occupant, by means of the "actual score." I have suggested three standard units of comparison, as will be seen on the card, viz. "rent per room," "rent per 100 sq. ft." of floor space, and "rent per 1000 cu. ft." of air capacity. Taking "rent per 100 sq. ft.," which is probably the fairest unit under all circumstances, it can easily be seen that, of two houses renting nominally at, say, $1 per month for equal floor space, if the "actual score" of one is 80 and the other 50, the "real rent" of the one is $1.25 and the other $2 for the unit of house accommodation compared with the real rent of $1 for a perfect house.

DWELLING HOUSE SCORE CARD

Applies to a Single Family or Household

State................City....................Street..............No. ....
Name of Owner...................... Name of Occupant...................
Name of Investigator............................ Date.................

Instructions for Discrediting when Depending on Judgment

Deduct from possible 6; very slight, 1; slight, 2; marked, 3; very marked, 4; extreme, 5.
Deduct from possible 3; very slight, $\frac{1}{2}$; slight, 1; marked, $1\frac{1}{2}$; very marked, 2; extreme, $2\frac{1}{2}$.

I. — DWELLING — 100 POINTS	Possible Score	Points Deficient	Actual Score
LOCATION — 18 Points	(18)	( )	( )
1. **General Character of Neighborhood**, villa, farm, residence, park.............................	3	....	....
(Discredit for factory, slum, neglected district)			
2. **Elevation**, high ground, sloping away on all sides.	3	....	....
3. **Condition of Street**, width (ft.)...., clean, smooth, hard, free from dust, sprinkled, flushed, free from refuse	3	....	....
(Indicate whether asphalt, block stone, macadam, cobble, wood, dirt)			
4. **Smoke**, free from (indicate source)	3	....	....
5. **Odors**, free from nauseous (indicate source)	3	....	....
6. **Dust**, free from (indicate source)	3	....	....
CONGESTION OF BUILDINGS — 26 Points	(26)	( )	( )
7. **Character of Dwelling — 10 Points**			
Detached...............................	10	....	....
Attached, separate entrance, discredit 1 point			
Attached, common entrance, discredit 2 points			
Flat (entire floor), discredit 3 points			
Apartment (2 or more on same floor), discredit 4 points			
Basement (over ½ above street level), discredit 5 points			
Cellar (over ½ below street level), discredit 6 points			
Additional discredits for flat or apartment without elevator, 2d floor 2 points, 3d floor 3 points, etc.			
8. **Sunlight — 16 Points**			
Height and distance of next building (use foot of its own window in case of flat or apartment, otherwise foot of lower window, as base line above which to measure height of next building).			

Direction (Ind. street or alley)	Height (feet)	Distance (feet)	Per Cent (Height -100)		
North........	......	....	....	3	....	....
South........	......	....	....	5	....	....
East.........	......	....	....	4	....	....
West	......	....	....	4	....	....

(If distance equals or exceeds height, no points deficient — if distance is less than height, actual score is same per cent of possible score as distance to height, *e.g.* if distance = 20% of height, actual score = 20% of possible score, etc.)

WINDOW OPENINGS — 11 Points	(11)	( )	( )

Rooms (Indicate kitchen, sleeping, bath, etc.)	Window Space (Sq. Ft.)	Floor Space (Sq. Ft.)	Per Cent Window Space (Floor space = 100)
1	....	....	....
2	....	....	....
3	....	....	....
4	....	....	....
5	....	....	....
6	....	....	....
Number of Rooms (including dark rooms) having window space less than 20 %..........			
Per Cent of same to total rooms			
Number of dark Rooms			
Per Cent of same to total rooms..............			

I.—DWELLING—100 POINTS	Possible Score	Points Deficient	Actual Score
9. Total Window Space, not less than 20% of total floor space .... (Discredit ¼ point for each deficiency of 1% —*e.g.* window space 16% of floor space, discredit 1 point, leaving actual score 4)	5	....	....
DISTRIBUTION OF WINDOW SPACE—6 Points			
10. Deficient Rooms, no room less than 20%...... (Discredit same per cent of possible score as per cent of rooms having window space less 20%, *e.g.* 6-room house, 2 rooms deficient, discredit ⅓ of 3 = 1, leaving actual score 2)	3	....	....
11. Dark Rooms, no room without window openings (Discredit same per cent of possible score as per cent of dark rooms, *e.g.* 6-room house, 1 dark room, discredit ⅙ of 3 = ½, leaving actual score 2½) **Notice**: dark room is discredited also above as "deficient room"	3	....	....
AIR AND VENTILATION — 13 Points	(13)	( )	( )
12. Heating Arrangements, adapted to secure circulation of fresh air such as open fireplace, hot-air furnace, stove (connecting directly with chimney in same room) .... (Discredit 1 point for steam or hot water, ½ point for each stove connecting with chimney in another room)	4	....	....
13. Temperature, adapted to secure even temperature, not excessive heat or cold, equal in different rooms .... (Discredit proportionately for each room without heating appliance)	3	....	....
14. Dampness, freedom from (indicate whether cellar, kitchen, sleeping rooms, other rooms) ...	6	....	....
STRUCTURAL CONDITION — 6 Points	(6)	....	....
15. Material. (Indicate whether wood, brick, stone, concrete, no decayed wood, walls, floors, ceilings in good condition) .... (Discredit ½ point for papered walls or ceilings)	3	....	....
16. Size of Rooms, height of ceiling, not less than 9 feet .... (Discredit ½ point for each foot deficient)	1	....	....
17. Floor Space, (no room less than 120 sq. ft.).... (Discredit proportionately for each room less than 120 sq. ft.)	2	....	....
HOUSE APPURTENANCES — 26 Points (Discredit total score in each case if appurtenance is not provided)	(26)	( )	( )
18. Bath. (Discredit 2 points for bath used in common)	4	....	....
19. Closet in Dwelling .... (Discredit 1 point for closet used in common, 2 for outhouse with sewer connection, 3 without sewer)	4	....	....
20. Sink. (Discredit ½ for sink used in common)...	1	....	....
21. Laundry. (Discredit ½ for common laundry)...	1	....	....
22. Running Water in House. (Discredit 1 point for common hydrant, 2 for hydrant outside, 3 for well outside)	4	....	....
23. Condition of Appurtenances, good material and workmanship, all pipes exposed	6	....	....
24. Quality of Water for Drinking	3	....	....
25. Quality of Water for Bath and Laundry.......	3	....	....
DWELLING TOTAL	100	....	....

COST OF HOUSING

Rent per month $......Rental value (if occupied by owner) $......
Unit of Comparison   Nominal Rent   Real Rent
Rent per room .... $..................... $..................
Rent per 100 sq. ft. .... $..................... $..................
Rent per 1000 cu. ft. .... $..................... $..................
               Probable income of family per month $.........

The foregoing applies solely to the house itself, or to the landlord as responsible for the house. But the conditions of health and the cost of housing are modified by the habits and circumstances of the occupants. These should be separated from the other problem by means of a separate score card. Here the problem of " congestion of occupancy " is paramount, and the unit of comparison is the " rent per occupant." The actual score on the " occupant " card becomes a coefficient of the actual score on the " dwelling " card, and this combined score gives the grading of the unit of housing accommodation as provided by the landlord and modified by the tenant. If, for example, two houses are scored 80 and 50, respectively, on the "dwelling" card, and the occupants of each are scored alike at 70 on the " occupant " card, then the combined dwelling and occupant scores are 56 and 35, respectively. If, then, the nominal or money rent is $2 per occupant, the real rents are $3.57 and $5.71 per occupant compared with $2 for the ideal or standard dwelling occupied by the ideal or standard tenant.

I wish to call attention to the pedagogical value of the score card as the basis of practical instruction in economics and sociology. This value has been conclusively demonstrated in our agricultural colleges, where the students begin their studies by using it on animals and cereals. It develops the student in his ideals of per-

DWELLING HOUSE SCORE CARD

II. — OCCUPANTS — 100 POINTS	Possible Score	Points Deficient	Actual Score
CONGESTION OF OCCUPANCY — 61 Points	(61)	( )	( )
Occupants, number			
Family, 10 years old and over, male			
" " " " " female			
Lodgers, Domestics, 10 years old and over, male			
" " " " " " " female			
Children under 10 years			
Total (Child under 10 as ½ person).............			
1. **Cubic Air Space** (average height of ceiling by total floor space), cu. ft.			
Cu. ft. per occupant........No discredit if 1000 or over	50	....	....
(Discredit 1 point for each 20 ft. below 1000, e.g. 600 cu. ft. discredit 20 points, leaving actual score 30)	11	....	....
2. **Sleeping Rooms per Occupant**			
(Discredit 1 point for each person in excess of number of sleeping rooms)			
CONDITION OF AIR AND VENTILATION — 18 Points	(18)	( )	( )
3. **Windows**, kept open to fresh air	3	....	....
Living rooms	6	....	....
Sleeping rooms			
4. **Temperature**, kept even, not excessive heat or cold	3	....	....
5. **Dust**, care in avoiding dust by sweeping, no home workshop	6	....	....
CLEANLINESS, care and attention, no rubbish, dirt, grease or refuse, — 21 Points	(21)	( )	( )
6. **Hallways**	3	....	....
7. **Floors**	3	....	....
8. **Walls**	3	....	....
9. **Plumbing**	6	....	....
10. **Yard**	6	....	....
OCCUPANTS TOTAL	100	....	....
Rent per occupant, nominal			
Real rent per occupant (compared with standard) $...			
$................			

fection, his accuracy of observation, and his power of judgment. These are the great essentials of scientific education, and they have been admirably stated by Mr. Craig in his book " Judging Live Stock." He says: " To formulate an ideal is absolutely essential, and in doing this it is imperative to familiarize one's self with the good qualities of animal life, correct conformation and the highest types, so that the least variation from these at once attracts the attention. When a distinct ideal, based on the best types and their highest qualities, has been formed in the mind, and this is supported by a discriminating eye, it is but another step to render a correct judgment."

What Mr. Craig says of agricultural education is true also of sociological education. The score card directs attention to details often overlooked. It requires consideration of their meaning and significance. It sets up standards of precise observation in place of vague or sentimental impressions of things in general. When perfected it will go far towards giving to home economics the character of a true science.

CHAPTER IV

AN IDEALISTIC INTERPRETATION OF HISTORY[1]

THE French are a nation of philosophers. Starting with a theory of the rights of man, they build up a logical system. Then a revolution, and the theory goes into practice. Next a *coup d'état*, an emperor.

The English are a nation without too much philosophy or logic. They piece out their constitution at the spot where it becomes tight, and their nobility gracefully gives up its ancient privileges in exchange for land values. They are practical, opportunist, unlogical.

The Americans are French in their logic and English in their use of logic. They announce the universal rights of man and then enact into law enough to augment the rights of property. They have had in their history three great periods of this philosophizing on innate and inalienable rights: the period of the constitution, the decade of the forties, and to-day.

The forties far outran the other periods in its unbounded loquacity. The columns of advertisements in a newspaper might announce on Monday night a meeting of the anti-slavery society; Tuesday night, the temperance society; Wednesday night, the Graham bread society; Thursday night, a phrenological lecture; Friday night, an address against capital punishment; Saturday night, the " Association for Universal Reform."

[1] Published originally under the title "Horace Greeley and the Working Class Origins of the Republican Party," *Political Science Quarterly*, Vol. XXIV, pp. 468–488.

Then there were all the missionary societies, the woman's rights societies, the society for the diffusion of bloomers, the séances of spiritualists, the " associationists," the land reformers — a medley of movements that found the week too short. Thirty colonies of idealists, like the Brook Farm philosophers, went off by themselves to solve the problem of social existence in a big family called a Phalanx. The Mormons gathered themselves together to reconstitute the ten lost tribes. Robert Owen expounded communism to the United States Senate and House of Representatives. It was the golden age of the talk-fest, the lyceum, the brotherhood of man — the " hot air " period of American history.

Fifty years before had been an age of talk. Thomas Jefferson and Thomas Paine had filled the young nation's brain with the inalienable rights of life, liberty and the pursuit of happiness. This second era of talk had also its prophet. Horace Greeley was to the social revolution of the forties what Thomas Jefferson was to the political revolution of 1800. He was the *Tribune* of the people, the spokesman of their discontent, the champion of their nostrums. He drew the line only at spirit rappings and free love.

This national palaver was partially checked by the fugitive slave law of 1850. The spectacle of slave-drivers, slave rescues and federal marshals at men's doors turned discussion into amazement. The palaver stopped short in 1854 with the Kansas-Nebraska bill. That law marked off those territories for a free fight for land between slave-owners and small farmers. On this land issue the Republican party suddenly appeared. Its members came together by a magic attraction, as crystals appear in a chilled solution. Not one man nor one set of men formed the party, though there are many claimants for the honor of first suggesting the name or calling the first meeting that used the name.   The fluid solution was there.   When the chill came, the crystals formed.   It was the fifteen years of revolutionary talk that made the party possible.   Men's minds had been unsettled.   Visions of a new moral world had come upon them.   Tradition had lost its hold and transition its terrors.

We hear nowadays of the " economic interpretation of history."   Human life is viewed as a struggle to get a living and to get rich.   The selfishness of men hustling for food, clothing, shelter and wealth determines their religion, their politics, their form of government, their family life, their ideals.   Economic evolution produces religious, political, domestic, philosophical evolution. All this we may partly concede.   But certainly there is something more in history than a blind surge.   Men act together because they see together and believe together. An inspiring idea, as well as the next meal, makes history. It is when such an idea coincides with an economic want, and the two corroborate each other, that the mass of men begins to move.   The crystals then begin to form; evolution quickens into revolution;   history reaches a crisis.

For *ideas*, like methods of getting a living, have their evolution.   The struggle for existence, the elimination of the unfit, the survival of the fit, control these airy exhalations from the mind of man as they control the more substantial framework of his existence.   The great man is the man in whose brain the struggling ideas of the age fight for supremacy until the survivors come out adapted to the economic struggle of the time.   Judged by this test, Horace Greeley was the prophet of the most momentous period of our history. The evolution of his ideas is the idealistic interpretation of our history.

Greeley's life was itself a struggle through all the economic oppressions of his time. In his boyhood his father had been reduced by the panic of 1819 from the position of small farmer to that of day laborer. The son became an apprentice in a printing-office, then a tramp printer, and when he drifted into New York in 1831 he found himself in the midst of the first workingmen's political party with its first conscious struggle in America for the rights of labor. Pushing upwards as publisher and editor, the panic of 1837 brought him down near to bankruptcy, but the poverty of the wage-earners about him oppressed him more than his own. " We do not want alms," he heard them say; " we are not beggars; we hate to sit here day by day idle and useless; help us to work — we want no other help; why is it that we can have nothing to do?"[1] Revolting against this " social anarchy," as he called it, he espoused socialism and preached protectionism. This was the beginning of his " isms." Not that he had been immune before to cranky notions. When only a boy of thirteen he broke away from the unanimous custom of all classes, ages and both sexes by resolving never again to drink whiskey.[2] When " Doctor " Graham proclaimed vegetarianism in 1831, he forthwith became an inmate of a Graham boarding-house.[3] But these were personal " isms." They bothered nobody else. Not until the long years of industrial suffering that began in 1837 did his " isms "

---

[1] Greeley, H., "Recollections of a Busy Life," p. 145.
[2] *Ibid.*, p. 98.
[3] *Ibid.*, p. 103.

become gospels and his panaceas propaganda. His total abstinence of 1824 became prohibitory legislation in 1850. His vegetarianism of the thirties became abolition of capital punishment in the forties. The crank became the reformer, when once the misery and helplessness of the workers cried aloud to him.

Greeley's " isms " are usually looked upon as the amiable weaknesses of genius. They were really the necessary inquiries and experiments of the beginnings of constructive democracy. Political democracy theretofore had been negative. Thomas Jefferson and Andrew Jackson needed no creative genius to assert equal rights. They needed only to break down special privilege by widening the rights that already existed. Jefferson could frame a bill of rights, but he could not construct a constitution. Jackson could kill a " monster " bank, but he could not invent a people's control of the currency. Negative democracy in 1776, in 1800, in 1832, had triumphed. It had done its needful work, but its day was ended when a thousand wild-cat banks scrambled into the bed of the departed "monster." Political democracy went bankrupt when the industrial bankruptcy of 1837 exposed its incapacity. It had vindicated equal rights, but where was the bread and butter? The call of the time was for a new democracy — one that should be social and economic rather than political; constructive rather than negative; whose motto should be *reform*, not repeal; *take hold*, not let alone; *faire*, not *laissez faire*.

But there were no examples or precedents of such a democracy. The inventor of a sewing machine or the discoverer of a useful chemical compound endures hundreds of failures before his idea works. But his failures are suffered at home. The world does not see them. Only his success is patented. But the social inventor must publish his ideas before he knows whether they will work. He must bring others to his way of thinking before he can even start his experiment. The world is taken into his secret while he is feeling his way. They see his ideas in the " ism " stage. To the negative democrat this brings no discredit: he has no device to offer. To the constructive democrat it brings the stigma of faddism. The conservatives see in him not only the radical, but also the crank with a machine that might possibly work.

Greeley's *Tribune*, prior to 1854, was the first and only great vehicle this country has known for the ideas and experiments of constructive democracy. The fact that the circulation of the newspaper doubled and redoubled beyond anything then known in journalism, and in the face of ridicule heaped on virulence, proves that the nation, too, was feeling its way towards this new democracy.

Naturally enough, Greeley was a puzzle both to the radicals and to the standpats of his day. The *Working Man's Advocate* [1] said of him:

If ever there was a nondescript, it is Horace Greeley. One night you may hear him make a patriotic speech at a Repeal[2] meeting. The next day, he will uphold a labor-swindling, paper-money system. . . . We should be sorry to be driven to the conclusion that such a man could be actuated only by paltry partyism.

The Abolitionists were incensed when he wrote to the Anti-Slavery Convention at Cincinnati:

[1] June 29, 1844, p. 3, c. 4.
[2] Repeal of the Act uniting Ireland with England.

If I am less troubled concerning the Slavery prevalent in Charleston or New Orleans, it is because I see so much slavery in New York, which appears to claim my first efforts. . . . Wherever the ownership of the soil is so engrossed by a small part of the community, that the far larger number are compelled to pay whatever the few may see fit to exact for the privilege of occupying and cultivating the earth, there is something very like Slavery. . . . Wherever opportunity to labor is obtained with difficulty, and is so deficient that the employing class may virtually prescribe their own terms and pay the Laborer only such share as they choose of the product, there is a very strong tendency to Slavery.[1]

The Whigs and protectionists used him, but dreaded him. The *Express* charged him with

attempting incessantly . . . to excite the prejudices of the poor against the rich, and in the general, to array one class of society against the other. . . . We charge the *Tribune* . . . with representing constantly that there is a large amount of suffering arising from want of employment, and that this employment the rich might give. We charge the *Tribune* with over-rating entirely the suffering of the poor . . . all of which tallies with, and is a portion of the very material, which our opponents use to prejudice the poor against the Whigs as a party.[2]

Two years after this attack by the *Express*, the *Courier* read him out of the party:

There can be no peace in the Whig ranks while the New York *Tribune* is continued to be called Whig. . . . The *principles* of the Whig party are well defined; they are *conservative* and inculcate a regard for the laws and support of all established institutions of the country. They eschew *radicalism* in every form; they sustain the constitution and the laws; they foster a spirit of *patriotism*. . . . The better way for the *Tribune* would be at once to admit

[1] *Tribune*, June 20, 1845; see "Documentary History of American Industrial Society," A. H. Clarke & Co., Cleveland, Vol. VII, pp. 211–216.

[2] *Tribune*, Aug. 5, 1845.

that it is only Whig on the subject of the Tariff . . . and then devote itself to the advocacy of Anti-Rent, Abolition, Fourierite and Vote-yourself-a-farm doctrines.[1]

These quotations give us the ground of Greeley's " isms " — the elevation of labor by protecting and re-organizing industry. Even the protective tariff, favored by the Whigs, was something different in his hands. The tariff arguments of his boyhood had been capitalistic arguments. Protect capital, their spokesmen said, because wages are too high in this country. Eventually wages will come towards the European level and we shall not need protection. Greeley reversed the plea : protect the wage-earner, he said, in order that he may rise above his present condition of wages slavery. The only way to protect him against the foreign pauper is to protect the price of his product. But, since capital owns and sells his product, we needs must first protect capital. This is unfortunate, and we must help the laborer as soon as possible to own and sell his product himself. " We know right well," he says,[2] " that a protective tariff cannot redress all wrongs. . . . The extent of its power to benefit the Laborer is limited by the force and pressure of *domestic* competition, for which Political Economy has as yet devised no remedy. . . ."

Here was the field for his socialism. It would do for domestic competition what protection would do for foreign competition. Protectionism and socialism were the two wheels of Greeley's bicycle. He had not learned to ride on one.

But the socialism which Greeley espoused would not

[1] *Courier and Enquirer*, Aug. 14, 1847; quoted in *Weekly Tribune*, Aug. 21, 1847.

[2] *Tribune*, March 27, 1845.

be recognized to-day. It is now condescendingly spelled " utopianism." He felt that the employers were victims of domestic competition just as were the laborers, and he assumed that they would be just as glad as the laborers to take something else. What he offered to both was a socialism of class harmony, not one of class struggle.

In the idealistic interpretation of history there are two kinds of idealism — a higher and a lower. Greeley's significance is the struggle of the two in his mind, the elimination of the unfit from each and the survival and coalescence of the fit in the Republican party. The higher idealism came to him through the transcendental philosophers of his time. The lower came from the working classes. The higher idealism was humanitarian, harmonizing, persuasive. The lower was class-conscious, aggressive, coercive. The higher was a plea for justice; the lower a demand for rights. In 1840 Greeley was a higher idealist. In 1847 he had shaved down the higher and dovetailed in the lower. In 1854 the Republican party built both into a platform.

Let us see the origins of these two levels of idealism before they came to Greeley.

Boston, we are told, is not a place — it is a state of mind. But every place has its state of mind. The American pioneer, in his frontier cabin, in the rare moments which his battle with gigantic nature leaves free for reflection, contemplates himself as a trifle in a succession of accidents. To him comes the revivalist, with his faith in a God of power and justice, and the pioneer enters upon a state of mind that constructs order out of accident and unites him with the almighty ruler of nature. This was the state of mind of Boston when Boston was Massachusetts Bay and Plymouth Colony.

But Massachusetts grew in wealth. Wealth is merely nature subdued to man. Capital is the forces of nature taking orders from property owners. God is no longer appreciated as an ally for helpless man. The revivalist becomes the priest and the protector of capital.

But now a new contest begins. Capital requires labor to utilize it. Labor depends on capital for a living. The contest is not between man and nature, but between man and the owner of capitalized nature. Boston saw the first outbreaks of the struggle in 1825 and in 1832. In the former year the house carpenters, in the latter year the ship carpenters, determined that no longer would they work from sunrise to sunset. They conspired together and quit in a body. In the former year the capitalists, with Harrison Gray Otis at their head, in the latter year the merchant princes whose ships traversed the globe, took counsel together and published in the papers their ultimatum requiring their workmen to continue as before from dawn to dark.[1] Losing their contention, the workmen again in 1835 began a general strike for the ten-hour day throughout the Boston district, only again to lose. Meanwhile the factory system had grown up at Lowell and other places, with its women and children on duty thirteen and fourteen hours a day, living in company houses, eating at the company table and required to attend the company church. While some of the ten-hour strikes of 1835 had been successful in Philadelphia and in New York, the working people of

[1] *Columbian Centinel*, April 20, 23, 1825; " Doc. Hist.," Vol. VI, pp. 76–81; *Independent Chronicle*, May 19, 23, 26, 30, 1832; " Doc. Hist.," Vol. VI, pp. 81–86.

New England were doomed to the long day for another fifteen years.

It was in the midst of this economic struggle that Unitarianism and transcendentalism, in New England, took hold of the clergy.   These movements were a revolt against the predicament in which the God of nature had unwittingly become the God of capital.   They were a secession back to the God of man.   At first the ideas were transcendental, metaphysical, allegorical, harmless. This was while the workingmen were aggressive and defiant in their demands and strikes.   But, after 1837 and during the seven years of industrial depression and helplessness of the workingmen following that year of panic, transcendentalism became pragmatic.   Its younger spokesmen allied themselves with labor.   They tried to get the same experience and to think and feel like manual workers.   Brook Farm was the zealous expression in 1842 of this struggle for reality and for actual unity; and after 1843 the Brook Farm representatives began to show up at the newly organized New England and New York conventions of workingmen, calling themselves also by the lofty name of " workingmen " delegates.

But this was not enough.   Reality demanded more than unity of sentiment.   It demanded reconstruction of society on the principle of unity.   At this juncture, 1840, Albert Brisbane came forward with his Americanization of Charles Fourier's scheme of social reorganization. Here was a definite plan, patterned on what seemed to be a scientific study of society and of psychology. Brook Farm welcomed it and tried it.   Greeley clothed himself with it as gladly as Pilgrim put on the armor after emerging from the slough of despond.   He opened the columns of the *Tribune* to Brisbane. He became a director of the North American Phalanx, president of the national society of Associationists (Fourierists), editorial propagandist and platform expounder. Total reorganization of society based on harmony of interest; brotherhood of capital, labor and ability; a substitute for the competition which enslaved labor in spite of the natural sympathy of the capitalist for his oppressed workmen; faith in the goodness of human nature if scientifically directed, — these were the exalted ideas and naïve assumptions that elicited the devotion of Greeley and his fellow disciples of the gospel of transcendentalism.

Two things disabused his mind. One was the actual failure and bankruptcy of his beloved phalanxes; the other was the logic and agitation of the workingmen. The higher idealism dissolved like a pillar of cloud, but it had led the way to the solid ground of the lower idealism. What were the origins of this lower idealism?

Three years ago, at Newcastle-on-Tyne, in England, in the company of a workingman official of a trade union, I visited the thousand acres of moorland belonging to the mediæval city and now kept open as a great playground within the modern city. My trade-union official showed me the thousands of workingmen and their families enjoying themselves in the open air. I asked him about the fifty or a hundred cows that I saw calmly eating grass in the midst of this public park. He explained that these cattle belonged to the descendants of the ancient freemen of Newcastle, who, in return for defending the town against the Scots, had been granted rights of pasturage outside the town. He said there had recently been a great struggle in Newcastle, when these

freemen wanted to enclose the moor, to lease it for cultivation and to divide the rents among themselves.   The
workingmen of the city rose up as one man and stopped
this undertaking.   But they could not get rid of the cows.

One hundred and thirty years before this time, in the
year 1775, Newcastle had seen a similar struggle.   At
that time the freemen were successful; they succeeded
in having the rentals from a part of the moor, which had
been enclosed and leased, paid over in equal parts to each
of them.   Thomas Spence, netmaker, thereupon con-
ceived an idea.   He read a paper before the Philosophical
Society of Newcastle, proposing that all the land of
England should be leased and the proceeds divided equally
among all the people of England.   He was promptly
expelled from the Philosophical Society.   He went to
London and published his scheme in a book.[1]   Two
generations later, in 1829, the book came to New York
and furnished the platform for the first workingmen's
political party.[2]   This party Americanized Spence by
amending the Declaration of Independence.   They
made it read: " All men are equal, and have an inalienable right to life, liberty and *property*."

George Henry Evans, also Englishman by birth but
American by childhood and by apprenticeship in a printing-office at Ithaca, started a paper, the *Working Man's
Advocate*, in 1829, and became the thinker of the workingmen's party.   Before he began to think he adopted
the motto of the party as the motto of his paper: " All
children are entitled to equal education;   all adults

---

[1] J. M. Davidson, "Four Precursors of Henry George," pp. 26 *et seq.*
Spence's book is reprinted by E. W. Allen (London, 1882), under the
title, "The Nationalization of Land, 1775 and 1882."

[2] *Working Man's Advocate*, June 8, 1844, p. 1, c. 1.

to equal property; and all mankind to equal privileges." He soon saw his mistake, as did most of the other workingmen. Every individual has a right to an unlimited amount of that kind of property which he produces by his own labor and without aid from the coerced labor of others. Such an unlimited right is consistent with equality, and *equal right* to property can therefore be asserted only as regards that which is not the product of his own or other's labor, namely, land. But the holders of the existing private property in land could not be displaced without a violent revolution. This Evans saw from the violent attacks made on him and the workingmen's party. But there was an immense area still belonging to the people and not yet divided. This was the public domain. There man's equal right to land could be asserted. He sent marked copies of his paper to Andrew Jackson in 1832, before Jackson's message on the sale of the public lands. The workingmen's party disappeared and was followed by the trades' unions of 1835 and 1836. The sudden rise of prices and the increased cost of living compelled labor to organize and strike throughout the eastern cities, from Washington to Boston. These strikes were for the most part successful; but the workmen saw prices and rents go up and swallow more than the gains achieved by striking. Evans pointed out the reason why their efforts were futile. The workingmen were bottled up in the cities. Land speculation kept them from taking up vacant land near by or in the West. If they could only get away and take up land, then they would not need to strike. Labor would become scarce. Employers would advance wages; landlords would reduce rents. Not for the sake of those who moved West did Evans advocate freedom of the public lands, but for the sake of those who remained East. This was the idea that he added to the idea of Andrew Jackson and Andrew Johnson. Theirs was the squatter's idea of the public domain — territory to be occupied and defended with a gun, because the occupant was on the ground. His was the idealistic view of the public domain — the natural right of all men to land, just as to sunlight, air and water. The workingmen of the East were slaves because their right to land was denied. They were slaves, not to individual masters, like the negroes, but to a master class which owned their means of livelihood. Freedom of the public lands would be freedom for the white slave. Even the chattel slave would not be free if slavery were abolished without providing first that each freedman should have land of his own. Freedom of the public lands should be established before slavery was abolished.

These views were not original with Evans. They were the common property of his fellows, born of their common experience, formulated in their mutual intercourse and expressed in the platforms of their party and the resolution of their trades' unions. Thus at the first convention of the National Trades' Union in 1834, one of the resolutions recited

that this Convention would the more especially reprobate the *sale* of the public lands, because of its injurious tendency as it affects the interests and independence of the laboring classes, inasmuch as it debars them from the occupation of any portion of the same, unless provided with an amount of capital which the greater portion of them, who would avail themselves of this aid to arrive at personal independence, cannot hope to attain, owing to the many encroachments made upon them through the reduction in the wages of labor consequent upon its surplus quantity in the market, which surplus would be drained off, and a demand for the produce of mechanical labor increased, if these public lands were left open to actual settlers.[1]

But it was Evans, mainly, who gathered these ideas together and framed them into a system. He and his disciple, Lewis Masquerier, worked out the three cardinal points of a natural right: equality, inalienability, individuality.[2] Men have equal rights to land because each man is a unit. This right is inalienable: a man cannot sell or mortgage his natural right to land nor have it taken away from him for debt, any more than he can sell himself or be imprisoned for debt. This right belongs to the individual as such, not to corporations or associations. Here was his criticism of communism and Fourierism. Establish the individual right to the soil, and then men will be free to go into, or stay out of, communities as they please. Association will then be voluntary, not coercive, as Fourierism would make it. Thus did the communistic agrarianism of Thomas Spence and of the Working Men's Party of 1829 filter down into the individualistic idealism of American labor reform in 1844.

When the labor movement broke down with the panic of 1837, Evans retired to a farm in New Jersey, but kept his printing-press. When the labor movement started up again in 1844, he returned to New York and again started his paper, the *Working Man's Advocate*, later changing the name to *Young America*. He and his friends organized a party known as National Reformers, and asked the candidates of all other parties to sign a

[1] *The Man*, Aug. 30, 1834.

[2] Reprinted in Masquerier, "Sociology, or the Reconstruction of Society, Government and Property," New York, 1877, pp. 68 *et seq.* — See "Doc. Hist.," Vol. VII, pp. 289–293.

pledge to vote for a homestead law. If no candidate signed, they placed their own tickets in the field. They printed pamphlets, one of which, "Vote Yourself a Farm," was circulated by the hundred thousand. In 1845 they united with the New England Working Men's Association to call a national convention, which, under the name of the Industrial Congress, held sessions from 1845 to 1856. The one plank in the platform of the New England Working Men's Association had been a demand for a ten-hour law, and the two planks, land reform and ten hours for labor, became the platform of the Industrial Congress. Through the New England Association the Brook Farmers and other Fourierists came into the land-reform movement.

It was in the latter part of 1845 that Greeley began to notice the homestead agitation. In the *Tribune* [1] he wrote an editorial beginning with his recollections of the workingmen's party which he had found fourteen years before when he came to New York. Now, he said, there had come into existence " a new party styled 'National Reformers' composed of like materials and in good part of the same men with the old Working Men's Party." He then describes their scheme of a homestead law and adds :

Its objects are, the securing to every man, as nearly as may be, a chance to work for and earn a living; secondly, the discouragement of land monopoly and speculation, and the creation of a universally land-holding People, such as has not been since the earlier and purer days of the Israelite Commonwealth. . . . Yet we are not prepared to give it our unqualified approval. The consequences of such a change must be immense. . . . We cannot see it lightly condemned and rejected. Will not those journals which have indicated hostility to this project oblige us by

[1] *Weekly Tribune*, Nov. 29, 1845, p. 5, c. 5.

some real discussion of its merits? Calling it " Agrarian," and its advocates " Empire-Club men " and " Butt-Enders " . . . does not satisfy us, nor will it satisfy the people. . . .

Evans, in his *Young America*, commented on this editorial, and especially on Greeley's assertion that the workingmen's measures had not sooner attracted attention because they had been put forth under what he called " unpopular auspices." Evans said :

All reforms are presented under "unpopular auspices," because they are presented by a minority who have wisdom to see and courage to avow the right in the face of unpopularity; and all reforms are pushed ahead by popularity hunters as soon as the pioneers have cleared the way. I do not mean to class the editor of the *Tribune* amongst the popularity hunters, but simply to express a truth called forth by his rather equivocal designation of that enlightened and patriotic body of men who, if the history of this State and Union be ever truly written, will be prominent in it as the "Working Men's Party." [1]

Five months later Greeley definitely committed himself to the workingmen's platform and to the reasoning with which they supported it.

The freedom of the public lands to actual settlers, and the limitation of future acquisitions of land to some reasonable amount, are also measures which seem to us vitally necessary to the ultimate emancipation of labor from thraldom and misery. What is mainly wanted is that each man should have an assured chance to earn, and then an assurance of the just fruits of his labors. We must achieve these results yet; we *can* do it. Every new labor-saving invention is a new argument, an added necessity for it. And, so long as the laboring class must live by working for others, while others are striving to live luxuriously and amass wealth out of the fruits of such labor, so long the abuses and sufferings now complained of must continue to exist or frequently reappear. We must go to the root of the evil.[2]

[1] *Young America*, Nov. 29, 1845.
[2] *Weekly Tribune*, May 2, 1846.

From the date when Greeley took up the measure, it advanced throughout the Northern states by bounds. He used precisely the language and arguments of the *Working Man's Advocate*.

The National Reformers and the Industrial Congress had worked out logically three kinds of legislation corresponding to Evans's three cardinal points of man's natural right to the soil. These were land limitation, based on equality; homestead exemption, based on inalienability; freedom of the public lands, based on individuality.

In order that the rights of all might be equal, the right of each must be limited. For the older states it was proposed that land limitation should take effect only on the death of the owner. Land was not to be inherited in larger quantities than 160 or 320 acres. Wisconsin was the only state in which this measure got as far as a vote in the legislature, that of 1851, where it was carried in the lower house by a majority of two votes, but was defeated on a final vote.[1] The struggle was exciting, and Greeley watched it eagerly. Then he wrote:

Well, this was the first earnest trial to establish a great and salutary principle; it will not be the last. It will yet be carried, and Wisconsin will not need half so many poorhouses in 1900 as she would have required if land limitation had never been thought of.[2]

The measure was brought up in the New York Legislature and was vigorously advocated by Greeley, but without action.

The second kind of legislation, based on man's natural right to the soil, was homestead exemption. Projects of

[1] J. G. Gregory, "Land Limitation, a Wisconsin Episode of 1848 to 1851," *Parkman Club Papers*, Vol. II.

[2] *Tribune*, March 27, 1851.

this class were far more successful than those looking to the limitation of holdings. Exemption legislation swept over all the states, beginning with Wisconsin in 1847,[1] but in mutilated form. The workingmen demanded absolute inalienability for each homestead, as complete as that of the nobility of Europe for each estate. But the laws actually enacted have not prohibited sale or mortgage of the homestead, as Evans proposed. They have merely prohibited levy and execution on account of debts not secured by mortgage. Voluntary alienation is allowed. Coercive alienation is denied. Greeley and the workingmen would have disallowed both.

Freedom of the public lands was the third sort of legislation demanded. Every individual not possessed of 160 acres of land should be free to get his equal share in fee simple out of the public domain without cost. The public domain, it was argued, belongs, not to the states nor to the collective people of all the states nor to the land-owners and taxpayers of the states, but to each individual whose natural right has not as yet been satisfied. America is fortunate in having this vast domain unoccupied. Here all the cardinal points of a natural right can be legalized without damaging vested rights : individuality, by private property without cost; equality, by limitation to 160 acres; inalienability, by homestead exemption. This was the idealistic vision in 1844 of the Republican party's first great act in 1862.

Greeley espoused all of these measures. He himself

---

[1] The legislation of Texas in 1829 and 1837 was entirely different in character and motive. Somewhat similar laws had been adopted in Mississippi, Georgia, Alabama, and Florida prior to 1845 as a result of the panic of 1837.

introduced a homestead bill in Congress in 1848. He urged land limitation and homestead exemption upon the state legislatures. The *Tribune* carried his message throughout the North and prepared the mind of the people for the constructive work of the future.

I might speak of others who helped to carry the workingmen's idealism into Republican reality. I will mention only Galusha A. Grow, the "father of the Republican party," and Alvan E. Bovay, the disciple of Evans.

Galusha Grow's first great speech in Congress, in 1852, on Andrew Johnson's homestead bill, was printed by him under the title " Man's Right to the Soil," and was merely an oratorical transcript from the *Working Man's Advocate*.

The other less distinguished father was Alvan E. Bovay. For him has been claimed the credit of first suggesting to Greeley the name Republican party, and of bringing together under that name the first little group of men from the Whig, Democratic, and Free Soil parties at Ripon, Wisconsin, in 1854.[1] Bovay had moved to Wisconsin in 1850. Before that time he had been associated with Evans and with the workingmen's party in New York, almost from its beginning in 1844. He was secretary, treasurer and delegate to the Industrial Congress. It was in New York that he became acquainted with Greeley. Bovay's speeches were reported at length in the *Working Man's Advocate* and *Young America*, and his letters frequently appeared in the *Tribune*. Whether he was the only father of the

---

[1] Curtis, "History of the Republican Party," Vol. I, p. 173. There were doubtless other spots of independent origin. See A. J. Turner, "Genesis of the Republican Party" (1898; pamphlet).

party or not, it is significant that it was these early views on the natural right to land, derived from Evans and the workingmen, that appeared in the Republican party wherever that party sprang into being. It is also an interesting fact that the workingmen were accustomed to speak of theirs as the true Republican party, and that Evans, in his paper in 1846, predicts that the National Reformers mark the beginning of the period when there "will be but two parties, the great Republican Party of Progress and the little Tory Party of Holdbacks." [1]

Greeley also took up the ten-hour plank of the workingmen's party. Prior to 1845, under the influence of Fourierism, he had opposed labor legislation. In 1844 he had written:

The relations of Labor and Capital present a vast theme, . . . Government cannot intermeddle with them without doing great mischief. They are too delicate, complex and vitally important to be trusted to the clumsy handling of raw and shallow legislators. . . . The evils . . . are Social, not Political, and are to be reached and corrected by Social remedies. . . . Legislation to correct such abuses can seldom do much good and will often do great harm. . . . [2]

His idea of the harmony of interests is seen in his hope that employers would reduce the hours of labor by agreement. "We do hope to see this year," he wrote in 1844, "a general convention of those interested in Factory Labor to fix and declare the proper hours of labor, which all shall respect and abide by. . . ." [3] And when the first Industrial Congress was about to assemble in 1845, he wrote:

[1] *Young America*, March 21, 1846, p. 2, c. 3.
[2] *Tribune*, Jan. 25, 1844, p. 2, c. 1; Feb. 16, 1844, p. 2, c. 2.
[3] *Ibid.*, Feb. 16, 1844, p. 2, c. 1.

An Industrial Congress, composed of representatives of Employers and Workmen, in equal numbers, ought to be assembled, to regulate generally the conditions of Labor. . . .   A general provision, to operate coextensively with the Union, that ten hours shall constitute a day's work, might be adopted without injury to any and with signal benefit to all.   . . .[1]

After the Congress he wrote again :

We should greatly prefer that a satisfactory adjustment were arrived at without invoking the aid of the law-making power, except possibly in behalf of minors.   We believe if the matter is only approached in the right way by those interested, discussed in the proper spirit, and pursued with reasonable earnestness and perseverance, that legislation will be found superfluous. . . . How many hours shall constitute a day's or a week's work should be settled in each department by a general council or congress of all interested therein, whose decision should be morally binding on all and respected by our Courts of Justice.[2]

But, with the failure of the Industrial Congress to bring in the employers, Greeley aggressively adopted the legislative programme of the workingmen and harmonized it with his theory of the protective tariff. Before this he had written :

If it be possible to interpose the power of the State beneficently in the adjustment of the relations of Rich and Poor, it must be evident that internal and not external measures like the Tariff, would be requisite.   A tariff affects the relation of country with country and cannot reasonably be expected to make itself potently felt in the relations of class with class or individual with individuals.[3]

Two years afterward, when New Hampshire had adopted the first ten-hour law and the employers were violating it, he wrote :

[1] *Tribune*, Sept. 30, 1845, p. 2, c. 1.
[2] *Ibid.*, Dec. 27, 1845, p. 4, c. 4.
[3] *Ibid.*, Aug. 2, 1845, p. 3, c. 1.

That the owners and agents of factories should see this whole matter in a different light from that it wears to us, we deem unfortunate but not unnatural. It is hard work to convince most men that a change which they think will take five hundred or a thousand dollars out of their pockets respectively is necessary or desirable. We must exercise charity for the infirmities of poor human nature. But we have regretted to see in two or three of the Whig journals of New Hampshire indications of hostility to the Ten-Hour regulation, which we can hardly believe dictated by the unbiassed judgment of their conductors. . . . What show of argument they contain is of the regular Free Trade stripe, and quite out of place in journals favorable to Protection. Complaints of legislative intermeddling with private concerns and engagements, — vociferations that Labor can take care of itself and needs no help from legislation — that the law of Supply and Demand will adjust this matter, etc., etc., — properly belong to journals of the opposite school. We protest against their unnatural and ill-omened appearance in journals of the true faith. . . . To talk of the Freedom of Labor, the policy of leaving it to make its own bargains, etc., when the fact is that a man who has a family to support and a house hired for the year is told, " If you will work thirteen hours per day, or as many as we think fit, you can stay ; if not, you can have your walking papers : and well you know that no one else hereabout will hire you " — is it not most egregious flummery ? [1]

The foregoing quotations from Greeley depict the evolution of the theory of the protective tariff out of the Whig theory into the Republican theory. The Whig idea was protection for the sake of capital. Greeley's idea was protection for the sake of labor. The Whigs did not approve of Greeley, but his theory was useful in 1840, and in that year they hired him to get out campaign literature. At that time he was a higher idealist, a transcendentalist, a zealot for harmony of interests, and believed that capitalists would voluntarily

[1] *Weekly Tribune*, Sept. 18, 1847, p. 5, c. 2.

coöperate with labor and need not be coerced by legislation. He was disabused of this notion when he saw the way in which employers treated the ten-hour movement. Whatever the workingmen had gained on this point, they had gained against the Whigs, through Jackson, Van Buren and the Democrats. Modifying his faith in harmony of interests, he took up legislation in behalf of class interests and rounded out a theory of labor legislation by the states to supplement protective tariff legislation by Congress. This became the Republican theory of protection in place of the dying Whig theory. True, the Republican party has not always lived up to this theory; but its defection is a further illustration of the American practice of using a theory of human rights to augment property rights. And, after all, it has been the Republican states that have led the way in labor legislation.

I have attempted to sketch the origin and evolution of the two species of idealism that struggled for existence in this epoch of American history. This biology of ideas exhibits both adaptation to, and rejection of, the contemporaneous economic development. The transcendentalism of New England, with its humanized God and its deified man, was rather a protest against, than a product of, the new economic conditions. As the years advanced and industrial anarchy deepened, the protest turned to reconstruction. But the tools and materials for the new structure were not politics and legislation, but an idealized, transcendental workingman. Transcendentalism resurrected man, but not the real man. It remained for the latter, the man in the struggle, to find his own way out. By failure and success, by defeat, by victory often fruitless, he felt along the line of obstacles for the point of least resistance. But he, too, needed a philosophy. Not one that would idealize him, but one that would help him win a victory. Shorter hours of labor, freedom to escape from economic oppression,—these were the needs that he felt. His inalienable " natural right " to life, liberty, land and the products of his own labor,—this was his philosophy. Politics and legislation were his instruments.

It is easy to show that " natural rights " are a myth, but they are a fact of history. It was the workingmen's doctrine of natural rights that enabled the squatter to find an idealistic justification for seizing land and holding it in defiance of law. " Natural right," here as always, was the effective assailant of legal right. Had it not been for this theoretic setting, our land legislation might have been piecemeal and opportunist like the English — merely a temporizing concession to the squatters on account of the difficulty of subduing them by armed force. Such an opportunist view, without the justification of natural rights, could not have aroused enthusiasm nor created a popular movement, nor furnished a platform for a political party. The Republican party was not an anti-slavery party. It was a homestead party. On this point its position was identical with that of the workingmen. Just because slavery could not live on one-hundred-and-sixty-acre farms did the Republican party come into conflict with slavery.

Thus has the idealism of American history both issued from and counteracted its materialism. The editorial columns of the *Tribune* from 1841 to 1854 are its documentary records. There we see the two main currents of idealism passing through the brain of Greeley and coming out a constructive programme for the reorganization of society.

CHAPTER V

ECONOMISTS AND CLASS PARTNERSHIP[1]

THE reason given by President Hadley why the economist should exert more influence in politics is that he represents the nation as a whole, and in the conflict of class interests it is important for social prosperity that there be one class of leaders who will keep in view the permanent welfare of the aggregate. The economist should not descend to be the spokesman of a class, like the politician, but he should retain his position as spokesman of all.

Whatever meaning may be given in practice to this statement, I have no doubt that all economists of standing have guided themselves by a sincere desire to promote the best permanent welfare of society. They would certainly be unworthy the name of *political* economists, and much more unworthy a hearing from the public, if they were not animated by such a desire. And it may turn out that, by a sufficient refinement of the definitions of " economist " and " class," we may reach the point where there will be no difference between our views. But, as it seems to me at present, there is a practical difference which will appear as I proceed.

[1] Discussion at the meeting of the American Economic Association, Dec., 1899, on the annual address of the President of the Association. The topic of President A. H. Hadley's address was "Economic Theory and Political Morality," and the general tenor of the address, as it seemed to me, is indicated in this discussion. Both papers, along with other discussions upon the address, are published in the *Proceedings of the Twelfth Annual Meeting*, pp. 45 ff.

The subject as introduced by President Hadley last year, and as now repeated, brings up the practical question as to the method by which the economist can acquire a positive influence on legislators, judges and executives in the formation and execution of laws.   In his former paper [1] he made the distinction between economists who devote themselves to social theory and the theory of utility and those who devote themselves to the practical questions of current politics.   Economists in our day had lost their influence in politics because they had turned from practical questions to theoretical questions. I take it that we are discussing the same question now. The question is not, what should be the position of the speculative philosopher, but of the practical economist. It is a question of method.

Taking this position, it seems to me quite plain that to have influence he must have the ear either of those who control legislation or of those who are striving to get control.   To do this his doctrines, and especially their practical application, must be in harmony with the interests of one side or the other.   Neither side will consult him on the ground of his claim to represent the nation as a whole.   They consult him because he is the one man who shows to the nation as a whole that the interests of that class are for the permanent interests of the whole.

Class Motives. — It will doubtless be agreed that, if the economist is to have influence, he must strike some dominant motive in the minds of those who listen to him, or he must educate such a motive.   There are two motives which pertain to this question — they may be

[1] " The Relation between Economics and Politics," *Economic Studies*, Vol. IV, No. 1, Feb., 1899.

called the motive of *patriotism* or public spirit, and the motive of *class interest*. These, I take it, are both different from *self-interest*. I would line up these motives along with those distinctions to which President Hadley has called our attention. I should say the motive of patriotism is the motive to promote " the permanent interests of the community," *i.e.* the motive corresponding to his " theory of prosperity." The motive of self-interest is the motive dominant in each of his two cats which struggle for one bird, each of his bosses who compete for one workman. The motive of class interest is midway. It is more than self-interest, because it means that the two bosses or the two cats must combine their forces, must for the time cease their individual struggle, and must join together for common action against another class. Class interest takes a man partly out of himself and gives him the spirit of sympathy and self-sacrifice for the other members of his class against whom he may hitherto have been fighting. Patriotism takes him still further from self-interest — it leads classes and parties to forget class struggles and to join together for common action against a national foe. Foreign war is the extreme case of the patriotic motive. It is found, however, at all times, but is not so spectacular.

All of these motives exist in different proportions in different individuals and in different proportions in the same individual at different times. Which is the most powerful? That depends on circumstances. When there is no national or class struggle at its crisis, then individuals settle back upon their self-interest. If, however, those who have common interests find themselves imposed upon by another class with common interests, then their class interest becomes a more powerful motive than self-interest. As a matter of fact, we find that economists have had their greatest influence at these critical points of class struggle, when they have helped to shape the legislation of a class just acquiring power. (Classical economists, 1805–1845, in England. Protectionist economists in United States, 1840–1900.)

In a free country the patriotic motive is the most powerful of all and dominates all others at periods of national crisis. The reason is because in a free country all classes have an equal share in government, and they feel that the nation is the guardian of all their other interests. If there is class domination, — if one class oppresses others, and the others have given up hope of getting justice and a share in the government, — then class interest or self-interest remains the dominant motive, and they will sullenly see their country defeated by foreigners. (Compare United States with Spain, Great Britain with India.)

Consequently only in those countries where the class struggle is recognized as such, and where the government has been organized in such a way as to give hope of fair play and justice to all the different class interests, is it possible to have this motive of patriotism which looks out for the general welfare. Failure to recognize the class struggle and to make a place for it means despotism of one class over the others. It is to the interest of the dominant class to refuse to recognize this struggle, and the economist who refuses to recognize it is playing into their hands. He is preparing the way for their despotic rule, and that means the crushing out of the spirit of patriotism in the excluded classes. If the economist truly represents society as a whole, he should strive to give the excluded classes a larger and more just legal share in government and industry. In that way he would cultivate the motive of patriotism, which is the motive to which, as the supposed representative of the whole, he must appeal.

Class Representation. — President Hadley has with deep insight connected in this discussion the two institutions of representative government and competition, both of which he asserts have broken down or are in process of disintegration. First, as to representation. I should hold that the break-down of the representative system proceeds from exactly the opposite cause from the one he mentions. It has broken down, not because it represents classes, but because it has ceased to represent classes. At the time of its greatest glory, of which he speaks so highly, representative government was the representation of an exclusive class, the corporations of merchants and manufacturers and the landowners. The wage-earners, numbering three-fourths to four-fifths of the present voters, were excluded, also Catholics, Jews, unbelievers. Such a parliament could indeed come together to confer, compare notes, educate the public and take united action. There are, it seems to me, two fallacies of historical interpretation in President Hadley's account of Parliament and Congress. The first is in seeming to hold that the King was above the party or class system, and the second in holding that representation of localities is identical with representation of classes.

1. He holds that the work of the early parliaments consisted in the creation of a " united public sentiment of the English people," and in rousing them to " resist the extensions of the royal prerogative to which, in the absence of such common action, they must separately

have fallen victims." I agree with this, but I would point out that what Parliament really did was to arouse the middle class and the excluded classes generally to unite against the dominant class, and that dominant class was simply the party of prerogative, or the court party, with the King as its boss. The King was not some *deus ex machina*, but he was one party to the class struggle. He shared his prerogative with his courtiers and defenders, in the form of monopolies, benefices, offices, privileges, tax exemptions, land titles and the like. The excluded parties and classes demanded a share of these privileges, a voice in the government, and they succeeded in the Bill of Rights, which in 1688 gave Parliament a veto on the King. That is, it gave the aristocracy and the corporations of the towns an equal voice with the king in framing laws. It meant the forcible admission of a subordinate class or party into sovereignty through their chosen representatives, and this is what is meant when we say that England was transformed from an absolute monarchy, or a despotism, to a constitutional monarchy. A constitutional government is one that recognizes the existence of antagonistic classes and opens up its framework to the equal influence of the two or three classes in the form of the mutual veto — the King with a veto on Parliament and Parliament with a veto on the King.

2. This brings me to what I consider the second historical fallacy, the assumed identity of representation of localities and representation of classes. When the representative system originated, it was primarily a representation of organized classes, and only secondarily of localities. The merchants' and manufacturers' guilds and corporations of the towns elected their representa-

tives in exactly the same way as a private corporation would now elect its president or attorney. They sent their leading men to Parliament, and if they did not have a member competent they chose an outsider from any part of the kingdom, just as they might choose a lawyer to plead their cause. Indeed, the early parliaments were strictly national conventions of merchants and manufacturers which sent a committee occasionally to the King with petitions, just as similar associations now petition Congress. They finally joined with the similar conventions of smaller land-owners, and the two together forced permanent recognition with a veto on the King, in the form of the House of Commons.

It happened that this representation of organized classes was also a representation of localities. The coincidence was an accident. It was because the suffrage was limited to a single class in each locality. Only the members of the corporations in the towns and the land-owners in the county could vote. Since that time universal suffrage has been adopted on the ground that the wage-earner should be represented. But the result has been simply to throw several antagonistic classes into the same constituency, and require them to elect one man by a majority vote who shall represent them all. This was easy enough when but one class voted by itself. It could then elect its own leading representative man. But to throw antagonistic classes into the same pen and require them to elect one man who should represent all, compels them to elect, not a man who represents a class, but a *compromise* candidate who represents none. The really leading class representatives have enemies in other classes and cannot get a majority. The compromise candidate has no bitter enemies, and he has no enthusiastic friends. He does not stand for principles or convictions. He is simply the tool of the boss. The boss is the man who is shrewd in manipulating these class antagonisms and in selecting those compromise candidates, who can get a majority out of conflicting interests. A system of this kind does not represent classes. It represents localities and irresponsible bosses. A truly representative assembly, framed on the basis of the early parliaments which President Hadley approves, would be one to which the different organized classes elected their own representatives as the older guilds elected their members of Parliament. Let the labor unions, irrespective of locality, come together and elect their members of Congress just as they elect the presidents and secretaries of their unions. They would then elect to Congress such men as Gompers, Sargent, Arthur, Debs and the like. These would be the true representatives of the wage-earning class. Let the bankers elect their representatives by themselves. They would elect men like Gage, J. Pierpont Morgan. Let the trusts elect theirs. They would elect Rockefeller, Carnegie, Havemeyer, Flint, or rather they would elect their great attorneys like Dill, Bourke Cockran, Joseph H. Choate. The railroads would elect Depew; the express companies would elect Platt. The Farmers' Grange would send its president, Aaron Jones; the Farmers' Alliance would send its president, Gardner; the Anti-trust League would send its president, Lockwood; and so on. In such a Congress these various interests might also send economists, men like Gunton, Hadley, Taussig, on one side, and men like Bemis, Ely, Henry George, on the other.

Such an assembly I should call representative in the original historical sense of the word. It would not be exactly suited to modern conditions, because the suffrage has been given to many classes which are not yet organized. But it illustrates the principle of true representation. There would be no compromise representatives. Each class would be represented by its ablest and authenticated spokesmen. There would be no opportunity for a boss behind the scenes, who could himself not get elected, yet who would be able to name the spineless trimmers who now pretend to represent the people.

Such an assembly would throw a very different light upon the question of compromise. As long as class antagonisms really exist, they will assert themselves, and the only alternative is civil war and class domination, or mutual concession. But it is all the difference in the world as to who are the men who make the concessions. It they are the real leaders of the different classes, then we may look for broad-minded, patriotic compromises. For the true leaders of a class must have two leading qualities : they must have tenacity of purpose, but they must also understand the claims of the opposing class. That is, they must be broad-minded and patriotic enough to see that civil war must be avoided, that other classes have rights, and that a point gained now is a new vantage ground for another point in the future. These are the the only kind of men that can permanently lead a class to victories. Labor unions have just such men as their leaders, and so do capitalists, and they are making these compromises every day in industry in the form of " trade agreements." What is needed is a representative assembly which will bring together these leaders with the leaders of all other classes, so that they can make similar compromises in politics.

But, on the other hand, President Hadley is right in criticising the present log-rolling kind of compromises. These are not true compromises.   They are made by men who represent nothing, who have no convictions, no principles, and are simply usurpers who have by their cunning gotten possession of our electoral machinery. Their so-called compromises are only secret dickers. The evil is mainly a mechanical one and requires a readjustment of governmental machinery, similar to that which was made in 1688 by the Bill of Rights, so that all classes will have their actually representative men in legislation.   As long as an economist does not recognize the existence of classes, he will fail to see the need of this readjustment of electoral machinery, which shall represent classes.

Class Competition. — President Hadley has drawn a valid distinction between competition of classes and competition of individuals within a class.   He has asserted that the kind of competition which economists would see perpetuated is that between individuals within a class, by means of which the other classes of society are benefited.   He says that modern civilized communities have so regulated the struggle for existence that third parties are benefited.   This is unquestionably true as far as it goes.   But I would ask, what is meant by the word " community " which he uses?   Is it " society as a whole " that has so regulated competition?   Society has not done so.   On the contrary, it seems to me that the competition of individuals within a class has been forced upon that class by the opposing classes in society. If a class were left to itself, its members would come to an understanding.   They would get rid of competition between themselves and would agree to exploit the other classes in common. Adam Smith says that capitalists are always in a tacit agreement to keep wages down to a minimum.   The way in which competition works seems to be as follows : Members of the same class are in competition with each other.   The weaker are crushed out. The number of competitors becomes smaller and smaller. Finally but one is left.   The entire institution becomes a monopoly.   The head man dominates his own class and dominates all other classes.   This phenomenon has occurred in every social institution.   Feudalism ended in the absolutism of the principal feudal proprietor, and we call the institution an absolute monarchy.   The church ended in the papacy.   Political parties have ended in the concentration of power in the hands of one man, or of the " machine," and we call it " boss " politics.   Business corporations have ended in concentration in the hands of a small number of directors of a monopolized corporation, and we call it a " trust."   The principle is universal.

1. When this monopoly stage of an institution is reached, there are three possible alternatives.   First, progress may stop.   The leaders of the class may hand down their power to successors.   In national government we call this " despotism."   In politics we call it " boss-ism."   In industry President Hadley would perhaps call it " trusteeism."   But it is the same in all.   It is rule by the monopolizing head of a single class, who distributes among his courtiers, supporters and henchmen, the prerogatives of his position, and in this way he attaches them to his interests.

Such a system of absolutism always finds its defenders.   But they always defend it upon the ground that it is the best thing under the circumstances for the nation as a whole. Bossuet was the eloquent court preacher to Louis XIV. He believed in hereditary absolutism. He thought the selfish wills of antagonistic classes could be crushed for the common good only by the absolutism of superior force. But he was a noble and fearless man. He saw that the power to protect was the power to oppress. He preached often on the " duty of kings." He turned to Louis and said, " O, King, use your power easily, for it is given to you of God for the welfare of men. Exercise it with humility. Do not forget justice, for God, who gives you irresponsible power over others, holds you responsible to Him. The greater your power, the more severely will He judge you at the last day."

I can understand such an attitude of mind. I can understand how the modern economist who sees that our representative government has broken down and has fallen into the hands of bosses; who sees that we are compelled to govern 10,000,000 Asiatics without their consent and without giving them a share in our government; who sees that the voters in our cities are better governed by Platt and Croker than by themselves; who sees also that our competitive system has broken down; that the managers of our great monopolies have become " trustees " in more than the " accidental application of this word," and that " they are able if they please to misuse this power to the detriment of others without being immediately overtaken by any legal or commercial penalty "; I can see how the modern economist who sees these new developments without seeing any democratic solution for them, should in a noble and fearless spirit become court preacher to the political bosses and the irresponsible trustees. He says to them : " Natural selec-

tion has preserved you as the survival of the fittest.   It
has given these Asiatics, these workingmen and farmers,
into your keeping.   Remember your position is one of
trust.   You are free from competitors.   There is no
legal penalty for abuse of power.   You are not responsible
to them.   I do not know what God will do in the matter.
But anyhow, be good to them.   Show them sympathy
and justice.   If you do not, I shall denounce you."

Now, in speaking thus I admit that I exaggerate the
position of President Hadley, as he views it.   But I see
no other outcome of his position, and in a question of
this kind we are all to be judged by the practical outcome of our teaching.[1]   I have no doubt that an economist who takes this position will accomplish great good
for society as a whole.   He will have an influence in
politics.   But notice that he will shut out from political
influence all the economists who do not have the ear of the
bosses and the trusts.   He is the defender of the institutions by which these men have gained power.   As such
he has their ear.   But he makes a distinction between
the good man and the bad man who possesses the power,
between their good and bad use of their power.[2]   As such
he is their needed critic.   But other economists who do
not indorse the necessity of absolutism or trusteeism, if
they are to have political influence, must get it through

[1] Since this was written, Mr. Baer, spokesman of the anthracite
railroads, is reported to have answered an inquirer: "I beg of you not
to be discouraged.   The rights and interests of the laboring man will be
protected and cared for, not by the labor agitators, but by the Christian
men to whom God in His infinite wisdom has given the control of the
property interests of the country."   See *Independent*, Aug. 28, 1902,
p. 2043.

[2] It will be noted that, since this was written, President Roosevelt
has clearly distinguished between good trusts and bad trusts in much
the pastoral spirit of Bossuet and Hadley.

those classes which resist these absolutist institutions.　If they can show that there is another solution to the problem, if they can show that there is a safe and rational method by which these excluded classes can share in the control of these institutions and by which the prosperity of the whole will be at the same time promoted, then the other classes will take up their arguments and will use them as the social justification of their class struggle.

In doing this, the other economists will also have an opportunity to emphasize the interests of the permanent welfare of society as paramount to class interest.　But the best work of both sets of economists as preachers of social morality will be done when they preach to their own class.　As long as their economic arguments are used in the main to justify one class against the others, the others will resent their moral exhortations as impertinent and hypocritical.

I said that there are two different methods by which the excluded classes can attack the privileged classes in their privileges.　One is by breaking down the monopolies and exclusive privileges of the dominant class and forcing admission for the *individual members* of their own class.　The other is by forcing admission as an *organized class*, through their representatives, into partnership with the monopolist and sharing with him by means of a mutual veto the government of the monopolized institution.

2. The former was the method advocated by Adam Smith.　Smith was the radical economist of his time. President Hadley says of Smith that " by showing the efficiency of competition as a regulator of prices and an increase of useful production, he furnished a powerful defence of the existing social order."　This is doubtless

a prophetic use of the term " existing." If Adam Smith defended the existing social order, it was existing *in posse* and not *in esse*. From beginning to end he attacked the ancient existing privileges of the dominant classes in English politics. These were two classes of what were really hereditary aristocracies. They were the corporations, or guilds, of merchants and manufacturers in the towns, and the landed aristocracy in the counties. The privileges and monopolies which he attacked were found in the laws which they had enacted for their own protection. These were the protective tariffs, bounties on exportation of corn, the statutes of apprenticeship, laws of settlement, laws against combinations of laborers and capitalists, the exclusive privileges of what he called " corporations, trades, crafts and mysteries," and the majority rule of these corporations by which they tied the hands of the minority. In making this attack, Adam Smith furnished the arguments by which the capitalist class was able to enlist the laborers and all the excluded classes in a successful attack on the existing dominant classes. The result was that the monopolies of the dominant classes were broken down by the attack of the excluded classes. Competition was henceforth forced upon the members of the dominant class, and, not only this, but the capitalist class secured admission to these privileged ranks on equal terms of competition. Thus the competition between individuals of one class for the benefit of society as a whole was itself the great aim and chief result of a class struggle. Had the subordinate class not been successful, then industry would have petrified in an hereditary caste system, as in India, and there would have been no prosperity of the whole.

3. The other method of democratizing an institution is to get admission as an organized class. This was done by the aristocracy and middle classes in the revolution of 1688 in the case of the national government, wherein Parliament was given a veto on the King, and all laws had to be henceforth approved equally by the King, the Lords and the Commons. This method is necessary where the monopoly cannot be abolished. Adam Smith was able to show how exclusive privileges could be done away with altogether. It was not so with the institution of government, which had to remain a monopoly and could not go back to feudalism.

We are in a similar position to-day respecting trusts and political parties. If these two kinds of monopolies can be abolished, then there ought to be economists who will show how to do it. The monopoly in politics, or bossism, may possibly be abolished by direct legislation or by proportional representation. If it cannot be abolished, then there will come laws like the Primary Reform laws recently enacted in several states, where the rank and file are legally admitted to a vote in the election of the boss. In the case of trusts, if they cannot be abolished, then the other remedy is to give the people a voice in electing the trustees. How this can be done, which method is suitable to different cases, are matters for economists to discover. Only those will attempt the discovery who see the need; that is, those who on the whole feel that the welfare of society will be best promoted by uniting the excluded classes for an attack on the privileged classes.

That this points to a radical difference between President Hadley's position and mine, and that our contention is not merely one of words, nor is it an obverse and reverse statement of the same position, is shown by the practical conclusions drawn. While he holds that there is but one form of government, namely, government by the boss of an institution controlled by such public opinion as the leading thinkers and preachers can bring to bear, I hold that there is another possible form, namely, government by the different interests and classes which hitherto were subject to the boss. This also is controlled more or less by public opinion, but it is essentially different from the former. If we must wait for public opinion, led by economists and social moralists, to control the bosses in industry and politics, then we are only waiting for a harsh despotism to become a paternal despotism. But if we recognize the social classes which are struggling for a share in these despotisms, then we can look forward, not to a persistent absolutism, but to a democratic government of industry and politics, where the subordinate and excluded classes gain a *legal* control over their rulers and are not forced to content themselves with the vagueness of merely *moral* control by public opinion. In other words, failure to recognize social classes means paternalism based on the survival of the strongest; while recognition of social classes means self-government based on legalized justice between classes.

I believe that the economist in working through social classes is working through the greatest of social forces. Class struggles are a condition that make for progress, and their absence indicates stagnation. At the same time, the economist does not represent a social class in the way that the lawyer, the labor leader or the politician does. He does not depend upon the class for election. He chooses his own ground. He is a pioneer.

He begins from the social standpoint, and works to the class standpoint. He sees that social classes are not permanent divisions in society. They are historical categories. They are temporary and shifting. They give way to new divisions. For this reason the economist may even create a class. At least he often unites different classes. This Adam Smith did. The later economists who followed Smith, like James Mill, Senior, Fawcett, were more closely allied to the capitalist class, because they attacked both the aristocracy and the laborers; and they were the economists who have had the strongest influence on politics, for they directly aided in abolishing the protective restrictions and poor laws of the aristocracy.

But Smith had not distinguished clearly between capitalist and laborer. At his time their interests had much in common, and he was able to show this and to bring them together. But he did not represent the nation as a whole. He did not represent the aristocratic classes. He attacked them. It may be said that he believed they stood in the way of the nation as a whole, and must therefore be sacrificed for the good of all. If that be so, I cannot see how he can be said to have represented them. They believed that they also stood for the good of the nation, and they resented any claim on his part to speak for them. To the aristocrats actually in the struggle it appeared that they were to be sacrificed for the good of upstart capitalists and the destruction of England. It remained for the succeeding century to answer positively as to which class was right. Adam Smith doubtless was honest, but so were the defenders of the existing order. In fact, they had prestige and history back of them, while he had only his arguments. He was not bitter nor partisan; he was only philosophical. But for this very reason he was compelled to see that the economic institutions of his time were framed in the interest of the dominant classes, and that these classes were but a part of, and actually stood in the way of, the nation as a whole.

As economists I believe we would stand on safer ground if, when our conclusions lead us to champion the cause of a class, or of a group of classes, or to expose another class, we should come squarely out and admit that it is so; not because the class interest is foremost in our minds, but because the class is the temporary means of bringing about the permanent welfare of all. We doubtless should always be guided by an honest striving for the welfare of all. We should never be blindly bigoted nor partisan nor committed irrevocably to a class position, with its bad as well as its good. We should be broadminded like Adam Smith. But we should admit that we differ among ourselves, and that our fundamental differences coincide in general with class antagonism in society. We are a part of the social situation. History alone will decide between us. Our present vision is limited. For this reason we ought to acknowledge that no one man is great enough and good enough to stand solely and at all times in practical politics for the nation as a whole, but that all men in a free republic are also moved by the same spirit of patriotism. We ought to acknowledge that the nation as a whole is represented by the accredited representatives of all classes; that no man can honestly represent a class in which he does not believe. It is out of the combined result of public-spirited men contending for their own convictions and authorized to speak for others whose convictions are the same, and who are capable of making concessions in the true interest of all, that all of society is truly represented. Not the individual economist, but the *associated economists*, represent the permanent interests of the nation as a whole.

CHAPTER VI

CLASS CONFLICT

Is it Growing in America, and is it Inevitable? [1]

THE present-day significance of the term " class conflict " is found in the apparent antagonism of employing
and wage-earning classes. There are other interests
that might be described as economic classes, but their
opposition does not lead to outbreak. Their differences
are compromised under forms of constitutional government. But a strike is incipient rebellion. It might go
to the limit of a general stoppage of industry, as it has
done in Belgium and Australia. Whether limited or
general, it is the revolt of a practically unpropertied class
against property rights. It is a kind of class conflict
not yet obviated by our forms of government, like the
contests of other classes or interests.

As nearly as I can make out from the census of the
United States, of the 24,000,000 men and boys engaged
in industry, 6,000,000 are farmers and tenants, 3,750,000
are farm laborers, 11,000,000 are other laborers, clerks,
and servants, 1,500,000 are professional and agent classes,
and 2,000,000 are other employers. There is no appreciable class conflict between farmers, tenants and farm
laborers. Over one-half of the laborers are sons of the

[1] Discussion before the American Sociological Society, Dec., 1906,
and published in the *American Journal of Sociology*, May, 1908, pp.
169–196. The syndicalist, or I. W. W. movement, was not in evidence
at that time, but it seems to justify some of the predictions.

farmers, destined to pass up into their fathers' position or out into other classes. The tenants are small contractors, interested more in prices and profits than they are in wages. The professional and agent classes are disinterested, or else interested in the classes to whom they cater. The field for a class conflict is the 11,000,000 other laborers and servants and the 2,000,000 employers.

But not all of these are in a position to provoke class feeling. In the thousands of small towns and villages the employer or the merchant and his help do the same kind of work side by side, and they have close personal relations, often that of father and son, like the farmers. The servants are individually attached to individuals of other classes. Many thousands of apparent laborers, like teamsters and pedlers, are also small capitalists. At the outside guess, not more than 6,000,000 wage-earners, and 1,500,000 employers and investors, are in the field where classes are forming. Two-thirds of the voting population are spectators. We call them the public. They may be forced to take sides, but they want fair play. The outcome depends on the way they are brought in.

While therefore only one-third are available for class conflict, yet they operate fundamental industries of our civilization, like railways and coal mines, or they command strategic points, like cities, the centres of population. Their importance is greater than their numbers.

Now, it must be noted that within this third of the population enormous industrial changes are going on. These tend to intensify the class conflict, but for the time being conceal it. The principal changes are the growth of corporations on the employers' side and the division of labor on the wage-workers' side. That corporations break down the personal ties that formerly held together the employer and his men has long been recognized, but this incidental effect is insignificant compared with the direct effect of the consolidated corporations and syndicates of the past ten years. By combining several corporations into one, by operating several establishments of the same kind in different parts of the country, by placing them all on a uniform system of accounting which shows at a glance every month the minutest detail of every item of cost, the modern trust is going further to alienate classes than did the simple corporation when it displaced the individual employer. The primitive competition of employer against employer is a children's game compared with the modern competition of manager against manager checked up every month by the cold statistics of cost. Under this system managers go down like tenpins, or up like Schwab. They "hire and fire" their employees, promote and derate their subordinates, with the precision of rapid-fire guns. Under their exact system of costs they measure a man as they do coal, iron and kilowatts, and labor becomes literally, what it has been by analogy, a commodity. If one be a scientist or an engineer one can but admire the marvellous results. The astounding reductions of cost, the unheard-of efficiency of labor, the precise methods of scientific experiment and tests, reveal a new field of conquest of the human mind. But if one talks with the workmen at their homes, one hears the grumblings of class struggle.

The system is perfected by the division of labor. Formerly a workman's efficiency consisted of two things, skill and speed. Division of labor has split up his skill into its constituent operations, and the progress of cost-keeping is carrying the analysis further than ever before.

Instead of the skill of one man, we have the grading of operations among a gang of men. Skill had to be measured by quality, by intelligence, by ingenuity, versatility and interest in his work. These human qualities are elusive and not yet measured even by modern psychology. But speed can be measured by quantity and a clock. Workmen now can be compared with each other and metered up like dynamos. The rise and fall of their energy each hour or day can be charted and filed away in a card catalogue for reference.

Immediately there follows a new science and art of industrial psychology. The efficiency of a steam engine is kept always at its maximum by feeding the coal with an automatic stoker. So the output of labor is kept at the top by adjusting the pay exactly to the motive and capacity. This is done by premiums and bonuses on output, instead of the cruder and more wasteful methods of paying the same price for every piece, and these premiums are nicely figured to the point where the workman will put out the maximum exertion for the minimum bonus. The psychology of the workman is analyzed and experimented upon as accurately as the chemistry of the different kinds of coal. A time-keeping department is created for this purpose, with experts, card records and a testing laboratory, and a new engineering profession springs up with industrial psychology as its underlying science. Wonderful and interesting are these advances in harnessing the forces of human nature to the production of wealth. The pioneers in this field, calling themselves " production engineers," may well be compared with the great inventors of the turbine and the dynamo in what they are doing to reduce cost and multiply efficiency.

But in doing so they are doing exactly the thing that forces labor to become *class*-conscious. While a man retains individuality, he is more or less proof against class feeling. He is *self*-conscious. His individuality protects him somewhat against the substitution of some one else to do his job. But when his individuality is scientifically measured off in aliquot parts and each part is threatened with substitution by identical parts of other men, then his sense of superiority is gone. He and his fellow-workmen compete with each other, not as whole men, but as units of output. The less-gifted man becomes a menace to the more gifted as much as the one to the other. Both are then ripe to recognize their solidarity, and to agree not to compete. And this is the essential thing in class conflict.

But it is significant to note that in the industries where the conditions described have gone farthest, there the class conflict is least apparent. Of the 6,000,000 wage-earners mentioned, possibly 2,000,000 are organized in unions. But the unions have practically disappeared from the trusts, and are disappearing from the large corporations as they grow large enough to specialize minutely their labor. The organized workmen are found in the small establishments like the building trades, or in the fringe of independents on the skirts of the trusts; on the railways, where skill and responsibility are not yet displaced by division of labor; in the mines, where strike-breakers cannot be shipped in; on the docks and other places, where they hold a strategic position. While the number of organized workmen shows an increase in these directions, it shows a decrease in the others. It is in these organized industries that the class conflict appears, and there the lines are drawing tighter. It is there that employers' associations are forcing employers into line and are struggling to do for the medium employer what the trust does without an association. But most of the unions in question are not unions of a class. They are unions of a trade or a strategic occupation. On the railroads they cater only to a third or a fourth of all railroad employees. They represent for the most part the first stage in the class struggle — that of the skilled workmen protecting themselves through apprenticeship against the inroads of unskilled. Other unions like the shoe-makers and mine-workers represent the second stage, that of an industrial class including all occupations. The first stage has been driven out of the trust; the second stage has not arrived.

And it does not seem likely, where a corporation has reached the position of a trust, that unionism will get a footing, no matter how class-conscious the workmen have become. The very division of labor, which tends towards class solidarity, offers means to circumvent it. It need not be repeated that a potent reason for the persistent class conflict of the past twenty years is the closing up of the great outlet for agitators, the frontier. But the division of labor offers a substitute outlet in the form of promotion. Promotion, where speed is the standard, has rich possibilities compared with old forms of promotion based on skill. Under the older forms workmen came into the various skilled trades by several side entrances of apprenticeship, and each trade had its narrow limits upward. Under the newer forms the workmen nearly all come in at the bottom, and the occupations are graded by easy steps all the way to the top. The ambitious workman advances rapidly, and with every step his rate of pay increases and his work gets easier. But he remains all the time a part of the gang, and his earnings depend on the exertions of those below him. As he approaches the head of his gang, he has the double job of a man who gets wages as a workman and profits on his fellow-workmen. He begins to be paid both for his work and for making others work. Quite generally it will be found that the head men of a gang are paid disproportionately high for the skill they are supposed to have. The difference is a payment, not for mechanical skill, but for loyalty. They keep their fellows up to the highest pitch of exertion, and they stand by the company in times of discontent. Their promotion is not a mere outlet for agitation — it is a lid on the agitation of others.

But there is still further room for promotion, when the workman becomes a foreman, superintendent or manager. Here he ceases manual work and keeps others at work. He gets a salary, often a bonus or a share in the profits, depending for its amount upon the work of his former fellows. Thus it is that a wise system of promotions becomes another branch of industrial psychology. If scientifically managed, as is done by the great corporations, it produces a steady evaporation of class feeling. I have often come upon fiery socialists and ardent trade unionists thus transformed and vaporized by this elevating process.

In some industries, like railroads and others, the straight line of promotion is as yet obstructed by cross trade lines, and it might seem that the situation is different from that herein described. In such cases a skilled trade or two, like the locomotive engineers, may be found which is organized and recognized by the employer on apparent class lines. But the situation is not essentially different. The true class conflict is really for the time prevented by elevating a strategic fraction of the class instead of promoting individuals. It is this kind of fractional organization, as already mentioned, that has been gradually eliminated from other industries with the growth of corporations and the division of labor.

Another line of promotion quite potent in drawing off leaders is politics. Class conflict in America is less persistent than in England and Europe, because the leaders find an outlet in salaried political jobs when the burden of agitation grows tiresome. If civil-service reform continues to make progress, this outlet, like free land, will gradually close, and the class struggle will become more intense.

While promotion at the top weakens class solidarity, immigration and women's labor at the bottom undermine it. Race divisions and their accompaniment, religious divisions, are injected, and to the inducement offered by way of promotion to exploit their fellows is added race antipathy toward those exploited. The peculiarity of class conflict is its occurrence within the dominant race. The bitterest class struggle now going on in America is that of the Western Federation of Miners, the most purely American of trade unions. In places where that union has been defeated the employers are bringing in the Italians and the Slavs, and the struggle is as much a defence against immigrants as an aggression on capital. In other industries like iron and steel, where the non-English foreigner is two-thirds of the force, those English-speaking workmen who have not been driven out have been promoted up to the higher positions, and both their race aversion and their superior jobs hold them aloof. In the iron mines of Minnesota, unlike the gold, silver and copper mines of the Rockies, the Western Federation meets greater difficulty in organizing the Americans than in organizing the immigrants. In still other industries, like the coal mines, where the immigrants are more Americanized and the Americans have not escaped their competition by promotion, race and religion have been fused and an economic class has emerged. Thus immigration has a threefold effect. At first it intensifies the conflict of classes in the dominant race. Next it shatters class solidarity. Finally, when the immigrants and their children are Americanized and promoted, they renew the class alignment. While immigration continues in great volume, class lines will be forming and re-forming, weak and unstable. To prohibit or greatly restrict immigration would bring forth class conflict within a generation.

The foregoing are some of the complex industrial conditions which must be taken into account in estimating the prospects of class conflict in America. There remains to be considered the question of politics. Class conflict inevitably compels the government to take a hand. The executive calls out the police, the militia and the army. The judiciary enjoins the strikers and orders the arrest and commitment of the leaders. The struggle terminates in favor of the side that controls the policy of these branches of government. Whether we like it or not, each side reaches out to get control. The contest is shifted to the field of practical politics. Here the great third party, the two-thirds of the voters, is sooner or later brought in. As long as organized labor can win by strikes or negotiation, it rejects the

political weapon. When strikes begin to fail and negotiation is fruitless, it turns to the elections. But strikes
are successful mainly in the early stages when employers
have not learned the tactics of organization. After
they have perfected their associations, after these associations have federated, and especially after employers
have consolidated in great corporations and trusts, their
capacity for united action exceeds that of organized
labor. Their tactics are directed, not so much toward
winning in strikes as toward preventing strikes and
disintegrating unions. By wise promotions, by watchful
detectives, by prompt discharge of agitators, by an all-
round increase of wages when agitation is active on the
outside, by a reduction only when the menace has passed
or when work is slack, by shutting down a plant where
unionism is taking root and throwing orders to other
plants, by establishing the so-called " open shop,"
— these and other masterful stratagems set up a problem quite different from what unionism has heretofore
met. It does not seem possible under such conditions
that organization will get a footing in the great consolidated industries. The only possibility appears to be
that in the event of some widespread social unrest or
depression of trade, the thousands of these employees
throughout the country will suddenly quit work, on the
impulse and without prior organization or concerted
action. Such an unlikely revolution would quickly end
in submission.

Neither does it seem possible that these thousands of
employees will turn to a socialist party. This is not
because they are not ripening for socialism. Nothing
is more surprising than the numbers of well-paid men
employed by the trusts and great corporations who say

in confidence that they are socialists. It is not their wages of which they complain, but the long hours, the intense speed and exertion, the two shifts of 12 hours six or seven days in the week, the Sunday labor sometimes continuing twenty-four hours in succession when the day and night shifts change. Their physical exhaustion and continuous work nullify the enjoyment of their good wages. But the very reasons that keep them from unionizing keep them from voting or discussing. They distrust politics, they think the socialist party has no chance, they are not willing to lose their jobs, they are in the minority, and the great mass of their fellow-workmen have but little time and strength to think and talk of anything except the gossip of their daily work. I do not look for a socialist party to recruit these voters — I look for a demagogue.

If we may judge from what has happened in two other English-speaking nations, Australia and Great Britain, a labor party may be expected. In Australia this party followed upon a series of widespread and disastrous strikes. In Great Britain it followed a supreme court decision that jeopardized the funds of trade unions. But a party formed on class lines cannot enlist more recruits than there are in the class. In this case, at the outside, it is one-third of the voters. Whether a socialist or labor party shall ever be able to reach even this number, depends on the attitude taken by the other two-thirds. If they demand fair play, and if they are able to enforce their demand, a class party will not attract even its own class. More inspiring to the ordinary man than the struggle for class advantage is the instinct of justice. But justice is not merely fair play between individuals, as our legal philosophy would have it, — it is fair play between social classes. The great constitutional safeguards which we have asserted since the time of Magna Charta have been adopted in order to place a subordinate class on an equilibrium with a dominant class. It is in this way that trial by jury has had to be reasserted whenever a new social class has emerged. And it is partly by restoring trial by jury that the great third class, the public, is now beginning to assert its right to hold the balance between two struggling classes. This beginning may be seen in the new constitution framed by the farmers of Oklahoma.

Class conflict may be growing, but it is not inevitable if this third class, which is not a class, is able to determine directly the issues. There are, indeed, serious obstacles in the way. The principal one is political. Between the public and the expression of its will are the political party, the party machine, and a legislature, executive and judges selected by these intruders. Here is a backstairs for manipulation, corruption and class legislation. But the public at large is too big and too exposed for the wire-pulling of classes. And it does not consent that one class shall have an advantage over another. It does not favor either radicals or reactionaries. When the public shall have more direct means of expressing its will, through direct nominations, direct election, initiative or referendum, then we may expect class conflict to subside. The class war in Colorado broke out because the legislature refused to carry out the will of the people as expressed in a constitutional amendment. A popular verdict may not always be just, but it insures non-resistance. It is not so much abstract justice that satisfies individuals and classes, as confidence in a full hearing, a fair trial and honest execution of the verdict. If these are guaranteed, the issue may be brought up again. Class antagonism will not disappear as long as there is wealth to distribute, but it can be transferred to the jury of the people. Then we may expect social classes to state their case in the open and to wait on the gradual process of education rather than plunge into battle.

I do not hold that this third class is disinterested and that its will is always right. Economically it stands apart as a class of consumers. It is interested directly in low prices for the products it purchases. The existing widespread movement for the regulation of corporations is a movement for reducing monopoly prices. If it is carried through, the consumers will be conciliated and satisfied. But they will be satisfied on the basis of existing wages, hours and conditions of labor. A movement of wage-earners for larger wages and shorter hours will then meet their hostility as well as that of the immediate employers. If the regulation of corporations on behalf of consumers is not accompanied with regulation on behalf of employees, the class conflict may become more intense and difficult. Time is the essence of prevention. It is not merely blind economic evolution that provokes economic classes into existence. It is class legislation in the past. The protective tariff has appealed to wage-earners and the public on behalf of manufacturers, but it has contained no provision, like that in the Australian tariff, by which the profits of the tariff should be shared with wage-earners. It has been left to them to get what they could by trade unions. With such an example of class legislation before them it is not surprising that, when unions are crushed by the great tariff-protected trusts, then the wage-earners should think of socialism. But it does not follow that the tariff should be abolished. It follows that when it is revised it should provide means to pass the protection along to the wage-earners as well as conciliate the consumers.

Other lines of legislation might be mentioned, which would tend to place social classes on an equilibrium. Whether they do so or not depends on whether they come before the whole people soon enough, on their merits and without the intermediary of political machinery. If this occurs, then no one class or part of a class will be big enough to swing all the voters. Like the waves on the ocean it may move up and down, but it comes back to the level of the massive bulk beneath.

CHAPTER VII

THE UNION SHOP[1]

THE open-shop controversy, in its extreme form, is peculiar to America. The British labor delegates, two years ago, were surprised to see the bitterness of the American unionist toward the " scab." This feeling has its roots in conditions and history peculiar to this country. For three generations the American working-man has been taught that the nation was deeply concerned in maintaining for him a high standard of living. Free traders objected that manufacturers would not pay higher wages, even if protected. Horace Greeley, who, as much as any other man, commended the " American System " to wage-earners, admitted the force of the objection, but he held that socialism, or, as he called it, " association," would share the benefits of the tariff with them. But this must come through the workmen themselves. Some of them tried it. The communistic experiments failed. They tried coöperation, education, politics. Neither did these seem to reach the high aims of protection. Meanwhile they were discovering the power of the strike. By this kind of association those who could hold together found themselves actually sharing the benefits of protection which Greeley mistakenly predicted for his fantastic kind of association.

[1] Address before the American Economic Association, Dec., 1904, and published in the *Proceedings*. Since that time, the "preferential union shop," so ingeniously contrived by Louis D. Brandeis for the needle trades of New York, has given practical force to the distinctions here noted between "closed shop," "open shop" and "union shop."

But the gains from strikes were temporary. The federal laws which protected manufacturers against the products of foreign labor permitted them to import the foreigners themselves. In many cases strikes were defeated by the immigrants, and in many more cases the immigrants went into the shops to share the gains won by the strikers, or gradually to displace them with their lower standards of living. With a unanimity never before shown, the unions entered the political field and got the Chinese exclusion acts and the alien contract labor laws. These theoretically rounded out the tariff system, and they somewhat lessened the pressure on the skilled trades. But the amount of immigration itself was not lessened. Rather have the laws been evaded, and the influx has swollen greater than before, while the sources have shifted to still lower standards of life. By a minute division of labor and nearly automatic machinery unknown in any other country, the skilled trades were split into simple operations and places created for the unskilled immigrants. The strike thus seemed likely to lose permanent results. The unions were unable in politics further to check immigration. Indorsing the tariff on products as a necessary first step, they were left to enact their own tariff on labor. The sympathies of the American public were with them, but these sympathies, lacking the historical sense, have recently somewhat declined, when it is found that the union theory is that of protection and not that of free trade. The British unions are protected by long periods of apprenticeship. The non-unionist is only another Englishman who can be talked to, and whose class feelings are strong and identical with those of the unionist. The employers are not protected by a tariff, neither have they imported foreign workmen. Division of labor is not minute, and the skilled workman is not directly menaced by the unskilled. But the American unions have very little industrial or racial protection. Apprenticeship is gone, except as enforced by them against the protests of employers. In order to enforce this and other measures needed to keep wages above the market rate, the unions found themselves compelled to enforce the rule that no one should enter the shop except through the union. Without this rule their efforts were nullified.

It naturally is objected that, in comparing the closed shop with the tariff, a corollary cannot be drawn from the laws enacted by government to the rules imposed by a union. The presumption is in favor of free trade, and only the sovereign power has the right to interfere, and that in the general interest. Where private associations restrict competition, the act becomes conspiracy. But here the unions found that public sympathy and judicial decision have made an exception in their favor. While a combination to put up prices is illegal, a combination to put up wages was gradually relieved of legal penalty. It was felt that the laborer was the weaker party to the bargain; that the same public policy which would keep down prices to the level of domestic competition would encourage the laborer to keep wages above the level of immigrant competition. Capital could take care of itself, and the capitalist who failed in competition would only drop into the ranks of wage-earners, but the laborer who failed had no place lower to drop. Consequently, while, on the one hand, the doctrine of protection to manufactures was gaining hold, on the other hand, its corollary, the exemption of labor from the conspiracy laws, was being established.

Some decisions went even further. Granting that it is not criminal conspiracy to quit work in a body in order to benefit their own members, it is not easy to draw the line at quitting work in a body to secure the discharge of a foreman or a non-unionist whose acts are injurious to the members. Though the decisions here are conflicting, yet there were early decisions sustaining this right, and so essential is it to their existence and so persistently have the unions asserted it, that, amidst conflicting decisions, many of them have established the union shop. Here the logic of politics has been with them, and the politicians have been more consistent than the manufacturers, for the high wages to which protection campaigners point are usually wages kept high by a closed-shop policy. Even the wages in unprotected industries like the building trades, which depend mainly on the closed shop, are offered as evidence of protection's benefits, while in the protected industries it is the closed-shop wages of tin-plate workers, moulders, blacksmiths, etc., and not the open-shop wage of woollen and cotton textiles, to which attention is directed.[1]

A curious flank movement has taken place in the use of the terms " closed " and " open " shop. As the unions originally employed the terms, a closed shop was one which was boycotted or on strike, and in which consequently the union forbade its members to work. An open shop was one where union men were permitted by the union to get employment if they could. To declare a shop open was equivalent to calling off a strike

[1] *Republican Campaign Text-Book*, 1904, pp. 86, 91, 223 *et seq.*

and boycott. The terms as now defined are different. The closed shop, instead of being non-union, is the union shop. And the open shop is declared open by the employer to admit non-unionists, and not by the union to unionists.

Yet, even from this new standpoint, the terms are not clearly distinguished. Many employers have what they call open shops, and yet they employ only union men. The union would say that these are union shops, whereas the public generally would call them closed.

The confusion arises from different points of view. The employer has in mind the contract or trade agreement with the union. He looks at it from the legal or contractual side. The union has in mind the actual situation in the shop. They look at it from the side of practical results. The agreements made in the stove industry, in bituminous coal mining, in three-fourths of the team-driving agreements, in railway machine shops and many others, are plainly open-shop agreements, where it is often even stipulated that the employer has the right to employ and discharge whomsoever he sees fit, only reserving that he shall not discriminate on account of union membership or union activity. Many agreements are silent on the question of employment and discharge, and in such cases the presumption is in favor of the employer's freedom in selecting his men.

It is evident that with these different points of view it is difficult to reach an understanding. Clearness would be promoted by adopting a use of terms which would bring out the above distinctions as they are found in practice. In doing so the closed shop would be viewed from the side of the contract, and would be designated as one which is closed against the non-unionist by a formal agreement with the union; the open shop as one, where, as far as the agreement is concerned, the employer is free to hire union or non-union men; the union shop as one where, irrespective of the agreement, the employer, as a matter of fact, has only union men. Thus an open shop, according to agreement, might in practice be a union shop, a mixed-shop or even a non-union shop. The closed shop would, of course, be a union shop, but the union shop might be either closed or open.[1]

The contention of some union defenders that the term " closed shop " is a misnomer, I do not agree with, if its use is limited as here proposed. They say it is not closed, because any competent man can get into it by joining the union. What they really mean is that the union is an open union, but this is another question, and an important one. Much can be said for a closed shop if the union is open, but a closed shop with a closed union cannot be defended. The use of terms above proposed makes it possible to draw these essential distinctions and to discuss each separate question of fact by itself and on its merits.

The historical steps were somewhat as follows. First, the union got the union shop by quitting work, or threatening to quit, in a body. Next they got the closed shop by a contract with the employer. If the employer would not make a closed-shop agreement, they either retained their original right to quit if he hired a non-unionist, or their open-shop agreement provided for negotiation whenever a non-unionist became

[1] The "preferential union shop," of the needle trades, works out a union shop.

obnoxious. In this way the open-shop agreement might mean, in individual cases, the union shop in practice.

Now the significant fact respecting the agreements just mentioned in the coal, stove foundry, railway shops and other industries, is that, while they are open-shop agreements, they are, on the whole, satisfactory to unions which in other branches of their work are most uncompromising for the closed shop. In all cases their satisfaction is based on three or four considerations. In the first place, the agreement is made, not with each shop, but with an association of employers, including the strongest competitors in the industry. It is to the interest of such an association to require all of its members faithfully to observe the agreement, because it places them all on the same competitive level as far as wages are concerned. The employer who would violate the agreement would get an advantage over the others in the largest item of his expenses. This the others, in self-interest, cannot permit, and consequently as long as he is a member of the employers' association, the union is relieved of the burden of enforcing the agreement, and the employers themselves, as a body, assume the responsibility of doing what the union could do only by means of the closed shop or the strike. If the employer persists in violating the agreement after his association has exhausted its powers of discipline, he is expelled, and then, being no longer protected by his fellow-employers, he is left to the tactics of the union.

In the second place, the agreement is made, not only for members of the union, but for all positions of the same grade, whether filled by union or by non-union men. No employer, therefore, can get an advantage, in lower wages or longer hours, by hiring a non-unionist.

No amount of protest or solemnity of promise, and, especially, no appeal to the Declaration of Independence
from those protected by a tariff that violates the Declaration, can persuade the unions that the employer wants
the open shop except to get his labor below the union
rate.   Some employers and some associations of employers, as in the machinery line and in iron and steel, have
been frank enough to admit this, when they insist that
their agreement with the union covers only union men,
and that they are free to make a lower scale of wages
for non-union men.   But, as a rule, an agreement cannot
stand for long on such an understanding, and very soon
it goes to pieces in a strike for the closed shop or the
dissolution of the union.   There have been isolated exceptions where the union is strong, and thinks that the
non-unionist, in order to get the higher rate of pay, will
join the union.   But, in general, only when the agreement covers the non-unionist as well as the unionist, and
when the employers show that they have the power and
the will to enforce it, can the union consent to the open
shop.   Even this takes time, for power and good will
are shown only through experience, and the workmen
have undergone many bitter experiences of dishonesty,
and many more experiences of inability, through the
pressure of competition or changes in management, to
live up to agreements honestly made.   The stove founders, the soft coal operators and others, after several years
of associated action, seem to have won confidence in their
ability and honesty of purpose in enforcing their open-
shop agreements, and for this reason, the unions, though
not entirely satisfied, are not driven by their more radical members to demand the closed shop.

In the third place, that clause of the agreement which

provides for the so-called arbitration of grievances covers all matters of discrimination as well as all matters of wages, hours and rules of work. By discrimination is meant all questions of hiring, discharging and disciplining both union and non-union men. In this respect it seems to me a mistake was made by the Anthracite Coal Strike Commission in its award as interpreted by the umpire, Colonel Wright. The Commission had awarded that no person should be discriminated against on account of membership or non-membership in any labor organization, and had provided a board of conciliation and an umpire to decide any disagreement that could not be settled by the parties concerned. Under this clause the umpire stated the principle involved as follows: " A man has the right to quit the service of his employer whenever he sees fit, with or without giving a cause . . . and the employer has a perfect right to employ and discharge men in accordance with the condition of his industry; he is not obliged to give a cause for his discharge. . . ."

The mistake in applying this principle of reciprocal rights lies in the fact that the union, under the agreement, had given up its right to strike. Having done so, it gives up its right to protect a member against discrimination or unjust discharge. In lieu of settling such a grievance by a strike the agreement sets up a tribunal to investigate and decide according to the facts. Of course, individuals retain their right to quit, and the employer retains his right to discharge, yet, since the union has abandoned its right to strike in view of the tribunal, the employer must be held to have abandoned his right to discharge a union man whenever the union alleges a grievance and appeals to the board. The employer always claims that discrimination was not intended, but this is a question of fact to be determined by the tribunal. Otherwise the most vital injury, one that concerns the very life of the union, is taken out of the hands of the board of conciliation and falls back upon the original remedy of the union — the strike. This is well understood in all trade agreements except the peculiar one in the anthracite coal industry. Every grievance or alleged grievance in the hiring or discharging of union or non-union men is taken up by the officers of the two associations and settled on its merits, under the terms of the agreement. Under no other condition could the union be assured against discrimination or unjust discharge; which is but another way of saying, under no other condition could it trust itself to an open-shop agreement. With this protection, the case of each non-union man can be taken up in conference by the officers of the two associations, and he can be disciplined the same as a union man for any acts injurious to the members of the union or menacing to the agreement.

These three conditions, I think, have been found essential in most open-shop agreements that have lasted for any length of time: namely, a strong and well-disposed association on each side; the same scale of work and wages for unionist and non-unionist; and the reference of all unsettled complaints against either unionist or non-unionist to a joint conference of the officers of the union and the association.

In describing these conditions I have indicated, conversely, certain conditions under which the union is forced in self-protection to stand for the closed shop. Such cases are those where there is no employers' association, or where the employers' association cannot control all of its members or all of the industry, or where the association is hostile or has a menacing, hostile element within it; as, for example, when it does not insist that its non-union or open-shop members shall pay the union scale. In these cases the maintenance of the scale and the life of the union depend on maintaining the union shop. Whether it shall be a closed shop or not, *i.e.* whether it shall be unionized by a contract in which the employer binds himself to employ only union men, and becomes, as it were, a union organizer, or whether, as far as the trade agreement is concerned, it shall be an open shop, depends on circumstances, and the same union will be found practising both methods, according to the locality or shop.

The closed-shop contract has recently been attacked in the courts, and in some cases overthrown, on the ground of illegality. Without branching into that side of the question, it should be noted in passing that such a contract usually carries a consideration. If the union has a label protected by law, this is a valuable consideration which the employer cannot be expected to enjoy unless he agrees to employ only union men, and consequently all label agreements of the garment workers, brewery workers, boot and shoe workers and others are closed-shop agreements. However, the main consideration to the employer is the enlistment of a responsible national authority on the part of the union to compel the local union or shop to fulfil its side of the agreement. The local union is moved by personal feelings, but the national officers have wider responsibilities and a more permanent interest in living close to the letter and the spirit of the agreements. This is the consideration distinctly stated in the agreements of the Typographical

Union with the Newspaper Publishers' Association, several of whose members have non-union or open shops, it being agreed that the national union will underwrite every closed-shop agreement made by a publisher with a local union. The same consideration is found in the longshoremen's agreements, in all label agreements, and though not always expressly stipulated, it is understood to exist, more or less, in all agreements whether actually underwritten by the national officers or not. If the employer wishes the national union to be responsible for its local members, he logically will agree to employ only members of the union. The open shop, by the very terms of the contract, leaves it to the employer to enforce the agreement by hiring non-union men, but the closed shop makes the national union responsible by requiring it to discipline the local union or even to furnish other union men. It is this consideration, more than anything else, that has led the stove founders and other employers' associations, under open-shop agreements, to watch without protest the gradual unionizing of nine-tenths of their shops.

There is no doubt that the object which all unions aim to reach is the complete unionizing of the trade. In support of this there are two kinds of arguments, one of which I should call sentimental, the other economic or essential. Certain of the economic arguments I have just indicated. But there are some places where these do not apply; and a union which relies solely on a sentimental argument cannot win the support of the public, which eventually makes the laws and guides the decisions. This sentimental argument holds that he who is benefited should bear his share of the expenses of the benefactor. The union which raises wages and shortens hours should be supported by all whose wages and hours are bettered, and the non-unionist, because he refuses support, should be shut out from employment.

An argument like this, if not backed by an evident necessity, falls under attack. Such is the case in government and municipal employment. The government fixes a scale of wages. In the United States this scale is considerably above the scale in similar private employment. Trade unions have doubtless taken the lead in establishing these favorable conditions, but they really depend, not on the unions, but on politics. They are the natural outcome of universal suffrage, and are not found to the same extent in countries or localities where the labor vote is weak or labor is newly enfranchised. Formerly the political party filled such positions with its partisans. The situation is no worse when the union fills them with its members. But competitive civil service, or civil service reform, is an advance on both partisanship and unionism. Government pays the scale to all alike. There is no competition of outsiders to force it down. The state can be a model employer, because its products do not compete on the market. The non-unionist or the aggressive employer is not a menace to the wages of government employees. If the government should let out its work to the lowest bidder, the union then could maintain a scale only by the union shop. But when the government hires its own workmen, the union shop is not needed. A strike would be absurd, and the appeal for fair wages must be made to the people at large, through their representatives. The appeal is ethical and political, and not to the judgment of a strike, and such an appeal is stronger when free from the onus of an exclusive privilege.

This is not saying that government employees should not be organized. In fact, the highest form of civil service in a nation committed to representative democracy is that where the public employees are organized in a union, so that all grievances can be taken up by their agents and " arbitrated " with the head of the department. This was demonstrated by Colonel Waring in the Street Cleaning Department of New York, and he showed that only by requiring his employees to join in a union could partisan politics be wholly shut out and the highest efficiency secured. But this sort of unionizing depends on a favorable administration and an enlightened public opinion, and not on the strike or the closed shop.

There is a class of private employment similar to that of government employment in the conditions which make the closed shop unnecessary. This is railway transportation. A railway company establishes a scale of wages for its higher classes of employees. This scale is uniform over its system, is paid to all alike, and is not nibbled down by dickers with individuals. When the railway brotherhoods accept such a scale, they know that it will be paid to non-unionist as well as unionist. Therefore they do not even ask that it be put in the form of an agreement, but are content that it simply be issued as a general order from the manager. They probably would take a different view if the company let out the hiring of employees to the lowest bidder among competing contractors, or even if they themselves tried to maintain a scale for section hands who are not protected by a long line of promotion. They certainly would refuse to work with a non-member to whom the company insisted on paying lower wages than the scale. The closed-shop policy on the railroads could be supported only by the sentimental argument, and the railway brotherhoods have recognized its futility when not backed by the economic argument. It is most significant that the agreements of the machinists' union for railway shops are likewise open-shop agreements, similar to the brotherhood agreements, issued as a scale of wages by general order for the entire system and making no mention of the union. This is also true of the machinists in government navy yards and arsenals, where the union has won several advantages for members and non-members alike. This is the union which, in general manufacturing, outside railway and government work, has been most bitterly assailed for its closed-shop principles, but it is evident, from the contrast, that these principles have been forced upon the union by the different character of the industry and the different attitude of employers.

The situation is different with street railways. Some of these companies are conducted on a large scale like interstate roads, and the unions are safe with an open-shop agreement. Others are conducted like shops, and the street railway union seeks closed agreements, and has been known in a few cases to go on strike against non-union men. This union is entirely different from the brotherhoods in that it admits to membership every employee of the company, including even the car cleaners, excepting only those who already belong to an old-line trade union. Its motormen and conductors are not protected by a long period of apprenticeship or slow line of promotion, like the locomotive engineers and railway conductors, and consequently their places can be filled by men fresh from the farm or from any other occupation or profession. In fact, the union contains ex-lawyers, ex-ministers, college graduates, and a variety of ex-talent that is unique. To them, therefore, the closed shop is often essential, and to the companies also it is an advantage, for the international union then guarantees the local contract.

The sentimental argument, of which I spoke as applied to government work, sometimes becomes more than sentimental when applied to private employment, even where the non-unionist gets the same pay as the unionist. There are always selfish and short-sighted members in a union. If they see a non-unionist enjoying the same privileges with themselves without the expense of union dues, and especially if the foreman shows a preference for the non-unionist, they too demand exemption from union burdens. Thus the union disintegrates, and a cut in wages or stretch in hours cannot be warded off. Experience is a hard teacher and has taught this lesson thoroughly. It is not a mistake that the persistent non-unionist in private employment should be looked upon generally as a menace.

Another fact regarding this sentiment is often overlooked. Being compelled to work together and help one another in the same shop, men's feelings toward each other are personal and intense. The employer in his office need never see the competitor whom he is trying to crush, and only their products meet on the market. He scarcely can understand that his workmen in the shop are also competitors of each other, but, in addition, are under enforced personal contact, and their sentiments cannot be kept down. What to him is business seems malice in them. Yet these feelings are really a factor in his cost of production, as much as the coal under the boiler or the oil on the bearings. It is not surprising that the open shop, even from the employers' standpoint, is not permanently practicable, and tends to become either union or non-union.

It would be possible to run down the entire list of unions, and to show in each case the industrial circumstances which make the union, or closed, shop necessary or unnecessary from the standpoint of maintaining wages. Wherever there is a large number of small contractors, as in the building trades or the clothing industry, an open-shop union cannot survive. The building trades in London, though less effective on wages than American unions, are nevertheless safe with their open-shop agreements, because, in addition to the fact that the unions are not compelled to protect the common laborer working with them, the master builder does not sublet his work, but has his own large establishment and permanent force, and hires all the trades directly. He takes up all grievances when they arise, including the grievance of the non-unionist. But in the United States the master builder has usually only an office force. He sublets all but the mason work to ten or thirty different contractors. These contractors often require little or no capital, and a mechanic to-day may be a contractor to-morrow. A non-union contractor, with his lower wages and imported labor, would soon drive the union contractor out of business. The building trades are therefore compelled to put their closed-shop policy foremost, and where they have been defeated in this policy, as in Chicago in 1900, they have soon regained all they lost of the union shop, even though working under explicit open-shop agreements.

In the clothing trades, the sweat-shop is simply the open shop; for the sweat-shop is the small contractor with fresh immigrants, long hours and minute division of labor, crowding into the market and underselling the shops where wages, hours and conditions are better. Such would unquestionably have been the outcome in the building trades had the unions not been able to enforce the closed shop. No amount of good will on the part of clothing manufacturers or master builders could stand against a market menaced with the product of open shops. It was through the open shop that the American-born tailor was displaced by the Irish and German tailor; that the Irish and German were displaced by the Jew and by Polish women; and that the Jew is now being displaced by the Italian. In the building trades the Irish, Germans and Americans have stopped this displacement by means of the closed shop. The Jew is vainly trying to stop it, and the Scandinavian in Chicago until recently had stopped it in one branch of the clothing trade. Each displacement has substituted a race with a lower standard of living. As soon as a race begins to be Americanized and to demand a higher standard, another still lower standard comes in through the open shop. This is the history of many American industries. Whether the conditions in the clothing trade are preferable, for the American nation, to conditions in the building trades, is a question open for differences of opinion. The difference, however, is not apparent among the workmen in those trades. The immigrant, the manufacturer, the consumer, may hold a different view, but if so, it should be understood that the question in dispute is that of the wages of those workmen. As things are, the union shop or closed shop is the wage-earners' necessary means to that end.

It is sometimes asserted that American unions, like the British unions, should place more reliance on reserve funds, benefit and insurance features, and that, with these attractions, they would not have been compelled to put forward so strongly the closed-shop policy. The British workman joins the union at the close of his long period of apprenticeship, and his motive is, not the coercion of the closed shop, but rather insurance against sickness, death, loss of tools and out-of-work. His union is like the American railway brotherhoods, which also rely on insurance and previous promotion. But the American unions do not have this period of apprenticeship to work upon, except as they have established it by the union shop. They are confronted by foreigners in language, modes of thought and standards of living, pressed on by necessities in a strange country, and eligible without previous training on account of minute division of labor. Should American unions wait slowly to build up their organization on the open-shop and insurance-benefit policies, they would be displaced by foreigners before they could get a start. The foreigners again would have to set up the union shop as soon as they in turn began to demand better conditions and were confronted by a new race of immigrants. This is exactly what they have done, and the union or closed shop in America is necessary to support those very insurance and benefit features which are proposed as a substitute for it.

That there are many serious problems springing from labor unions is evident. But they would properly be discussed under other headings. The present dis-

cussion is not merely of their good or bad methods —
it is of their existence and their power to raise wages.
Under a different order of industry or a socialistic policy
of government, unions might be superfluous. Their existence and their methods arise from the nature of the
industry and the attitude of employers. A method necessary in the building trades or coal mines may be superfluous on the railroads. Their methods also arise from
the universal human struggle for power. No institution
or individual can be trusted with absolute power. Constitutional government is a device of checks and balances.
Employers' associations are just as necessary to restrain
labor unions, and labor unions to restrain employers'
associations, as two houses of Congress, a Supreme
Court, a president and political parties, to restrain social
classes. Progress does not come when one association
destroys the other, but when one association destroys
the excesses of the other. This kind of progress is going
on in the several industries mentioned above. There
the open-shop question has never been even considered
or mentioned, or else in course of time it has become
only an academic question, because the employers'
association takes up and remedies every real grievance,
or disproves every fictitious grievance, that provoked
the union into existence, and does not permit any of its
members to " smash " or undermine the union. The
bad methods of the union are gradually reduced by discussion backed by the power of organization, and its
good methods are encouraged. Education improves
both parties; mutual respect succeeds suspicion. In
those industries it is accepted that protection to capital carries with it protection to labor; that fair profits
imply fair wages; that well-disposed associations on

each side shall together discipline the non-unionist the same as the unionist; that the employers, having lost despotic control of their labor, regain a nobler control through coöperation with the union; that the opposition to non-unionist is not based alone on sentiment or malice, but on economic necessity; and that a question, which only stirs up class hatred in the field of pronunciamentoes and abstract rights, works out a peaceable solution when men acknowledge the facts and their mutual rights.

CHAPTER VIII

UNIONS OF PUBLIC EMPLOYEES[1]

The subject is: Should public employees organize as trade unions? Should they organize for the sake of getting increased wages, reducing the hours of labor, getting fair treatment in matters of discipline, including promotion and discharge? A trade union is an organization with such purposes. The subject does not concern beneficial or social organizations, which may possibly take up questions of wages and hours, but do not exert pressure. The related question is, Should such an organization, with these purposes in view, be affiliated with the labor movement in general? Should it belong to central bodies? Should it seek the support of other unions in promoting its own purposes?

There are certain features of public employment which require a distinction in methods. Methods may differ at some points, owing to the difference in character of public and private employment. If employees organize for improving wages, hours and conditions, it follows that, as a final resort, they have the power of quitting work in a body. But, if I understand the trade union movement, a properly organized union has, preliminary to going on strike, a constitutional requirement that the differences shall be submitted to arbitration. This is the difference between unionism and syndicalism.

[1] Address before the Women's Trade Union League at Chicago. See *Union Labor Advocate*, Oct., 1907, pp. 140–143.

Here, the methods of public and private unions are alike.

But an organization of public employees should not rely upon the strike, in the first instance. It may be that on Russian railroads a strike is the proper procedure and the only one which can be adopted. But, in our western civilization it is not necessary that these unions should strike, because they have another weapon — politics. The organizations of public employees, through universal suffrage, have the support, as a rule, of the wage-earning voters, and, if they can make it plain to the voters that their demands are just, then eventually they can bring about the changes which arbitration in their case would decide to be fair.

Another difference between organizations of public employees and those of private employment relates to the open and closed shop, so called. The reasons advanced for the closed-shop policy in the case of private employment do not hold good in the case of public employment. The private employer is subject to competition. He is trying to get his labor as cheaply as possible. If there is an agreement between a union and a private employer, and it is possible for him to employ men who are not members of the organization, it naturally follows that secret agreements or concessions will be made with those non-union employees which will gradually cut below the scale which the union has established. In the ordinary competitive lines of employment it is scarcely possible for a trade union to maintain its scale of wages without insisting that all of the employees shall belong to the union. Such insistence is necessary in order to protect the employer from his competitor. He is not free to do as he pleases, even though he seriously intends to pay the union scale of wages.

But the situation in the case of the public, as employer, is different. The city, or state or nation is not subject to the competition of private employers; it establishes a scale of wages for the different grades of service, and it pays that scale of wages out of revenue derived from taxation, if necessary. The management of the public service is governed by a scale of wages and hours which has the effect of law, and it is not driven to reduce the price by indirect methods. Consequently, the essential condition which is sought to be secured by the so-called closed shop in private employment is secured by law in public employment for both union and non-union employees.

There are two lines of argument which trade unionists usually put forward for the closed shop: One, an economic reason. It is simply a necessary means — unfortunate perhaps, but necessary — of securing the actual payment of a scale of wages agreed upon. The other is a sentimental reason. The trade unionist feels that a man who is getting the advantages which the unions have secured in high wages is an ungrateful man, greedy and selfish, if he does not pay union dues and help out the organization. This sentimental reason cannot stand alone. Every one of us gets advantages in society that we do not pay for. We receive advantages which others have secured for us. If we do not contribute in a proper way to promote the common advantage of our fellows and ourselves, that is something which must be left to our private judgment, influenced by the opinion of our fellows.

With the proper organization of public employees

the open-shop principle is not a menace to the union organization. Recognition of the union, and dealing with it as such, which are essential to this public organization, make it to the advantage of every man in the service to go into the organization as soon as he is employed in the department.

This being the starting-point, I will take up certain objections usually brought forward against organizations of employees in public service. One of the objections is that it interferes with the discipline of the department; that it prevents that freedom in handling the employees which is necessary for efficiency of the service; that it introduces arbitrary plans of promotion, grading and so on, which interfere with the best interests of the public service.

As far as my observation goes, I find that a proper organization of public employees works in exactly the opposite direction; that not only does it not interfere with the efficient management of the service, but it is a protection for the service against one of the greatest evils by which public employment is menaced in democratic communities; namely, the interference of the politician.

When Seth Low was elected mayor of New York, some ten years ago, he appointed as his commissioner of street cleaning one of the most eminent engineers in this country, Colonel George E. Waring. When Colonel Waring came into the street-cleaning department, he found political chaos. There had been and was still in existence a remnant of an old organization of the Knights of Labor. There were other organizations purely local. But, common to all these organizations was the fact that they were linked in some way with ward politicians, or, as they are called in New York, district leaders. If the Knights of Labor wanted to secure an advantage for any member, they went to the Tammany politician, who went to the commissioner of street cleaning, or to the mayor, and secured the desired promotion, or relaxation of discipline or release from punishment. Waring found this situation in the department of street cleaning. People who object to the organization of public employees might very properly object to the kind of organization which he found. It was not *bona fide* labor organization, although it was an organization of labor. It was an affiliation between so-called labor unions and the Tammany politicians.

The first thing that Waring did when he came into the department was to propose that a single organization of all employees should be recognized as a part of the administration. He instructed all of the street cleaners, the drivers and sweepers, to organize their local unions at the several stables, — forty-one of them. Then these stables, or " locals," were to elect forty-one delegates to a " general committee," which should represent all of the employees. This general committee, then, should elect a committee of five, whom he called " spokesmen." The spokesmen were to meet in joint session, whenever necessary, with five superintendents or heads of departments, named by Waring himself. The ten were known as the " Board of Conference." Then, if any street sweeper or driver had a grievance, instead of going to his district leader, a Tammany politician, he brought up that grievance in the secret union meeting of his fellows at the stable where he reported. If his fellow-workmen indorsed his grievance as a legitimate matter which they would stand for, then their delegate on the committee of forty-one brought it before that committee, and if that committee indorsed it as a legitimate grievance which should be remedied, it was handed on to their five spokesmen, who brought it before the Board of Conference.

There is a full report of the two years' operation of that system.[1] We find that, in the second year, of some 1100 grievances which were brought before the committee of forty-one, about 830 of them were turned down by the men themselves in their secret union meetings. That is, nearly four-fifths of the " kicks " were found to be unwarranted by their fellow-workers. Their fellow-employees would not stand for their alleged grievances.

See what a fruitful field was taken away from the politician. Here were 1100 grievances which the politicians might have taken up and carried to the head of the department. But the men themselves, when it was once perceived that their union was to be held responsible, would not allow them to be taken up. Then of the 270 grievances which were referred to the Board of Conference, every one was settled except one. There was but one case that was not settled either by the men themselves or by the Conference Board. This case came up to Commissioner Waring, and he, after hearing it, decided in favor of the employee.

I consider that this invention of Commissioner Waring in the street cleaning department of New York is the most important practical contribution that has been

[1] Published as a supplement to "Municipal Affairs," June, 1898, pp. 226–234. This important document was not printed officially by the city, but has been made available through the public spirit of the Reform Club, of New York.

made to civil service reform in a democratic government. It practically did almost all the work that a civil service commission usually is required to do. At the same time, it had the advantage over a civil service commission in that it was self-governing. It involved only the men in the department and did not rely upon an outside committee of reformers to interfere in the management of the department. It allowed Commissioner Waring and the superintendents to promote men and discharge men, to do as they pleased in the management of the department — always under the check that the man thus disciplined could bring his treatment as a grievance before his fellow-workmen and have it taken to the highest court provided within the department. It gave freedom to the superintendents and the management of the department, which civil service reform does not do, and, at the same time, gave justice to the workman, which civil service reform attempts to do. But it was done by men directly interested in the department, who were conversant with all the details and had all the knowledge necessary to a proper decision. I should think that such an organization of a public department could go still further towards self-governing civil service, and be made the examining board for admission to the service, as well as grievance board for suspensions and dismissal.

As everybody now knows, if he is familiar with the history of New York, this particular measure of Colonel Waring's brought up the most inefficient department of the city government to the highest point of efficiency. It elevated the street-cleaning department from a scramble for spoils to an efficient municipal administration. It took it entirely out of politics, eliminated the ward boss, and it is not surprising that Tammany Hall, when it returned to power, abolished the system.

Tammany politicians and similar politicians are opposed to labor unions. They are ostensibly the friends of labor. They espouse unions. They advocate the cause of labor. But when we get down to the fine points and discover just what kind of labor organization they want, and what is to be accomplished by it, we find that they are like other employers. They do not want a kind of labor organization that interferes with their management. The politician necessarily must be opposed to the organization of municipal employees if he is going to make anything out of the public service for himself.

It is an interesting fact that, about the same time that Colonel Waring was introducing his system in New York, in another part of the world a similar system was being introduced. In New Zealand, in 1894, and in Victoria and New South Wales afterwards, there was introduced in the government railway service and in the post-office and telegraph service, the so-called system of " appeal boards." These appeal boards, in New Zealand,[1] were simply a system by which the employees of the service elected their representative, the government elected its representative, and a third person, a judge of one of the courts, was designated as the presiding officer. In the government service, if an employee of the service has a grievance, he brings it to his representative on this appeal board. He can be represented there by a fellow-employee. Lawyers are not admitted. This fellow-employee may be the secretary of his union, or

[1] "Government Railways Act, 1894 and 1896. Orders in Council." New Zealand *Gazette*, Sept. 23, 1897.

any person in the service competent to represent him in the settlement of his grievance. All the cases of discipline in which a grievance is alleged are brought before this board.

This system is not as democratic as Colonel Waring's, but it is more than a mere coincidence that these two things happened in different parts of the world at the same time. The explanation is that, both in Australia and in this country, we are attempting a new experiment in the world — running a government by universal suffrage. It is an easy matter for the governments of England and Germany, whether in cities or nation, to maintain discipline in the departments, because the workingmen have little political influence. But we are trying to run the public service with hired help that is a partner in running it. In England it does not matter so much, because the municipal councils, until the last few years, have been solely of the employing class. I got pretty well acquainted last year with several town councils of England, and they were made up mainly of just the same class of men as I should have found had I visited a manufacturers' association or attended a meeting of an employers' association. They were not politicians — they were business men. They ran the government of the cities in the way business men would run private corporations. They dealt with employees much on the same basis, and the workingmen had no appeal. If the men have a grievance, they must do the same as the employees of a private corporation. They must organize and strike.

But in this country, with universal suffrage, the workingman in public employment does not need to strike. He forms a clique and goes in with the politicians. He has the suffrage. We cannot get away from organization. These employees will organize, in one way or another. The real solution is, not to try to destroy the organizations of public servants, but to give them official recognition, to give them a part in the administration of the department, and then to hold them to that responsibility.

Another example: British administration, as I have said, has been free of political influence on the part of employees. But in the past eight or ten years the wage-earners of England have been taking an active part in politics. They have elected wage-earners to the town councils and to Parliament. England is just beginning to have that clash of interests in city and national government with which we have been familiar for half a century or more. Hitherto, it has been a simple matter, with only the employers elected, to have business-like administration in cities. But, since the trade unions and the employers are together trying to operate the government, their town councils are becoming conventions for class struggle instead of harmonious boards of business directors. They are beginning to have the same inefficiency that we are familiar with.

But I found one city, Manchester, where, in the municipal tramways department, the management has changed the policy of class struggle. Instead of undermining and displacing the union, it has recognized the union of tramway employees. It has made the union a branch of the administration. It takes up with the officers all questions of wages, hours and discipline. These are settled by trade agreement and arbitration. The general manager tells me of the great advantage gained. Formerly a town councillor would approach the manager, asking for the appointment of a certain man, or an advance in wages for another or less severe discipline for another, — for it is not true that city government in England is free from political or personal favoritism. The manager could not know whether the alderman's request had merit in it or not. But, now, when a claim comes from the union, he knows that it is something real, for it comes from all the men. He takes it up with the union and settles it. The alderman has lost his opportunity.

So it is when modern democracy comes forward to operate public undertakings. The employees have political influence. This is a serious menace to good administration, unless the organizations that inevitably spring up are given official recognition and made a branch of the administration.

There is another side of the question. While it is important that these organizations should be encouraged and recognized, it is also important that they should not dominate. No class of people can be trusted with absolute power. The best of people see their own interests more clearly than they see the interests of others. People become broadminded by coming against others who are as powerful as they are.

The British unions have had an experience. An organization known as the Municipal Employees' Association had brought in thousands of public servants, like nurses and common laborers, who had never before had a union. Its platform read: " No strikes, but to operate through the ballot box." This was well enough for the unorganized workers. The association was admitted to the town councils of labor unions and to the national Trades Union Congress. It grew rapidly and began to take in employees who were eligible to existing organizations. It set up its motto of an industrial union — " All Municipal Workers in One Society." It began to encroach on other unions. It took away their members, because it could get better wages for them through' politics than through strikes. But how was it doing this? It was building itself up on the labor vote of the very unions which it was destroying. The others protested, and the Trades Union Congress, by a vote almost unanimous, adopted the following resolution : " That any method of organization which seeks to divide workmen employed by public authorities or private employers from their fellows in the same occupations employed by private firms is detrimental to the best interests of Trade Unionism, and that the Parliamentary Committee use its best endeavors to prevent the spread of such methods of organization." [1]

The conclusion is this : if municipal or public employees secure for themselves better wages and better conditions than the best wages and conditions in outside employment, then they separate themselves out from the labor movement and become a privileged class. They cease to belong to the labor unions, because they depend, not upon labor organization, but upon politics. It is political influence which they hold as a club over legislative officials, and not the labor organization formed to lift up labor as a whole. If municipal or public employees secure special privileges and are advanced beyond the same class of labor in private employment, they lose their interest and their willingness to pay dues and to support the organization of labor in general. The British trade unions have hit upon the proper rule,

[1] *Proceedings*, Trades Union Congress, 1906, pp. 164, 167.

that the wages and conditions of the employees of private concerns and the wages and hours of public employees shall rise and fall together. The trade union scale, in the case of organized labor, and the scale paid by the best class of employers where there is no union, should be the same as that paid in public employment. That is to say, the trade unions of England have taken the ground that there should be no special privileges given to public employees; that if they want their wages raised and their hours reduced, they must join the general labor movement and help to get wages increased and hours reduced for labor in general; that they may reasonably expect always to be at the head of the procession and to have the wages and hours which the best grades of private employers are paying, but that they shall not be permitted to go beyond that and become a privileged class, with better wages than those the employees of private concerns are securing on the outside.

The difficulty is this: A legislator, a town councilor, an alderman is elected by a plurality vote. It may take only a few votes one way or the other to cause his defeat. A compact organization of employees may effect that result. Consequently, an organization of municipal employees holds a club over the alderman that is disproportionately great. It is not the proportion they bear to the total vote, but the proportion they bear to the margin between the two parties. The real trouble is that there is no method of referring these demands of public employees to the common sentiment of labor organizations in general. They are allowed in many cases to operate on their own initiative and with the tacit sanction of other labor unions. But now the Trades Union Congress, in self-protection, prohibits these organizations of public employees from using the labor vote as a means of getting for themselves privileged positions over and above what labor in private employment has.   This is a sound principle from the standpoint of public efficiency and public administration.   It applies in America, as in England.   Then, when public employees organize and affiliate with the unions of employees in private service, we have labor organizations on a rational economic basis, going forward and improving conditions in both public and private employment.

CHAPTER IX

RESTRICTIONS BY TRADE UNIONS[1]

SOME employers say, " We should have no objection to trade unions if they would organize to increase production instead of restricting production." Economists and critics have shown that unions, by their restrictive policies, stand in the way of progress. The unions, in deference to a public opinion that judges measures mainly by their effects on production, defend themselves by denying that their policies are restrictive.

But their arguments are indirect; they look towards the ultimate effects of unions, and not to their immediate effects. Ultimately, the unions may be said to increase production when their policies force employers to adopt labor-saving devices; but this is plainly an indirect result brought about by the employer to counteract the direct result of the union. Ultimately, also, their social effects may contribute to social progress by shortening the hours of labor and maintaining more expensive standards of life; but these, again, are indirect results, preceded by policies which, so far as production is concerned, are essentially restrictive. In truth, the characteristic policies of unions imply restrictions of some kind upon employers.

[1] *Outlook*, Nov., 1906. See also "Report on Regulation and Restriction of Output," prepared by the author and others under the direction of Carroll D. Wright, and published as *Eleventh Special Report* of the Commissioner of Labor, 1904. (Government Printing Office.)

The success of unions has come about only as they have abandoned the field of production and have confined themselves to distribution. It is with the distribution of wealth that they are necessarily concerned, and the irrepressible conflict of capital and labor is found in the difference between production and distribution. In modern industry it is the employer — the one who assumes the risks of business — upon whom the responsibility of production is placed. To meet this responsibility, he offers inducements to the other factors to join with him, — to the capitalist or land-owner he offers interest or rent, to patentees he offers royalties, to experts and managers he offers salaries, to workmen he offers wages. It is his business to combine these factors and to afford inducements such that each will yield its largest and best contribution to the joint product. But with the other contributors the first question is the return they will get from their productive energies, and a trade union is simply a combination to get a larger return.

Such a combination, in the nature of the case, can operate only by means of obstacles placed in the way of the free action of employers. As individuals the several contributors can secure the return they wish, only to the extent to which they can hold back in the bargain, and this is limited by the freedom which the employer has of turning from one to another. As a combination they direct their efforts towards limiting this kind of freedom, and this is the primary object underlying all the restrictions of a trade union. The aim is mutual protection — or perhaps joint aggrandizement — and the methods are restrictive in the same sense that a protective tariff on imports is restrictive. In both cases some of the arguments advanced may be fallacious, such as the argument that by restricting trade you increase the amount of work to be done.

I do not hold that protectionism and trade unionism are parallel in all respects. One is the policy of government, supposed to stand for all of the people; the other is the policy of individuals acting for themselves. But even here it is conceivable that government might adopt this policy and relieve individuals of enforcing it, as government has already done in the case of factory protection and child labor, and as government has done in Australasia along the entire line of trade union policy. The essential parallel is the fact that both lines of industrial philosophy proceed along restrictions on freedom of trade and bargaining, and that neither is primarily an agency for the production, but rather an agency for the distribution, of wealth. If they increase production, it is because they set other forces at work to overbalance their restrictions.

Consider the changes necessary in the character of a union if it should direct its energies to the production of wealth. It would in so far cease to be a trade union, and would become either a society for technical education, or an association for sharing profits, or a coöperative association.

It might be well for unions to give more attention than they do to the technical or trade education of their members. But, apart from incidental instruction in their trade journals, their efforts in this direction are confined almost solely to securing opportunity for apprentices to learn all branches of their trade. And here, strangely enough, it is only by way of restrictions the most onerous to employers that the apprentices are granted such opportunities. The union restricts the number of apprentices to the shop and restricts the ratio to journeymen; it requires three, four or five years of apprenticeship, and enjoins the journeymen to aid and instruct the apprentice. It prohibits the employer from keeping the apprentice at one operation, but requires that the employer shall change him to another machine, say, every six months. The object is two-fold: the number of apprentices is limited in order that the trade may not be overcrowded and wages reduced; and an all-round education of the apprentice is stipulated in order that the union man may become a better mechanic than the non-union man. These are un-doubted restrictions on the employer; they prevent him from specializing his workmen and adopting that minute division of labor which the economists set forth as a fruitful instrument of wealth-production. But it is evident that they are necessary to the existence of the union, that their motive is self-protection, and that, by way of a method immediately restrictive, their ultimate result is to raise the general efficiency of the union mechanics.

As regards profit-sharing, evidently the offer must come from the employers. It is one form of the induce-ments which they offer to their managers and workers to engage more actively in the production of wealth. It scarcely needs an association of the workmen, and, if it did, such an association would not be a trade union.

The only other form that a union could adopt in order, as an association, to promote production would be that of a coöperative society or corporation. In-deed, this is what several organized trades in the United States have done at one time or another in their history.

The experiments have either failed or have been disasters if they succeeded. When the union takes the risks and responsibilities of production, it becomes, not a coöperator with the employer, but a competitor. Herein is failure. If it succeeds, then it raises up in its own ranks an element interested in profits rather than wages. This element becomes exclusive, treats its fellow-members as employees, hires outsiders if it can get them cheaper, and, sooner or later, goes over to the other employers or is expelled by such remnant of the union as survives. The moulders and the coopers have furnished illustrious warnings of this kind to unions not to engage in production, with its motive of profits.

By painful experiment, or by the experience of others, the unions have generally come to the point of confining their attention to wages, — that is, to distribution, — leaving to employers the questions of production. This may be unfortunate. The resulting policies may seem unreasonable. If so, it is because industrial conditions have separated those interested in the production of wealth from those interested in its distribution. The labor union is a protest on the part of the latter. Its policies are necessarily restrictive, but the restrictions vary in extent, partly with the extent to which the separation has been carried, partly with the extent to which the union dominates. Where the separation has been bridged by conciliation, or where the union has been weakened or suppressed, the restrictions have been lessened, but their essential restrictiveness remains in the very protective nature of the trade union itself.

The methods of unions cannot be understood except in terms of conflict. This is true not only of strikes, but also of the methods used to retain the winnings of strikes. The conflict continues after the strike is won. Consequently, to the experienced members, more important than wages is the preservation of their union. New and inexperienced unions fall in pieces after a strike is won. Their members have a juvenile faith in promises. But with experience they learn that it is the union rather than the promises that they must rely upon. Take the minimum wage. The employer agrees to pay not less than a certain amount by the day or hour. But the agreement is not a contract in law. It cannot be enforced in court. It has probably been made under duress, — that is, under a strike or threat of a strike. Furthermore, it applies only to the union members. If the employer agrees to pay it to non-members, and if he lives up to his agreement, the state of conflict ceases and the union need go no further. This is the case with the railroad brotherhoods — the engineers, firemen, conductors and trainmen. They deal with corporations conducted like governments. Their scale of wages is like a legislative enactment fixing a uniform rate of pay for government employees over a vast area. The scale is issued as a general order from the highest authority to all subordinates who hire and discharge these classes of employees. The positions themselves are well defined — there is but one man, and no chance to divide up his work among a set of helpers. The superintendent is not expected to pay less or to pay more, nor to change his force in order to get cheaper help. Years of experience have shown the railway brotherhoods that they can rely upon a promise so far removed as this one is from the ordinary treatment of labor as a commodity fluctuating upon demand and supply. A successful strike or threat is as good as a contract. Consequently the brotherhoods do not go further and demand that irritating restriction so naturally resented by employers, the " closed shop."

But take the building trades. Here the cardinal principle of unionism is the refusal to work with non-union men. The employer is restricted to those who are willing to join the union and whom the union is willing to admit. Waiving questions of law and ethics, look at the economics. Here is an industry decentralized to the furthest extent. A general contractor agrees to put up a building. He lets out most of the work in ten to thirty subcontracts by competition to the lowest bidders. These subcontractors have little or no capital; their work is narrowly specialized; labor is their largest item of cost; they tend to become simply brokers on the labor market; their jobs last for but a few days or weeks; they hire men by the hour and lay them off on the half-hour, according to the weather or the supply of material or the progress of other trades. Here is the ideal labor market from the standpoint of demand and supply. It is like that of the bulls and bears in the wheat-pit, while railroad employment is like the market for postage-stamps. It is not surprising that building mechanics are extreme and peremptory in their restrictions. Their minimum wage would be impossible if labor could be thrown in and out of this market at the will of the struggling brokers. Hence their insistence on the one great restriction that supports all others — the closed shop. Their members they can control — they can fine, suspend or expel the one who works for less than the minimum. But if the contractor is free to employ the expelled members, their discipline is gone. The contractor who can import and hire outsiders can get the contracts, and the others must do the same or lose the business. Sentiment is excluded, and the benevolent contractor must come down toward the level of the lowest. Under these conditions the closed-shop restriction is the necessary protection of the minimum wage.

Take machinery and the division of labor. The superficial effects of its introduction are well known. It increases the production of goods and decreases the cost. But in this statement there are hidden two entirely opposite effects. One is the increase in the output of the workman, the other is the substitution of cheap labor. Perhaps no mechanical invention has worked a greater revolution than the invention of the linotype in the printing trade. It has increased the speed of the operator at least fivefold. But it made possible a three months' apprenticeship of girls in place of a three years' apprenticeship of boys. Yet this substitution did not occur in newspaper offices, because the Typographical Union was able to prevent the introduction of women. Consequently men were transferred to the machine, reducing their hours of labor from ten or twelve to seven or eight per day and increasing their wages. At the same time the cost of composition was reduced 80 per cent, and the size of papers was increased and their price was reduced. The benefit of the invention was thus distributed among the four parties to the transaction — to the inventor in royalties, to the publisher in profits, to the public in prices, to the printer in wages. Thus the machine came in on its merits as a means of increasing speed and not as a means of substituting cheap labor.

The cigar-making machines are different. They

increase the rate of output not more than 50 per cent, and there are good cigar-makers whose speed on hand work is equal to that of the machine. The profit on these machines has come from the substitution of girls at $7 for men at $18. These machines come into the trade, not as labor-saving, but as wage-saving, devices. The benefit goes to the inventor, the manufacturer and the consumer, but not to the workman. The Cigar-makers' Union has resisted them, and, though permitting its members to work on them, refuses to grant the union label to manufacturers using them. It may be said that the union made a mistake and should have welcomed these inventions as the printers welcomed the linotype. But there is a difference between welcoming a machine that lightens your work and welcoming one that takes your job. And the public, which, in its desire for cheap products, sees no distinction between an invention that shares its benefits with the workmen and one that makes their daughters their own competitors, is not a disinterested critic of the workman's restrictions on machinery. The linotype in newspaper offices is an exception to the rule. Skilled workmen in general have seen machinery and division of labor make way for girls and immigrants. The union opposition has been a losing fight. They have the consolation of cheaper products, but this they cannot realize if they are displaced by cheaper labor.

So much for the introduction of machinery. When once introduced, instances may be found where unions stand in the way of its unrestricted output. These restrictions apply, however, to machines whose speed depends mainly on the work of the operator, and not to automatic machines. Thus the machinists' union holds to the one-man-one-machine tradition of the craft, but it interprets the rule to apply only where the machine requires constant attention. The disagreement with the employer grows out of the fact that this line of division is indefinite, and is continually moving forward as machines become more automatic. The bituminous mine workers hedge the undercutting machines about with many rules, limiting the number of " runs " in a day, limiting the number of hours per day, increasing the number of men to the machine, and reducing the differential between the price per ton for pick mining and the price for machine mining. These rules tend to transfer much of the benefit of machinery to the wage-earner, giving him more wages for less work. They also restrict the introduction of the machines by lessening the profits on them, but this must necessarily occur to a certain extent in any case if the gain of a machine is shared with the wage-earner. Some of the miners' restrictions are unjustifiable, because they go further than needed for this purpose.

Doubtless the most familiar and widespread criticism of unions is the one that they hold back the ambitious and energetic workman and prevent him from making the most of his abilities. I have examined a number of cases where this charge is made, and have usually found that it is one half of the truth. The other half is in the circumstances of modern industry which take away from the more energetic workman the fruits of his energy and drive the slower workman beyond the point of endurance. In the first place, the criticism is seldom made by employers whose emphasis is on the quality of their product. Such employers are sometimes found to encourage the union, and even openly to agree with it, in limiting the amount of work to be done in a given time. If they can succeed in this, they can increase the expenses of their competitors who emphasize quantity instead of quality. In the building trades the " legitimate " builder often looks with favor on the union rules which restrict the speed of workmen employed by the " speculative " builder. The limitation seldom affects his own work, because men cannot do good work if they hurry. A similar division between employers is found in the clothing trade, in pottery and in almost every trade where the quality of the work depends on the care of the workman and not on automatic machinery. Even in non-union establishments the same is true. The manufacturer of a widely advertised cigar prohibits his girls from earning more than seven dollars a week, when the best of them could earn ten or more at the piece rates paid. In these cases the restriction on output is necessary if the manufacturer cares to uphold the reputation of his product.

The illustration shows the double meaning of terms when we speak of the " ambitious," the " capable," or the " skilful " workman. " Ability " may mean ability to reach a high speed and thus turn out a great quantity of product, or it may mean ability to improve and to maintain a good quality of work. Modern industry, with its world market, its stress of competition and its lack of responsibility to the consumer, has run to cheap products, low costs and enormous speed of workmanship. A partial reaction is occurring, as seen in laws against adulteration, and in the large development of proprietary goods and advertised trade-marks, and there is a sentimental reaction in the arts and crafts movement. This is from the standpoint of the consumer and the manufacturer. From the standpoint of the workman the reaction appears in the effort to restrict speed.

It is minute division of labor and extreme specialization that have brought forth this high speed of modern industry. The skilled mechanic who turns from one operation to another may be competent, but he is not expeditious. When his work is split up and specialized, two important changes occur. Wages are changed from a time basis to a piece basis, and the foreman can inspect the quality of output. Piece rates intensify the workman's motive to exertion by keeping the reward always in sight, and employers are surprised to find that the output is increased far beyond what they thought was possible. The men's earnings are often doubled and trebled; and the employer, ignorant of industrial psychology, concludes that they had been cheating him. He " cuts " the piece rate. But the men exert themselves still more, and then comes another cut, and so on. In a large establishment, with twenty thousand or more piece rates, the workmen learned from a remark of the proprietor and the acts of the foreman that, no matter how much they exerted themselves, they could not expect to earn more than $2.65 a day. In one department of seventy men there were four ambitious ones who paid no heed to the hint, but strove to increase their earnings above that limit. The foreman used them as a gauge on the others, and when he found a piece on which their earnings were excessive he cut the rate for all. At last the others organized a union, compelled these four to join, and adopted a rule that no man should earn more than $3 a day. All of them began to earn about $2.98 a day. Then the employer cried out that the union restricted output, which was one-half the truth, for they had both increased the output and restricted it. The restriction began with the employer.

This is not an exceptional case. It is an old story, and ought not to need repetition; but I have heard a great employer deny, in the presence of a large audience, that the piece rates in his establishment had been cut, when I knew of my own observation that it had been done under circumstances similar to the above — so ignorant and far removed from their workmen are the heads of great corporations. I am not defending restriction of output, much less denying it; I am explaining it. Unions are often compelled to resort to it, and in some cases, like the one above, they are organized for that purpose alone. The policy is forced on them in self-protection, at first against their wishes, but afterwards accepted as something so self-evident that they do not recognize it as a restriction. As long as industry is conducted on prevailing standards, unions will spring up, will restrict or regulate output, will be " smashed," and will again spring up. The prevailing standards really crush ambition, except for the very few who can become foremen, by holding up a reward and then snatching it away as soon as the workman is able to reach it. Instead of appealing to ambition, such standards rely on coercion; and employers are prone to mistake the feverish energy of unorganized workmen for loyalty when it is really fear. In times of prosperity the speed of both union and non-union workmen is less than in periods of depression. The whip of unemployment rather than the hope of reward is the inducement to ambition offered by business methods.

There is another fact of some significance regarding restrictions. Nearly all of the typographical unions have removed restrictions on the output of the linotype machine, but there remain a few " locals " which limit their members to one-half or two-thirds of the unrestricted speed. In visiting some of the restricted newspaper offices I was surprised to see gray-haired men. This suggested a comparison of ages, and the returns from a dozen offices showed that in the unrestricted offices only 2 per cent of the operators were over fifty years of age, while in the restricted offices 15 to 20 per cent were over fifty. The Government Printing Office, under civil service rules, shows 22 per cent of the employees over fifty, and 2 per cent over seventy years of age, — a proportion about the same as that of the male population at large. This grievance of premature old age arises from every industry conducted on modern principles. Wage-earners are at their highest mark of earning ability between the ages of twenty and forty. Above the latter age, when the professional or business man is just entering his prime, the wage-earner is declining and soon is discharged or transferred to lighter and less remunerative work. He must give way to a younger man who can keep up with the pace. But trade union and civil service restrictions protect him. Freed from overexertion in his earlier years, he holds on in the advanced years. These facts will be viewed differently according as our standard is production or distribution. May it not be that some future generation will look back with gratitude on the heresy that justifies restriction of output?

Some of the foregoing restrictions are supported by irritating shop rules which interfere with the employer's efforts to improve his plant and management. In the interest of industrial progress and the increase of production, the employer should have a free hand in these particulars. But there is one form of restriction that is free from this objection; namely, restriction on the hours of labor per day. Here is the logical line of compromise. The bricklayers have recognized this principle perhaps more than any other American union, for they have yielded to the employer on nearly all points of management and have concentrated their demands on high rates for short hours. Compared with the London bricklayer at twenty cents an hour for nine hours, the New York bricklayer at seventy cents for eight hours is the cheaper workman; for not only is his exertion much greater, but his employer has specialized his work, has arranged an unremitting flow of brick and mortar, and lays him off at any half-hour. Not a minute of his precious time is wasted, nor a stroke of his arm permitted to lag. What is true of the bricklayers is true approximately of most American unions, compared at least with their European brothers. By restricting the hours the employer gets unrestricted output per hour.

CHAPTER X

UNIONS AND EFFICIENCY[1]

In a recent article one of the foremost efficiency engineers of the country, referring to the adoption of the system of scientific management in industrial establishments, predicts that it will mean " for the employers and the workmen who adopt it, and particularly those who adopt it first, the elimination of almost all causes for dispute and disagreement between them."

The spokesmen of organized labor seem to take a different view of the matter. Their attitude is partly one of hostility, partly of suspicion. Are the principles of trade unionism and scientific management in irrepressible conflict? Can one survive only by crushing the other, or is their opposition an accident due to imperfections which may be corrected, so that both can flourish together?

It is sometimes argued that trade unions would be of greater advantage to workingmen if they would make the production of wealth their main object and abandon altogether their restrictive policies. But I consider that production is the business of the employer, and that, if a union turns itself mainly to production, it can do so only by becoming its own employer; that is, by becoming a coöperative society.

As a matter of fact, modern trade unionism is a survival of all kinds of experiments in organization, includ-

[1] *American Economic Review*, Sept., 1911.

ing coöperation, politics and joint membership of employers and workmen; and it has survived only to the extent that it has chosen to enforce policies that restrict the employer. Labor has never been able to compete with the employer, as coöperation requires. Those coöperative societies which have succeeded, like the coopers and moulders, have done so by becoming employers, and are now simply successful corporations employing hired labor. Those which have failed did so after leaving around them the wrecks of other wage-earners hired by regular employers; for they kept their heads above water only by generously failing to pay themselves full wages in order that they might cut prices, and thereby they weakened the ability of competing employers to pay full wages. Thus a labor organization that devotes itself to production travels a disastrous circle. It fails, whether it succeeds or fails.

Conscious of the futility of trying to cope with the employer on his own ground, modern trade unionism contents itself with trying to tie his hands. Its policies are necessarily restrictive. If it cannot prevent the employer from doing as he pleases at some point or other, it is something besides a trade union. The real questions are, whether its restrictions are injurious or beneficial? to whom? and who is to decide?

Again, it is sometimes charged that unions are organized mainly to foment trouble, especially strikes. The fact is, that unions came into existence after periods of strikes, and were thought by workmen to be the means of getting their demands without strikes. The modern idea of a permanent trade union began with the ideas of negotiation, arbitration and trade agreements, with their permanent joint boards and periodic joint conventions for the settlement of differences. Experience had shown that it was not difficult to win strikes in periods of prosperity, but it was impossible to retain the fruits. Consequently, to the experienced unionist, the preservation of his union has come to be more important than winning strikes.[1] And nearly all of the restrictive policies of which complaint is made spring from the effort to preserve the union. The irrepressible conflict, if there is one, between unionism and scientific management will be found at the points where management weakens the solidarity of unionism. Other points of conflict are incidental. These are irrepressible. The real question here is this: Can scientific management deal scientifically with organizations as well as individuals? Is there a science of industrial organization as well as a science of engineering details?

The history of the stove moulders and stove foundrymen will assist us.[2] Long before management became a science the stove foundrymen had practised its principles. For forty years, prior to 1890, they were working out the problem of efficiency details. Competition forced them to learn by experiment and to spread by imitation what science learns by observation and measurement, and spreads by propaganda. They learned to subdivide labor so that a three-dollar man would be kept on three-dollar work and never be permitted to turn his hand to what a dollar man could do. They had, of course, some crudities which science would

[1] This conviction first became dominant in labor organizations in the decade of the fifties, both in England and the United States. See "Documentary History of American Industrial Society," Vols. VII and VIII, period of 1840–1860.

[2] See *Bulletin of Labor*, No. 62, Jan., 1906, U. S. Bureau of Labor, article by Commons and Frey on "Conciliation in the Stove Industry."

eliminate, such as piece-rates instead of premiums, prizes and bonuses; but these differences I consider unessential, for they agreed on the essential thing of playing on the motives of individual workmen to stimulate output, regardless of the effect on other workmen and other employers. The consequence was that for forty years every step towards greater efficiency and greater output per man brought a cut in prices of stoves; and every cut in the price of stoves took away by so much the employers' reward for enterprise; every loss of profit forced employers to cut the piece-rates of wages; every cut in piece-rates forced the wage-earners to greater output for the same earnings; and so on, around the vicious circle of futile efficiency.

Now, that circle is very familiar to wage-earners in every business. It is so familiar that they take it as a matter of course, and therefore usually fail to state their case against efficiency, or their case for restrictions; just as it might not occur to them to explain an aëroplane disaster by the attraction of gravitation. Even where monopoly or special privilege prevails, and competition does not force friendly employers into the ranks of hostile employers, the thing that is equally plain is the infinite capacity of stocks and bonds to absorb every gain from the efficiency of labor. The sugar trust, the steel trust and other trusts that might be mentioned are not hopeful inducements to wage-earners to take an interest in scientific increase of output. Fear or greed may coerce or induce exertion, but somewhere along the road ahead of them, they see the bonus foreman, the profit-sharing superintendent and the absentee stockholder ready to relieve them of their increased product.

As regards the stove moulders, they tried coöperation

as early as 1847 and often thereafter, in the vain endeavor to avoid strikes. Along with this they became the most persistently violent and restrictive of all labor organizations, or rather of all attempts to form a permanent organization. To prevent employers from cutting piece-rates and in order to build up a compact union, they established the rules that apprentices should be limited; that no man should be allowed to work with the aid of helpers; that no man should be allowed to earn more than a fixed wage set by the union. And then, to enforce these rules, they fined and expelled the violaters and established and violently enforced the other rule that union men should not be allowed to work with non-union men. Finally, this anarchy of individual efficiency brought its correction in the form of a representative government in control of the industry. This is the trade agreement, or joint conference system, that has preserved industrial peace in the stove foundry business for over twenty years. It governs the employer as firmly as the employee. The employer who cuts a piece-rate is expelled from the employers' association and is left alone to defend himself against the union. The union has removed its restrictions on output, and every man is left to earn as much as he wishes, without the fear of menacing his own or others' wages. It required some fifteen years of the agreement system to bring about this final result, so inveterate and abiding had been the distrust by the union of the employer's power or will to restrain himself from seizing upon the efficiency earnings. Many of the other rules of this interesting system of industrial organization are worth while to the student of industrial efficiency. Throughout these rules run the two conflicting principles — efficiency and restriction — both of them brought into a kind of equilibrium by the higher principle of organization.

I do not mean to say that the trade agreement system of the stove industry is the only form of organization that scientific study and ingenuity can work out for modern industry. Nor do I mean to say that in that system the participants have themselves as yet worked out all of the problems and yoked organization to efficiency so that they will always run lovingly together; nor that the consumer will not ultimately demand a voice in their councils. Nor do I mean to say that efficiency engineers are not taking into account the problems of organization as well as individual output, nor that the hostility of unions is a discriminating and reasoning hostility. What I do mean to say is this: the employer's business, as business now goes on, is to attend to the increase of efficiency; the wage-earner's business is to sell himself to do the employer's bidding for a period of time. The two interests are necessarily conflicting. Open conflict can be avoided in three ways: by the domination of the employer, as in the steel trust to-day; by the domination of the union, as in the iron industry prior to the Homestead strike; by the equal dominion of the two interests, as in the stove foundry business to-day. The first and second methods do not solve the problem; they suppress it. The third meets it in the same way that similar conflicts are met in the region of politics; namely, a constitutional form of organization representing the interests affected, with mutual veto, and therefore with progressive compromises as conflicts arise.

Foregoing are certain general bearings of the question. They indicate the fields for investigation. It is the business of science to work out the details and to combine details into workable systems. I have suggested the comparison of the early empirical systems of efficiency with the modern scientific systems. The modern systems are certainly a great advance on the early ones. All of them have this fact in common, that they recognize the principle of a minimum wage, which the old theory of wages disregarded. Here it seems that the long struggle of organized labor has received the sanction of science, and that the principle of efficiency is to be abandoned when it is not adequate to support the standard of living. The unions have contended that the minimum wage is not the same as a maximum. They permit the employer to pay more than the minimum if he wishes to do so. Now comes the scientific engineer and takes them at their word and does it in such a precise and mathematical way that there can be no doubt of his devotion to truth. It seems illogical in the unions to stand out against a system so carefully based on what they themselves have fought so long to get. Perhaps their ground of dislike is only sentimental. Indeed, they do not like the engineer's quite impersonal methods of investigation and recommendation. They know that he is hired by the employer to advise him how to get the greatest output at the least cost. The engineer studies how to economize the forces of nature embodied in physical capital and the forces of human nature embodied in men. He can hardly make the same distinction between the two that the workman makes. The stop-watch, the special slide rule, the speedometer, the time-testing laboratory, have the same use applied to both. The " fatigue curve " is unfeelingly figured out so as to show the speed at which each human machine should run in order to insure its longest life and greatest efficiency.

The older theory of labor, when the merchant was in control, was resented by the workman as a commodity theory, for it looked upon the price of labor as governed by demand and supply, like the price of anything else. The engineer's theory is rather a machinery theory, for it looks upon labor as an ingenious and necessary device, governed, indeed, not by laws of physics, but by laws of psychology. This device has certain fixed charges which must be met in the fashion of maintenance, repairs and depreciation, by a minimum wage to support a standard of living. Over or under this, each individual differs from others, not perhaps in load, slippage, friction and other physical details which machinery takes over, but in the psychological motives that induce attention, continuity, watchfulness. Compensation is the inducement that evokes these motives, and compensation should be as nicely adjusted to each detail of psychology and effort as is the adjustment of an electric current to the machine it is fed into. The blacksmith's bonus should be greater than the machinist's, because the blacksmith has to be induced to carry a greater load. And it is by nice experiment and comparison that the precise point is determined where the maximum ratio of output to ingo lies.

This theory and this practice are certainly more illuminating and hopeful than the commodity theory, but somehow they still lack something needed to arouse the approbation of the man investigated.

I am inclined to think that the lacking thing in the theory is the fact that it will be the employer, the foreman, the superintendent, and not the scientific engineer, who will carry it out in practice. The minimum wage is not so much a conclusion of science as an adjustment to circumstances. It represents the balance of two forces that are continually changing. If the wage contract were an ordinary contract enforceable at law, the engineer might install his system, tie it up and then go away until the contract ran out. But the wage contract is practically a new contract every morning. The employee can quit, and the employer can discharge him, at any moment. The new employee may be taken on, or the old one taken back, at a different rate. Even without a conscious purpose to violate the promise, a period of unemployment is certain to break the connection between old and new employees, old and new contracts. If there is no authority and no bargaining power able to require that the new contract shall run the same as the old one, only good faith and self-interest will be left to decide it. This is as much as to say that the union man cannot conceive of a minimum wage without a union or a statute to enforce it.

The minimum wage requires as its counterpart a system of extra pay for greater efficiency. The attitude of unions toward the bonus system is hostile. Strong unions even stake their existence on forcing the issue against it. Even the Locomotive Engineers, the least chargeable of all unions with restrictive policies, required the Santa Fe railroad officials to abandon it after a few months' trial. At the conference when this decision was reached, the heads of the organization avowed their willingness to coöperate, but said, "So far as this prize system that you have at the present time, we are all afraid of it. We are afraid of the principle behind it."

And one added in regard to the machinists, who had been defeated in their strike against the system, " I do not believe, had the old class of men remained here with their organization, that it ever would have been possible for you to put the bonus system in among the machinists in your shops." [1] This attitude of the engineers, the most favorable of all unions toward the policies of their employers, standing by the Santa Fe railroad for three or four years while it defeated the machinists and installed the system in its machine shops, but ready to invite the fate of the machinists in order to get rid of the same system applied to themselves, is conclusive of the hostile attitude of organized labor. In this case, also, the engineers were standing against the least objectionable form which the bonus system has taken. It was not the form but the " principle behind it " that they resisted.

Reduced to its last analysis, the " principle " of the bonus system is the principle of individual bargaining instead of union bargaining. Union bargaining means more than the formal negotiations at the time when the schedule of wages is made up. It means continuous oversight of each individual contract, and ability to require that it conform to the schedule. Its machinery must be something like that of a purchasing department with its testing laboratory to determine whether each delivery of goods comes up to the specifications. The fear of the unionist is the fear that his organization cannot cope with the infinite number of little variations from the schedule, or with variations that the schedule does not provide for.

The different bonus schemes differ materially in the

[1] *Machinists' Journal*, Dec., 1910.

degree to which they permit these variations. The earlier ones of Taylor, Halsey, Rowan[1] and others, differed but little from piece-work. A bonus was figured on each piece above the standard number of pieces expected for the minimum wage. On certain days or pieces the man might make a bonus; on other days or pieces he would make less than the expected number. This close calculation works out into something like a task system, for the man who does not make a bonus is more expensive than others and is the first to lose his job. On the other hand those who make bonuses set the standards for comparison with others. In this way each individual is continually carrying on a bargain with his foreman, setting up his record of output as the claim on his job, while competition forces all to meet him with as good a bargain. The later systems, especially the Emerson cumulative system, eliminate the accidents and fluctuations of the earlier systems by figuring the bonus on a man's entire work for a month, rather than on each separate job or piece.[2] But they retain, of course, the essential feature of the individual bargain.

How difficult it is for a union to cope with these individual differences may be seen even in the collective bargaining of the strongest unions. The employers argue from the record of, say, the ten best men and the employees from the record of the ten poorest men. The place where the minimum wage, or the piece-rate, or the bonus rate, shall be placed, is partly a matter of evi-

[1] See description of earlier systems in *American Economic Association Studies*, Vol. I; also Commons' "Trade Unionism," p. 274.

[2] See description of Emerson's system in *Engineering Magazine*, series of articles, 1910–1911.

dence, partly a trial of strength. The evidence is seldom conclusive and, since laborers generally are the aggressive party, seeking higher wages, shorter hours and better conditions, the evidence is not enough to carry their point. This is a reason why arbitration by a disinterested third party is distasteful to them. And, since each side puts up only its strongest evidence, neither can be trusted to act on the evidence of the other, however scientific, except when confronted by equal bargaining power of the other. Even the exact methods of the efficiency engineer are only a more precise form of evidence and are not enough to settle a question which turns so much on matters of opinion and feeling governed by the bargaining power of the parties. To the extent that the individual bargain enters, the laborers, as a whole, are not able to make advance against the employer's defensive position. It is this fact, that so much depends on bargaining, and that bargaining is the daily contact of employer and employee, whereas efficiency records and standards are merely data for comparisons in bargaining, that gives occasion for the efficiency engineer often to explain the failure of his system by the " failure of employers to act on his recommendations." The fundamental defect is the failure to investigate, first, the bargaining relations; then to organize these relations in such a way that conflicts of opinion and interest will be furnished a channel for expression and compromise; and then, last of all, to work out the standards and records under the direction of and subordinate to this organization of the bargaining parties. I do not pretend to say how this shall be done. It also is a matter for investigation in each case. I only contend that the individual bargain should be eliminated as far as possible and the collective bargain substituted.

Trade unionists, in this matter, are not different from non-unionists. The trade unionist has merely secured power to do what the others would like to have done. I know of one huge " trust " which succeeded long ago in driving out organized labor, but which finds in all of its shops an inexplicable arrangement that prevents any man from earning more than a certain amount of money at piece-rates. Perhaps scientific management and the bonus system would break down this apparent conspiracy, but I should expect it to recover after the men became familiar with the new devices. Nothing is more surprising often to employers and the merely scientific man, than the unanimity with which thousands of unorganized laborers will suddenly turn out on strike at the call of a few hundred organized laborers. It is their desperate recognition that the day of individual bargains is gone for them. And it would seem that a great corporation, representing thousands of stockholders speaking through one man, might be able to anticipate unionism by finding some means of scientific organization of labor before installing scientific management. In lieu of this, they wait until a union is formed, and then complain that it is hostile to efficiency. The example of the stove moulders, which I have given, shows that their hostility to efficiency is the hostility to methods that take them at a disadvantage in their power of protecting themselves. When once they are guaranteed assurance, as in the foundry business, that this will not be done, they respond as reasonably as other people.

There are many attractive and important contributions which the efficiency engineers are making towards the solution of labor problems. Their careful study of the human element in production is notable, appearing in the greatest variety of applications under the name of " welfare work." They are bringing forward issues that merely obstructive unionism will be compelled to meet in a spirit of coöperation or else go down. On the other hand, it is an uninformed opinion that persists in holding that the opposition of organized labor to industrial efficiency is merely obstructive and unreasoning. Organized labor is rather the organized expression of what labor in general would express if organized. To meet the avowed hostility of organized labor is to meet the instinctive hostility of nearly all labor, based on experience. It is not enough merely to adopt clever devices of compensation designed to separate laborers into individual bargaining units, for it is exactly this separation that competitive conditions are forcing laborers, as well as capitalists, to overcome. It is also necessary to adopt methods that will recognize the mutuality and solidarity of labor and to convert this craving for harmony and mutual support, as well as the impulse of individual ambition, into a productive asset.

CHAPTER XI

EUROPEAN AND AMERICAN UNIONS[1]

THE labor movement in America, compared with that in Europe, has shown remarkable peculiarities. These have, in the main, grown out of different economic and political conditions. Perhaps the most striking difference is that brought about by universal suffrage. It was not until 1867 that suffrage was granted to artisans in Great Britain, and not until 1885 that it was granted to agricultural laborers. But the suffrage became nearly universal in the northern states of the Union before 1830, and the first activity of the laboring people turned upon the utilization of their newly found political rights. This began in 1829, when the first labor party was formed, and in 1834 the first labor politician, Ely Moore, of New York, was elected to Congress. As a result of this participation in politics by the wage-earning class, the older political parties have contended for their influence, and have made concessions to the labor vote. This has tended at all times to break up the solidarity of the labor movement. Leaders, like Ely Moore, are lifted out of the labor movement and transferred to an independent position on a salary in the political field. At the same time, there have been but meager civil service requirements, and, consequently, labor leaders have received administrative appointments which rendered them independent of their labor constit-

[1] *Chautauquan*, April, 1911, pp. 247–254.

uency. The result has been that politics has drawn off the labor leaders and has continually weakened the solid front which has characterized the labor movement in England for sixty years.

This explains one of the interesting differences between American and European unionism, namely, the part played by professional men and representatives of the middle classes. In the British labor party of to-day we find such men as Macdonald, Snowden and others, university or professional men, coming into the labor movement by the way of socialism; but in America at no time has there been any leadership of unionism by professional men. There have been such men as Henry D. Lloyd, outspoken defenders of the unions, but never leaders in their councils. The professional element in the American labor movement has been that of men who were labor leaders first and lawyers and politicians afterwards. This has been characteristic from the time when Ely Moore became the friend of Andrew Jackson to the present time. In other words, the " intellectuals " of the British unions, and the same is more generally true of the continental unions, have come from outside the labor movement. In America the " intellectuals " have been a product of the movement itself.

The second peculiarity having a similar effect has been that of abundance of land. It was not until about 1890 that it became generally impracticable for wage-earners to leave the cities of the East and to create for themselves independent means of livelihood in the West. Since 1890, workingmen moving to the West find employment at some times more congested than in the East. Consequently, labor now rebounds to the East, intensifying class solidarity. But prior to the last decade or two there could be no solid labor movement, for the most ambitious and aggressive of the labor leaders, dissatisfied with their economic condition, could readily abandon their fellows and find an independent subsistence in the West. Thus the labor movement has been one of waves, depending upon the fluctuations in industry and the cost of living. The two periods of greatest inflation and rapid rise of prices culminated in 1835 and 1865. Each was caused by an inflation of paper currency. Prices rose so much more rapidly than wages that wage-earners were unable to escape to the West. They were perforce compelled to organize, and with the most astonishing success they forced wages up above anything that European unions could boast. But their success was short-lived. The ensuing depression disintegrated their forces, and their leaders went West or were drawn off by the political programme offered to them by the leading parties.

Another peculiarity of the American labor movement is a result of immigration and the variety of nationalities and races that must be brought together in a single organization if the movement is to be a success. Immigration did not show its effect until about 1850. Then we find the first indications of two languages in union meetings: German and English. No understanding of the American movement, compared with that especially of England, can be acquired until one perceives the importance of race and language. These underlie the strenuous demand of American unions for the closed shop, as compared with the relative indifference of English unionists on this subject. The closed shop is essentially labor's application of the protective tariff principle. The older nationalities have often created organizations denying the right of non-unionists to work alongside in the trade, with the most startling results in the different levels of wages in the same locality. Up to the decade of the fifties, it would scarcely happen that a skilled laborer, such as a bricklayer, would receive wages more than double the rate of pay of a common laborer. This is true at the present time in England, where, in general, we might find a bricklayer getting twenty cents an hour, with a common laborer getting ten cents an hour. But during the past sixty years the bricklayer in America has pushed his wages up from, say, two dollars a day of ten hours to five or six dollars for eight hours; while common labor has been able to advance only from a dollar for ten hours to a dollar and a half or a dollar seventy-five for the same number of hours. In other words, by means of the closed shop, this class of skilled labor has been able to increase its wages three-fold, or 200 per cent, measured by the hour; while common labor has increased only 50 or 75 per cent. The discrepancy has not been as great in other industries, where the closed shop has not been so successfully maintained, but the difference in all cases is far greater than that between European organized and European unorganized labor.

On the other hand, the advantage of a common race and a common class feeling, particularly among British and German wage-earners, has made it possible for unions to hold their ground without serious menace from non-unionists. The non-union Englishman is much more opposed to taking the job of the union Englishman than a non-union Italian to taking the job of a union Irishman. It is, therefore, on this question of races and immigration that the real class conflict in

American industry has occurred; for the backward or alien races have been made the instruments of employers to reduce the wages of the older nationalities. The hostility to immigration, exhibited by American unionists, is simply evidence of their attack upon the instruments used by their employers to defeat their demands, and the remarkable thing about American unionism in the last fifteen years has been its capacity to bring together in one organization many different nationalities. This is most strikingly the case among the coal-mine workers, and, in such cases, the newer races of Slavs and Italians have been able to advance their pay often 100 to 200 per cent; whereas, older races of skilled miners have advanced perhaps 50 per cent. In other words, an equalization of wages occurs in both countries at different levels and in different degrees. In Europe, skilled labor tends to approximate to that of unskilled on account of class solidarity and common language. In America, unskilled labor is lifted towards the wages of skilled labor when the two are brought together by the closed shop within the same union.

Another peculiarity of American labor movements is our federal system of government and the constitutional supremacy of our judiciary over labor legislation. On account of the fact that we have some fifty different legislative bodies enacting labor laws on entirely different levels of pressure, and as many different courts declaring these laws unconstitutional, labor has been compelled to organize over a wide area, to solidify its organization, and to enact, by the power of organization, uniform laws which our federal system and our written constitutions have prevented the states from enacting. The real beginnings of labor legislation came after the labor movement of the sixties and the Knights of Labor of the eighties. Almost all of this legislation has been declared unconstitutional in one state or another, and, consequently, we find that a union like the mine workers, unable through the law to secure weekly payments or prohibition of the trucking system and company houses, proceeds over a wide range of states to enact such laws by mutual agreement with employers after a strike. Thus, uniformity of legislation, which is brought about in European countries by a single legislature enacting laws for the entire country, is brought about in America by a single union forcing agreements with employers for an interstate competitive area.

This condition also explains in part the insistent demand of American labor for the exclusive policies of the closed shop, and explains certain peculiarities regarding the national organizations of labor. In England, the Trades Union Congress, organized in 1867, is really the national organization of the trade unions for legislative and parliamentary purposes, and out of the Trades Union Congress has grown the labor party of the past ten years. But in the United States, where labor laws are enacted by the several states and not appreciably by the Federal government, the organization of labor for legislative purposes is the State Federation of Labor. Any one who compares the Trades Union Congress of England with the American Federation of Labor misses the point. His comparison should be made with the state federations of labor. The American Federation of Labor is really similar to the British Federation of Engineering and Ship Building Trades or to the more recent General Federation of Labor, organized with a fund to support the unions in case of strikes. The prime purpose of the American Federation of Labor is to protect each union against dual organizations in its effort to legislate for the entire country through strikes and boycotts. The prime purpose of the state federations is to induce the state legislatures to enact labor laws. The Trades Union Congress of Britain does not seriously concern itself with the conflicts of dual organizations which are admitted to its councils, and it has no strong executive committee with power of discipline over conflicting unions, and no body of organizers endeavoring to enlist non-unionists in the ranks of organization. These matters, so vital to the American Federation, are left in Great Britain to the General Federation, or to the several district federations, or to the several unions. Of course, where the Federal government in America has jurisdiction in matters of interest to labor, such as restriction of immigration, hours of labor on public works and the use of the injunction by federal courts, the American Federation of Labor takes an active legislative part similar to that of the Trades Union Congress. But this is not its primary purpose, although there are indications that it will more and more be forced, in resisting the federal courts, to press for congressional legislation restricting the courts.

In this sense, a comparison of the Trades Union Congress of Great Britain, following the Taff Vale decision, with the American Federation of Labor, following the use of the injunction, is instructive. The Trades Union Congress, formed primarily for parliamentary purposes, was able, after the Taff Vale decision, to unite with the socialists and to elect labor members to parliament; but the American Federation of Labor has been unable and unwilling to start an independent labor party, because political contests would disrupt the unions in their economic contests. The Trades Union Congress can go ahead in politics, while the General Federation of Labor and the other federations remain intact in the struggles with employers. Following the British analogy, a labor party in America should be started by a National Federation of State Federations of Labor.

A comparison of the status of trade unions before the law in England and America will emphasize further this distinction. It was not until 1875 that British trade unions secured a legal standing that would free them from a charge of conspiracy. But the American unions were relieved of this charge by the decisions of the courts as early as 1842, following their aggressive political movements of 1830 to 1836. In England, by the time of the Taff Vale decision in 1901, the legislation of 1875 was practically nullified, and in 1906 the unions, through the labor party and the Trades Disputes Act, secured almost complete immunity from attacks as organizations. In America, after the astonishing and unique movement of the eighties through the Knights of Labor, based mainly on the use of the boycott, the courts, although adhering to their precedents relieving the unions of the charge of conspiracy, introduced the notion of malicious conspiracy and the method of the injunction as a means of prohibiting it. The boycott has never been used to an appreciable extent by British unions, and, in fact, would probably create such popular hostility that it would be destructive of the unions. On the other hand, in America, the boycott has been as powerful as the strike. Such unions as the brewery workers, hatters, printers, cigar makers, and garment workers, have their strength mainly in the support of fellow unionists who refuse to purchase the products of non-union labor. It is the boycott which explains the significance of the doctrine of malicious conspiracy, that is, a conspiracy designed, not " to benefit one's self," but " to injure the business of another." It will be seen, therefore, that the effort of the American trade unions to secure that immunity which the Trades Disputes Act has given to British trade unions, involves an effort to sustain the practice of the boycott which the British unions have not practised. In fact, we must look to Germany, with its powerful socialist movement, in order to find that complete legal immunity of trade unions in the use of the boycott which is essential to the existence of so many American unions.

CHAPTER XII

LABOR AND MUNICIPAL POLITICS[1]

NEITHER municipal ownership nor private ownership have accomplished the good results in the United States that should be expected of them, and both are far behind what both have accomplished in Great Britain. I attribute this backwardness mainly to the infancy of the movement for municipal ownership in the United States. The American people have never seriously studied in detail the financial, political, administrative and labor conditions necessary to make municipal ownership a success, because they have never had thrown upon them the responsibility and necessity of making it a success. The question has not yet been big enough to attract attention, and all the energies of the people in municipal government have been consumed in fighting the private corporations which have possession. We are in precisely the same position that British municipalities occupied 40 years ago in the gas business, and 15 to 30 years ago in the street car and electricity business. And the two most noticeable facts regarding the movement in Great Britain are the

[1] Summary of investigations made for the National Civic Federation in 1905 and 1906 and printed in Volume I of its "Municipal and Private Operation of Public Utilities," pp. 88–112. Some ten cities and twenty-four municipal and private plants were visited in Great Britain, and some fourteen cities and fifteen plants in the United States. The visiting party was selected so as to represent the "pros" and "antis" of municipal operation.

steady improvement made in municipal operation after municipal ownership had passed the fighting stage and had become a settled policy, and also the great improvement in private ownership and operation during the same period. In comparing the two countries, I have been impressed by this fact more than anything else, that successful private operation follows successful municipal operation. The private companies in Great Britain have learned to accept and act upon a view of their public obligations which we have found to be utterly foreign and inconceivable to the managers of similar private undertakings in the United States. This is seen most strikingly in the fact that the British companies were willing that our engineers should make a physical valuation of their properties for comparison with their capitalization and their earnings, whereas the American companies would not permit such a valuation. Many of the British companies also for years have been subject to complete publicity of their accounts and examination of their books by public auditors and accountants, thus furnishing information that we were not able to get in America. This kind of information is essential both from the standpoint of the prices paid by consumers and that of the wages paid to employees, because it enables us to know whether prices are as low and wages are as high as the companies can reasonably afford. Another instance of the higher view of their obligations held by British companies is the many precautions they have taken to conciliate their employees and to prevent the necessity of strikes. In every case this higher view has come about because the companies have before them the menace of municipal ownership, if they do not live up to their public obligations. They cannot afford to have strikes, because they would at once arouse into action the demand for municipal ownership. They cannot afford to keep their accounts private, because in order to head off municipal ownership they must let the people know just how much profit they are making. The consequence is that many of the vices which we have found in private ownership in the United States, and which were formerly found in Great Britain, have been largely eliminated in that country. And at the same time the vices and crudities of municipal ownership which we have found in the United States have been largely eliminated in Great Britain through experience and through the accurate comparison which can always be made with private ownership.

My interpretation requires that at least for some time to come, both private ownership and municipal ownership be carried along side by side in the same country, that each municipality have full power and home rule to change from one to the other according to its judgment of which it is that offers the better results in the given case; and that in this way the defects of both municipal and private ownership in the United States may be gradually eliminated and both may be brought to the higher level occupied by both in Great Britain.

Monopolies and Politics

I take it that the key to the whole question of municipal or private ownership is the question of politics. For politics is simply the question of getting and keeping the right kind of men to manage and operate the municipal undertakings, or to supervise, regulate and bargain with the private undertakings. The kinds of business that we are dealing with are essentially monopolies performing a public service, and are compelled to make use of the streets which are public property. If their owners are private companies they are compelled to get their franchises and all privileges of doing business, and all terms and conditions of service from the municipal authorities. And in carrying out their contract with the municipality they are dealing continually with municipal officials. Consequently it is absurd to assume that private ownership is non-political. It is just as much a political question to get and keep honest or businesslike municipal officials who will drive good bargains with private companies on behalf of the public and then see that the bargains are lived up to, as it is to get similar officials to operate a municipal plant. We do not escape politics by resorting to private ownership — we only get a different kind of practical politics.

Since these businesses are monopolies of public service and must make use of public property, the question of municipal ownership is entirely different from that of other kinds of business. A private business that has no dealings with municipal officials and is regulated by competition has no place in this investigation except by way of contrast. We have found that this difference between the two kinds of business is not always appreciated by certain classes. These are the socialists and the public utility corporations. The socialists are opposed to private competition in any form and would extend public ownership to all kinds of business. The public utility corporations and their defenders naturally seize upon this position of the socialists to confuse the issues respecting their own kind of business. The public

at large is misled for a time until the distinction comes
to be one of practical importance.   This attitude of the
several parties to the controversy was most clearly
brought to our attention in Glasgow, where public
ownership has been extended to all of the businesses
occupying the streets.   Following the municipal tramways of 1894, many projects were brought forward for
further municipalization, including banking, housing,
insurance, tailoring and baking.   Councillors were
elected favorable to these proposals, and the voters,
inspired by the remarkable success of the tramways,
were not critical in their inspection of these new enterprises which the council was contemplating.   In the
midst of this socialistic tide, two anti-municipal ownership associations were organized — the Citizens' Union
and the Rate-Payers' Federation.   They started an
active agitation, and, along with other influences, the
tide of municipalization has been checked or stopped.
We were led to believe that from these two associations
we could secure information that would correct the
universal indorsement of municipal ownership found
elsewhere in Glasgow, but were surprised to find that
both associations indorsed all that had been done in
municipalizing tramways, electricity, gas and water.
They only opposed the municipalization of other undertakings competitive in character.   No more conclusive
indorsement of the success of municipal ownership in
Glasgow could have been brought to our attention, but
at the same time nothing more conclusive could be
offered to show that the general public cannot be permanently deceived by the fallacy of the socialists and
the dodge of the franchise corporations in confusing competitive business with monopolistic public-service busi-

ness. The essential difference is that the public-service business is in politics, whether operated by a private company or by a municipality, but the competitive business does not depend on politicians for its profits.

In Wheeling, West Virginia, the gas employees take part in the primaries of the Republican party, and the motormen and conductors of the street car companies are given leave of absence on pay to work in the primaries of both the Republican and Democratic parties. Even the officers of the street railway employees' union take part in this kind of traction politics on behalf of their employers. The councilmen and aldermen nominated and elected in this way control the municipal gas works, and they control the franchises and contracts of the private companies. The " City Hall Ring " is just as much a ring of the political tools of the private corporations as it is a ring of municipal politicians.

In cities other than Wheeling the convention system prevails instead of the direct primaries, and consequently it was not found that the wage-earners of the private companies took a similar active part in political campaigns. But in Syracuse, Allegheny, Indianapolis and Philadelphia, where municipal employees are named by politicians, it was found also that street car, electric, gas and water companies had employed men on the recommendation of councilmen, mayor or chairman of a political committee. This practice was carried furthest by the street car companies of Syracuse and Allegheny. In Chicago, where a most rigid civil service law is enforced, no evidence of political appointments could be found in the municipal electricity or water departments during recent years, but men were hired on recommendation of aldermen by the private electrical companies at the time when their contracts were before the council for renewal.

There is a distinction which has been found in all of these cases between political appointments in municipal undertakings and political appointments by franchise corporations. The alderman or mayor who secures the appointment of a political supporter on a municipal job exerts himself just as much to retain that man in his job as he did to get the appointment for him. But both he and his supporters take a different view when the appointment is secured with a street railway, gas or electric company. The alderman then says, " I get the job for you, but you must make good; I cannot keep the job for you; the company has the right to discharge you if you don't do your work." It is for this reason that the private company has an advantage over the municipal management under the spoils system, for it can get rid of a political appointee after trying him out and finding him inefficient. This explains also why it is that the employees of a franchise corporation, even though they get their appointments through politicians, are nevertheless found to take an active part in organizing themselves in a trade union, but where they depend on the politicians for retaining their jobs and improving their wages and conditions they do not look to a union for protection. Where the politicians' support stops after appointment, as in a private undertaking, they are more likely to protect themselves by organizing a union. The result is similar in a municipal undertaking when civil service reform releases the employee from depending on a politician. The trade unions in Chicago have no difficulty in organizing the workmen who have been appointed through the Civil Service Commission, but

they are not able to get the " hold-overs " who came
in through political pull.

Curiously enough, the politician profits more in
some respects by the appointments which he secures for
his supporters with a franchise company than he does
by those on municipal jobs.   Since all parties understand that the alderman's influence stops after appointment, there is no ill feeling on the part of his supporter
if he is discharged.   He and his family and friends
continue to be the supporters of the alderman who has
done his best for them, and his discharge at the same
time makes room for the alderman to name another
man, who also with his family and friends become supporters.   It is different in municipal employment,
where it is expected that the politician who gets the job
for his follower will keep it for him.   If he is removed
from that job he loses confidence in the ability or good
faith of the politician.   On account of these differences
in the attitude of workmen, politicians and managers,
the private corporation in politics is more efficient from
the standpoint of its stockholders than the municipal
undertaking in politics, and at the same time the capable
politician can build up his organization just as effectively
under one system as under the other.   Where civil
service rules are enforced, as in the Chicago Electric and
Water departments, this political influence is excluded,
but there is no way of preventing a private corporation
from hiring its employees on the recommendation of a
politician.

There are other differences which operate to the advantage of the private corporation.   Its employees are
more minutely specialized, and a few positions of a permanent, semi-political character are created which are

kept distinct from the technical and administrative positions, whereas in the municipal undertaking, without civil service rules, a larger proportion of the positions are likely to be semi-political. The municipal undertaking is compelled to keep a few sub-managers, foremen and inspectors who are familiar with the layout of the plant and distributing system, and such positions have been found to be permanent, while the other positions are subject to political vicissitude. In the private corporations investigated the political positions are found not so much in the operating department as in the legal department, and among the directors, presidents and highest officials. These make the bargains directly, by means of a cash consideration or otherwise, with the political managers. Only where nominations are made by direct primaries, as in Wheeling, has it been found that the rank and file of the employees are retained on account of this political influence.

Under the convention system of nominations the principal activity of private corporations was found to be that of contributions to the expenses of campaign committees and candidates. It is difficult to see that it is necessarily dishonorable or corrupt for any citizen to contribute according to his ability toward the expenses of his political party in conducting a campaign. The education of the voter respecting the issues is of the greatest importance and requires corresponding expenditures. But for some reason these contributions are looked upon as strictly confidential, and it was only through the accident of my personal acquaintance with certain participants in Syracuse and Indianapolis that any information on the point was given to me. This shows a contribution of $2000 in Syracuse by two directors of a franchise company to the Democratic campaign committee, in a municipal election. It shows contributions at Indianapolis by a franchise company in the municipal campaign of 1903 of $300, and in 1905 of $1500 to the Democratic committee, and in 1905 of $5000 to the Republican committee. In 1905 one company paid $10,000 to the Republican committee, and $2000 to the Democratic committee, and another paid $17,000 to the Republican committee. The Republican administration, elected in 1905, has to deal with important franchises and contracts renewable during its term.

Efficiency of Municipal Operation

Whatever weakens or corrupts city government in its admitted duties of protecting the health, property, life and morals of its citizens, also weakens or corrupts it in operating public utilities or in regulating the private operation of those utilities. We cannot separate the question of municipal or private operation from the question of honest and efficient city government in every other department. The municipal corporation is a unit, and the supply of either water, gas, electricity or transportation is only a single department of its work, and is good or bad to the same extent that the other departments of police, fire, health, parks and taxes are good or bad. When we investigate the politics and labor of these four public utilities, we are investigating the whole question of municipal government. If the conditions are such that the city does not operate or regulate these utilities satisfactorily, we find that it does not do anything else satisfactorily. This fact is abundantly demonstrated when we take up one by one the several factors that go to make up the total political life of a city.

First is the suffrage. In all of the Northern cities of the United States the suffrage is on the universal manhood basis. In the Southern cities it is restricted by education or poll-tax requirements, and in British cities by tenant, lodger and household limitations. These restrictions bear most heavily on the wage-earning classes, amounting to the exclusion of one-fourth to two-fifths of the wage-earners. But the classes excluded are the casual and irregular laborers, the pauperized and indifferent workers, the hoodlum and hooligan elements. These are mainly the unorganized laborers, so that in England the trade unions have the field to themselves, more than they have in the United States, for entering upon a political movement. They are not compelled to make alliances with political bosses who know how to get these unorganized voters. In two Northern cities, Indianapolis and Syracuse, definite information was obtained of bribery of the voters. In Indianapolis the bribable voters are largely the colored element of the town, and in Syracuse the hoodlum, immigrant and colored element of the down-town precincts. Among these voters a large part of the campaign contributions is distributed.

Next to the suffrage are the qualifications of the councillors, aldermen and city officials. In the British cities only the councillors are elected, one each year, holding three years for each ward. The councillors select the managers and city officials. Most important of all, the councillors and aldermen are not required to live in the wards they represent and many of them live in the suburbs. One-half to four-fifths of the councillors and aldermen live outside the wards they represent, and the proportion is strikingly larger in the working-class wards, which elect two-thirds to nine-tenths of their councillors from outside. Many inquiries were made as to the reasons, on the part of voters, for this indifference as to the place of residence of their candidates, and the explanation that seems adequate is the absence of campaign and corruption funds and the inability of councillors to find jobs for their constituents. The councillor in Glasgow who is most active in pressing for jobs in the municipal service lives in the ward which he represents, among constituents in need of employment. Furthermore, councillors and aldermen are unsalaried. This freedom of choice makes it possible to elect both the leading business men and the leading labor men to govern the city. Not only do we find eminent bankers, financiers and employers of labor in the councils, but we find the secretaries and officials of trade unions, most of them living outside the wards they represent. The absence of such leaders and truly representative men from American city councils is the most discouraging fact brought to our attention. We have not found any of the leading business men corresponding to those in British cities. The largest delegation of wage-earners which we found was in the city of Wheeling, where they number fourteen, but not one of them was an official or representative of a trade union, although the unions are stronger in Wheeling than in the other places visited. There the wage-earning councillors were largely the employees of corporations whose owners were interested in the public utility corporations. Their campaign expenses were paid from those sources, and their successful qualities were those of a good "mixer" with the voters, and obedience to their employers in casting their votes as councilmen. In other cities not provided with the direct primary system of nominations there were practically no wage-earners in the council.

In American cities the form of organization has been found to be most complicated. Authority and responsibility are scattered here and there in a mayor, a commission, a superintendent, a council, a committee of the council, or even two committees, sometimes a joint committee of two branches of the council, a civil service commission, and so on. The finances and accounts of municipal undertakings are mixed with those of other departments. Scarcely any system that we have investigated would for a moment be recognized as satisfactory for an effective business management. The voters are unable to tell who is responsible or what exactly are the financial results. The one preëminent advantage of private operation is centralized control by one man, subject to a board of directors. This is also the form of organization of the British cities, where a committee of the council takes the place of the board of directors, and the manager, selected by the committee, holds his position not for a fixed term, but permanently, or until removed. The American system most nearly corresponding is the commission system of South Norwalk and Detroit, which permits the selection of men from any part of the city and retains a number of them when others drop out.

The foregoing statements refer only to the legal or formal organization of British and American cities. The real political influences behind this formal organization are found in the conflicting interests of the voters who elect or control the city officials. In both countries the interests that are most important in deciding the results are those of the saloon keepers, real estate owners, political parties, trade unions, municipal employees, business classes, contractors and franchise corporations.

In both countries the saloons, known in England as the "public house," or "pub," are regulated by the municipal council. This compels them in self-protection to take a part in politics. In some places, like Glasgow, their candidates make a pretence of standing for working-men, and they appeal to the labor vote in support of labor measures in the council. In other places, like Liverpool, the large brewery interests enter the field as capitalists, and elect their partners to the council. In American cities the saloon interest is an important wheel of the political machine. In any case their candidates are elected, not for the sake of efficient government, but really in order to weaken the government that endeavors to regulate their private business.

Much less evidence was found of real estate dealers and speculators in British cities than in American cities. Owing perhaps to the system of landed property and the jealousy of the landed interest, real estate speculation is very quiet and subdued in British cities. The councils, outside London, are almost exclusively of the commercial, manufacturing, professional and labor classes. The purchase and sale of sites either by a council or by a company, and the selection of routes, are so jealously controlled by the landed interest intrenched in the House of Lords, that land speculation in connection with public utilities does not greatly influence the local councils.

In all of the cities visited in Great Britain, except

Glasgow and London, it was found that national political parties managed the municipal elections. The exception in Glasgow is mainly owing to the fact that there the
Liberal party is so overwhelming that the Tories have
no chance. Even the committees that manage the
municipal undertakings are selected so that the dominant
party of the council has majorities. In two places, however, Leicester and Birmingham, an eminent financier
of the opposite party is elected to the head of the finance
committee. Party politics in itself is not a barrier to
successful municipal operation. The part taken by the
working classes in the election of councillors in England
is divided into two stages. The few labor members
elected ten to twenty years ago came in as members of
the Liberal party and they retain that allegiance. They
are first Liberals and secondarily trade unionists. The
second stage is that of the Labor party of the past five
years, in which the trade unions have joined with one
wing of the socialists. The object of the Labor party
has been that of getting legislation to protect the funds
of trade unions from attachment by the courts. It has,
however, organized local branches for municipal elections. Much the largest number of candidates put up
by the Labor party are the salaried officials of the unions,
who, if elected, retain their union position. They are
not usually " organizers " or " agitators," for the
British unions do not have such salaried positions, but
they are the official secretaries who are at the same time
the experienced negotiators with employers. A much
smaller class of so-called " labor councillors " are the
socialists, who are generally small merchants, employers
or professional men, with a programme more radical than
that of the trade unionists. Finally, there were found

a half dozen political adventurers of the "fakir" type, not nominated by the Labor party, but taken up by the Liberals, Tories or public-house interests to draw off the vote of the Labor party. In general, while some criticism was heard from aged councillors or from old-line trade-union Liberals, to the effect that the new labor movement was deteriorating the character of the councils, yet the criticism was confined to the lack of business and financial capacity, to the inability to take "broad" views of municipal business, and to the efforts to find municipal work for applicants. With the exception of the half dozen adventurers, no criticism is made of their integrity or earnestness and sincerity of purpose in urging the cause they advocate; while in the case of the trade-union officials there was a general agreement on the part of all classes that they brought a kind of intelligence and a point of view that was needed in the council's deliberations as a large employer of labor.

Organizations of Municipal Employees

The increase in municipal ownership in Great Britain has, of course, brought an increase in the number of municipal employees, and this has caused apprehension in certain quarters. Generally the chief officers of the municipal enterprises take the ground that they and other employees should not vote in municipal elections, and they openly set that example to their subordinates. Some of them go even so far as to advocate the disfranchisement of municipal employees in municipal elections. This has also been advocated by some of the councillors. However, such a proposition is no longer seriously considered. If the vote of municipal employees is a menace, the remedy must be looked for in directions other than disfranchisement. It goes without proof that such a remedy is needed, for municipal employees sooner or later cast their votes for candidates who promise or have secured a betterment of their conditions, regardless of its effect on the enterprise as a whole. Omitting disfranchisement, there are two directions in which such a remedy can be found, first, a limit to be set beyond which municipalization shall not go, and second, the attitude of the public, and especially of the workmen in private employment.

Although there are doctrinaire and socialistic elements that set no limit to public ownership, the overwhelming sentiment of those now in control of the municipal councils places a limit at the point already reached by cities like Glasgow, Manchester and Leicester. With this practical agreement there is no prospect that the number of municipal employees will be materially increased beyond the proportion reached in Glasgow, where their voting strength is possibly one-sixteenth of the total. The total number employed by the London County Council and the London Borough Councils is about one-fourteenth of the registered voters.

The natural tendency of municipal employees to better their own condition by use of their political strength is seen in the growth of the Municipal Employees' Association. This is a spurious form of trade unionism which has sprung up with the growth of municipalization, and nothing of its kind has been found among American unions. It has gained affiliation with other unions in the Trades Union Congress and in local Trades Councils. Its platform is simple enough: to prohibit strikes, to oppose councillors at the polls, if they stand in the way of granting its demands, and to call on other unions for help in the elections. Its demands are in excess of anything that other unions have been able to secure from private employers or even from municipal corporations. It invites into membership all employees of municipalities, and since they are nearly all eligible to other unions, evidently the aim of this organization is to separate a privileged class of workmen, and to do this through the political power of those whom they abandon. It weakens other unions while building on their support. With even a minimum of intelligence in the other unions such a parasitic union would be repudiated. Such has been the fate of the Municipal Employees' Association. As long as its membership was small the consequences of its policy were not observed, and its demands received the uncritical assent of others in the general approval of all efforts to raise wages. But with its rapid growth during the past two years, the unions of unskilled workmen, who suffered first from its competition for members, brought their protest to the Trades Union Congress in 1906, and that body, after careful deliberation, repudiated the methods of the Municipal Employees' Association, and all similar organizations of public employees, by the practically unanimous vote of 1,196,000 to 42,000. It is thus promptly settled, before this organization had reached 15,000 members throughout Great Britain, that the trade-union world is clearly opposed, both in sentiment and self-interest, to the creation of a privileged class of municipal employees. As far as the regular trade unions are concerned the principle of trade-union wages, rising and falling in municipal employment the same as in private employment, is accepted in its full significance.

Our investigations have shown that the proper method of dealing with employees is the most difficult and critical problem of municipal ownership. The appointment, promotion and dismissal of employees and the wages to be paid offer peculiar opportunities for political and personal influence inconsistent with efficiency. Civil service reform, so-called, has been found in its highest perfection in the city of Chicago, but it is evident by comparison with a less perfect device in Syracuse that its integrity depends on the political influences that control the mayor and the heads of departments. If the head of the department is independent of politics, as shown in Cleveland, Detroit and South Norwalk, the civil service commission is not needed. The Chicago system is a temporary bulwark built around the departments until such time as the chief officer himself can also be protected from political selection. This is the case in British cities where the idea of a civil service commission is unknown. But even there, especially in the Sheffield tramways, appointments have been made on the recommendation of councillors. The experience of Glasgow is instructive. Fifteen years ago the practice of hiring employees on the recommendation of councillors was universal in all departments. But with the growth of municipal ownership it has almost disappeared. This is partly because several thorough investigations of alleged favoritism have been made by the council; partly because public-spirited business men have exposed the evil, have made it clear to the voters, and have been elected to the council on the issue of driving out favoritism; and partly because the adoption of the minimum wage policy of the labor members has stopped the practice of councillors' unloading and pensioning their old employees on the municipal pay-roll. The only remnant of the practice discovered after a thorough investigation in Glasgow was in the unskilled work of the tramways, and this came about through the effort of that department during the industrial depression of 1905–1906 to aid the city government in finding work for the unemployed. The pressure for employment during the depression was enormous, and all managers were besieged by hundreds of applicants. A card of introduction from a councillor secures at least the privilege of filling out an application blank, and this amounts to a limited preference over those who do not have such cards, but the managers follow up the application by a thorough examination before making appointments. In other places all charges of favoritism were carefully investigated, and they were found to be baseless, except in the case of motormen and conductors at Sheffield. These are selected on the recommendation of councillors. The Manchester Tramways Committee, at the beginning of its organization, recognizing the possible evil, adopted a rule instructing their manager not only not to pay attention to letters from councillors, but to give preference to applicants who have no such recommendations.

Our investigations have shown that the strongest safeguard for a manager against the pressure of outside recommendations is the recognition of organized labor within his department. Wherever we have found a class of employees organized and dealt with as such through their representatives, we have found those positions exempt from politics. This follows from the nature of labor organization, which cannot survive if individuals are given preference on political, religious, personal or any other grounds than the character of the work they do. Even in the politically honeycombed municipal undertaking of Allegheny, the union of electrical workers stopped the practice of paying assessments by its members for political campaigns. The success of the civil service system of Chicago is owing more than anything else to the fact that organized labor has one of the three members on each examining board. The manager of the Manchester tramways ascribes his freedom from interference by individual councillors to his recognition of the union that holds 90 per cent of his motormen and conductors.

Private Companies and Municipal Councils

The foregoing is a review of several interests which have been discovered as tending to weaken the efficiency and integrity of municipalities in the operation or regulation of monopolies, together with the factors that tend to correct these evil tendencies. In inquiring into the part played by all of them, including saloon keepers, real estate speculators, party politicians and municipal employees, the most impressive fact in Great Britain is the absence of any political " machine " which could bring them together and line them up under a centralized control. Whatever corrupting or incapacitating tendencies there may be in these several interests that come into conflict with good administration, each works by itself, and there is no permanent interest or class of manipulators which thrives by marshalling them together in a perpetual onslaught and undermining of the city government. Public-spirited and independent citizens are not compelled to enter into bargains nor to make promises to a political organization, which would dis-

gust them with a position on the Town Council. This
absence of a powerful machine is mainly due to the fact
that there are no great financial bargains at stake, such
as municipal contracts or franchises, whose owners
have a direct interest in breaking down city government.
None of the menacing factors above mentioned is large
enough, and all of them combined cannot gain enough,
to warrant them in making large contributions to an
expensive organization for the control of elections and
appointments. The brewery interest is practically the
only interest of financial importance whose profits can
be menaced by acts of the Council, but the menace to
it is based on moral, and not financial, grounds. In
resisting this menace it does not directly attack the
business integrity of the Council, but, more important,
there is no opportunity for it to make an alliance with
contractors and franchise speculators who could increase their profits and make sharper bargains with the
city if the councillors were weak or corrupt, or under
the control of a machine which they must support.
The absence of powerful financial opponents of good
government leaves the way open for business men to
enter the councils and to attack abuses or defend the
interests of the city without risking their private business
or antagonizing their social circle. The eminent bankers,
financiers and merchants who serve the cities as aldermen on the finance committees are free to do so because
neither they nor their clients or business associates
are interested in stocks which might be depreciated if
they helped the city to drive a good bargain. These
men are often the directors in large manufacturing, railway and other private companies. Councillors and
aldermen on the gas, water, electricity and tramways

committees are even stockhloders and directors in private gas and water companies of other towns. It would be impossible for such men to act conscientiously on the great board of municipal directors, and to give the town the same kind of service as they give to their private companies, if they or their business associates were interested in companies which had business relations with the Council. Neither could the medium and smaller business men and employers afford to accept positions on the councils and take the independent stand they do, if the bankers and large business men on whom they depend for credits and sales were interested in the stocks of franchise companies. With these great antagonistic interests out of the way, the business men of the town find, not only that their private business is not menaced, but that the conditions of all private business are greatly improved, if they lend their abilities to the improvement of municipal business. The time which they take from their private affairs is often not even a business sacrifice. The honor and distinction of public service on the council is really an advertising asset in their private business. It would be a liability if they were called upon to antagonize large financial interests.

I do not hold that the contrast in American cities gives evidence that the private corporations which we have investigated have taken the initiative in corrupting and weakening the municipal councils. The initiative has just as often come from corrupt officials who " hold up " the corporations. The real question is not, Who is to blame? or, Is it blackmail or is it bribery? but the real question is, What is the situation that compels officials, campaign committees and corporations to resort to blackmail and bribery? Plainly by comparison of American and British cities the answer is found in the enormous profits at stake on municipal elections.

It is the absence of a political machine and its financial contributions that also makes possible the election in British cities of remarkable groups of Labor councillors. With but few exceptions the labor members are representative of the best elements of the trade unions. Although they lack the financial experience of business men they contribute a valuable knowledge of labor conditions on which successful management of municipal undertakings depends. Men of their integrity and earnestness have the opportunity to come forward because the trade unions are not undermined nor their leaders bribed by the paid agents of a political machine. And the financial interests that would profit by the election of weak or dishonest labor candidates are not powerful enough to sudsidize the astute agents needed by the machine for the purpose.

A contrast with this situation appears in two of the places visited where private companies operate public utilities. The municipal council of Newcastle-on-Tyne is decidedly inferior in quality and ability to others, and two of the leading financiers on the council declared that their only reason for remaining in the position is the election which the council gives them as corporation representatives on the Tyne Improvement Commission. The presence of private gas, electricity and water companies, with their representatives in the council, prevents the leading business men from interesting themselves in the success of the municipal government, while an equivocal class of labor agitators takes advantage of the situation to get elected to the council.

Sheffield, also, with its influential gas company, is the only town visited where the employees in the tramway and street departments are appointed through the influence of councillors. In that town there is a peculiar inducement for the eminent business men in charge of the gas company to look with approval on the election of inferior councillors, because the council elects three of its members as directors of the company. The strength of the company is seen in the incompetency of these municipal directors, who are kept in ignorance of essential details in its affairs. With councillors of this inferior type and with the indifference of business men to the management of municipal affairs, the result is seen in the absence of any protest against practices which are undermining the municipal undertakings.

Certain effects of the municipal ownership movement in Great Britain on the private companies are evident. The Sheffield Company, under the far-seeing management of Sir Frederick Mappin, has directed its policy for many years with the distinct purpose of meeting the arguments for municipal ownership. To avoid agitation it has refrained from going to Parliament for permission to increase its capital stock. Consequently it has distributed its large surplus profits in the form of reduced prices for gas and betterments to its plant. Most instructive of all is the attitude of the companies toward their employees. With the sentiment of municipal ownership ready to explode, the companies cannot afford to risk a strike. The Newcastle gas company has met this situation by a willing recognition of the gas workers' union and by a resort to arbitration through which wages have been materially raised. The South Metropolitan Company has developed its co-partnership scheme with astonishing shrewdness and careful attention to details, so that every disaffected workman is silent or dismissed. The Sheffield Company, although its president had openly attacked and wrecked trade unions in his private business, contented itself with gradually undermining the gas workers' union, through the payment of wages and bonuses superior to those paid by other private employers of the district, and even in the case of unskilled labor, superior to those paid by the municipal corporation of Sheffield.

Trade Unions and Wages

The influence of wage-earners through their unions upon the conditions of municipal employment in the United States has been complicated through the presence and activity of practical politicians. In the municipal enterprises investigated, except South Norwalk and Richmond, the eight-hour day has been established for the past ten or fifteen years for all employees, whereas, in the private companies the hours are longer or have more recently been reduced for a portion, but not all, of their employees in the more skilled branches of work. This advantage in municipal undertakings has been brought about, not by a definite labor party, but by the influence of wage-earners as voters upon the municipal officials.

A curious contrast, however, presents itself in the wages paid by contractors on municipal work. While the larger cities in their own employment reduced the hours several years before similar reductions were made by British municipalities, yet, unlike the British municipalities, provision was not made requiring contractors on municipal works to observe the hours and wages paid by the municipalities themselves. It has only been within the past five or six years that a definite movement was undertaken by the wage-earning element to extend these provisions to contractors, and this, on account of adverse decisions of the courts, led to the adoption in New York of a constitutional amendment in 1905 stipulating that the prevailing rate of wages should be paid by contractors on the work of the State or its subdivisions. This clause has recently been adopted by the city of Chicago. The hand of the politician is seen in formerly omitting contractors from requirements respecting wages and hours, since by this device he was able to win both the wage-earners and the contractors to his support. But with the more extensive organization of wage-earners and their independence of the politicians, the contractors are placed on the same basis as the municipality.

In only one case investigated in the United States is there a formal trade agreement between the union and a municipal department, namely, that of the electricity department of Chicago, but since permanent appointments in that and other departments of Chicago are controlled by the Civil Service Commission, the effect of this agreement is to control only the temporary or sixty-day appointments. The unions, however, are recognized by the Civil Service Commission to the extent that an officer of the union concerned is appointed as one of the three members of the examining board which passes upon applicants for municipal positions. The other two members are employers or technical experts selected by the commission outside the municipal service. The consequence of this arrangement is that the unions are satisfied that the civil service law is honestly ad-

ministered, and, at the same time, the non-union workmen are protected against discrimination. In Great
Britain there are two undertakings, Birmingham gas
and Manchester tramways, which have trade agreements with the unions, and in all other places the same
result is reached by the provision requiring the payment
of trade-union rates of wages.

The municipal undertakings in both countries are
necessarily " open shop," in the sense that employment
is open both to union and non-union men. In the case
of the more skilled trades this usually results in the
employment of union men, depending partly on the attitude of the manager. This attitude is favorable to the
unions in all of the British municipalities except Liverpool and is favorable in the American cities of Cleveland,
Detroit and Chicago. In these places the managers
consult the union officers in arranging wages, hours
and conditions of work. The three American places
mentioned are those where the political machine, supported by the contractors and franchise corporations,
has been eliminated from the control of the city government by a popular revolt against the corporations. But
in Allegheny, Syracuse, Wheeling and Indianapolis, where
a combination of politicians and franchise corporations
is in control of the municipal government, the attitude
is distinctly hostile to the unions, and appointments and
promotions are made with reference to the political
adherence of the employees. The exception to this
statement is found in the Allegheny electric undertaking
to the extent that the Electrical Workers' Union has
organized the linemen. In this case appointments are
not made on political grounds and the linemen do not
pay the assessments required of other employees. Of

the private companies investigated in Great Britain, all of them except one were hostile to union labor. The exception is the Newcastle gas, which has had open-shop agreements with a gas workers' union during seventeen years. In the United States all of the private companies are hostile to union labor. Most of the companies in both countries protested that they were not hostile, while only one asserted positively that it was, but the acts and policies of all, except Newcastle gas, as shown by our investigations, demonstrate their hostility.

Minimum Wages

In the matter of wages and hours the principal effect of municipal ownership is seen in the unskilled and un-organized labor in both countries, in that of street railway employees in Great Britain, and in that of gas workers and electric workers in the United States.

The policy of all of the British municipalities is to place the minimum wages of common labor at the level paid by the best private employers for similar work. This is about 15 per cent to 40 per cent higher than other private wages for the same class of labor in the same locality. The greatest difference, that of Leicester, was the result of arbitration, brought about through the organization of common labor in that town. In this case those private employers who recognized the union paid the same wages as the municipality. In one locality, Sheffield, the minimum wage paid by the gas company is higher than the minimum paid by the munic-ipality and other private employers, and the gas com-pany at Newcastle pays its organized common labor the same minimum as the municipality, but all of the electric and tramway companies pay less for common

labor doing the same kind of work than the municipalities in which they are located.

In the United States the minimum paid for common
labor by the private companies is, in all cases except
Atlanta, lower than that of the municipality, and the
minimum paid for common labor by municipal undertakings is higher than that of private companies of the same
locality. The correspondence runs as follows : Syracuse,
municipal $1.50 for eight hours, private $1.50 for ten
hours; Detroit, municipal $1.75 for eight hours, private
$1.80 for nine hours; Allegheny, municipal $2.75 for
eight hours, private $1.75 for ten hours; Wheeling,
municipal $1.85 for eight and nine hours, private $1.85
for ten hours ; Cleveland, municipal $1.76 for eight hours,
private $1.75 for ten hours; Indianapolis, municipal
$1.60 for eight hours, private $1.50 for ten hours;
Chicago, municipal $2.00 for eight hours, private $1.75
for ten hours; New Haven, municipal $1.50 for eight
hours, private $1.50 for nine hours; Richmond, munic-
ipal $2.00 for nine hours, private $1.20 for nine hours;
Atlanta, municipal and private $1.00 for ten hours.

These are the minimum rates and not the average
rates, nor the highest rates paid for unskilled and usually
unorganized labor. In this respect the municipalities,
both in Great Britain and the United States, have
adopted the trade union principle of the minimum wage
for that class of labor which ordinarily has no union,
and all of the familiar arguments for and against the
theory of the minimum wage as applied to trade unions
can be brought forward as applied to the municipalities.
Against the minimum wage theory is the criticism that
it shuts out from employment the old men who are
not worth the minimum wage. The private companies

investigated, which pay less than the minimum, of course, justify it on the ground that the Italians, negroes and others employed are not worth the minimum, but the trade unionist usually tells them that by paying the minimum they would attract better workmen. So far as our investigations have gone, they show that in municipal employment this has been the case. Since the adoption of the minimum wage policy, enforced sometimes by civil service rules, the quality, character, physique and efficiency of the common labor employed by municipalities has been greatly improved, and municipal employment has ceased to be looked upon as an old-age pension for laborers worn out in private employment. This is a hardship to individuals to the same extent that trade unionism is a hardship to individuals. But from the standpoint of the municipality it is a gain, because more competent laborers are employed, and municipal employment is clearly distinguished from municipal charity. The aged and inefficient laborers, discharged from private employment, and unable to secure municipal employment, must, of course, be supported from the public treasury, and it is a significant fact that the movement for old-age pensions as a substitute for the poor-house in Great Britain has been strengthened by the minimum wage policy of the past ten years, which has relieved municipal employment of its poor-house features.

In all of the occupations where organized labor was found, the policy of all of the municipalities investigated, except South Norwalk, is that of paying the trade-union rate. This is also, of course, a minimum rate and the conditions are the same as those governing private employers of the locality who recognize the union. A few cases of individuals were found where the city was paying individuals less than the unions, but these were cases in which the union had granted a permit to work below the scale on account of old age, or were cases over which a dispute as to the character of the work was in process of adjustment, or where, as in Chicago, wages in private employment had been advanced after the municipal budget had been voted and the latter could not under the law be changed until the next fiscal year. We have not found any instance, except that of the Municipal Employees' Association in Great Britain, above mentioned, where the unions have demanded higher minimum wages of the municipality than those paid by union employers. Individuals, both in municipal and private undertakings, get higher wages than the union minimum.

Outside the ranks of unskilled labor in Great Britain the principal difference between wages in municipal and private undertakings is found in the case of the motormen and conductors on tramways. This has been brought about by a reduction in the hours of labor in municipal employment, so that in two municipal undertakings, Glasgow and Manchester, the hours have been reduced to 54 per week, and in two others, the Liverpool and London County Council, to 60 per week, while in the three private undertakings the hours are 70 per week. Since the wages have not been decreased the result is seen in the rate of pay per hour. Taking the London County Council Tramways and the London United Tramways, where comparisons can fairly be made, since both are in the same town, the wages for motormen are 4.2 per cent, and for conductors 30 per cent higher on the municipal than on the private system. Outside London, considering the local levels of wages, the municipal undertakings pay higher wages than the private undertakings. This difference is not owing to the change from horse to electrical traction, since the wages on the municipal undertakings were advanced when the municipality secured possession, which in the case of Glasgow was six years before electrical traction was adopted. The private companies, although paying less than the municipalities, have also advanced their rates of pay with the introduction of electrical traction. The same is true of the traction companies in the United States, although our investigations have not included a survey of these companies, and we are unable to make a statistical comparison.

In the case of gas workers employed by the municipalities and private companies in Great Britain it has been found that, with the exception of the South Metropolitan Company, there is not much difference between the wages paid in the two classes of undertakings. The differences observed in this occupation grow out of the amount of work required of the stokers. On account of the severity of the work it is the practice both of the private companies and the municipal undertakings in the United States to require the stokers to work actually only one-half of the number of hours for which they are paid, the other half being available for recreation. This is true also in three of the municipal undertakings in Great Britain, while in the fourth, Glasgow, the stokers work five hours out of the eight instead of four. In this respect Glasgow is on the same basis with the most favorable of the private companies, Newcastle, where, on account of the presence of a strong labor organization, the stokers also are on the basis of five hours' work for eight hours' pay. In the other two private companies, which have succeeded in destroying the labor organizations that formerly existed, the amount of work required of the men has been increased to a greater degree than the increase of wages. So severe was this hardship on the employees of the South Metropolitan Company that in two of the stations they voted to accept the proposition of the company to return to the twelve-hour day and to forego the advantages of the eight-hour day, which they had secured through their union in 1889. By increasing slightly the total amount of work in the twelve-hour shift they increased their total daily wages, but the cost of labor to the company is the same on the twelve-hour basis as it is in the other stations on the eight-hour basis. Measuring their wages, however, by the hour, the men on the twelve-hour basis receive the lowest rates of pay of all the private and municipal undertakings. This twelve-hour system, resulting from the smashing of the union and the overwork of the employees, is approved in some quarters as a " genuine example of coöperation."

At the other extreme the least amount of work required of stokers is in the municipal undertaking at Manchester, and there the reduction in the amount of work has been criticised as indicating a detrimental influence of trade unions upon the municipal undertaking. A question of this kind must be decided according to the opinions of the investigators. Looking at the severity of the work it would be unwarranted to say that the stokers in the Manchester municipal undertaking are doing a smaller amount of work than should be fairly required of them. An important consequence of the policy of the Manchester municipality, in its effort to avoid overworking the stokers, is seen in its effort greatly to improve the equipment of the plant in order to reduce the amount of labor required, the net result being that the labor cost in Manchester is not greater than in other places.

In the United States the gas workers are on the twelve-hour day at Richmond and Atlanta, but in the municipal plant at Wheeling all employees have the eight-hour day, while with the private company at Philadelphia the shift men in the retort house were placed on the eight-hour day when the company took possession. They had worked twelve hours under municipal ownership. The wages paid by the Richmond municipal plant, all of whose employees are whites, are 90 per cent to 100 per cent higher than the wages paid to negroes who do similar work in the Atlanta private undertaking, and the wages paid to white mechanics and apprentices at Richmond are 30 per cent to 120 per cent higher than those paid to the corresponding white employees by the Atlanta company. In one occupation, that of the bricklayer, the wages in the two places are the same.

In the electric industries in Great Britain, outside of employment of unskilled labor, there does not appear to be any material difference in the rates paid by the municipalities and the private companies taken as a whole. It was not possible to make an exact comparison on account of the differences in classification and the wide range of wages, depending partly upon the size of the undertaking. Such differences as were found to exist between municipal and private undertakings might be explained upon the basis of the differences in the level of wages in the several localities.

In the United States in all cases, except South Norwalk and Detroit, the wages paid by the municipal electric undertakings are materially higher than those paid by the private undertakings of the same localities. The widest difference is found in Allegheny and in Chicago. The only positions in which the private electrical companies of Chicago pay as high wages for similar work as the municipal undertaking is that of a small number of their wire-men, who work alongside the other organized building trades of the city. Their other wire-men doing the same work get less pay.

In the matter of " welfare work," or provision for the comfort, cleanliness and recreation of employees, the best conditions were found in the works of the Commonwealth Electric Company at Chicago, the municipal water-works at Cleveland, the Philadelphia gas-works, the municipal gas at Leicester, municipal trams at Glasgow and Liverpool and South Metropolitan gas at London. The worst conditions were at Wheeling and Richmond municipal gas and Sheffield private gas. In general, the buildings and works constructed during the past four or five years both in private and municipal undertakings, show a great improvement over the older buildings and works, in the provision for baths, lavatories, lunch and cooking rooms, recreation rooms and grounds. Taking the entire list of properties visited, the best under one form of ownership is equalled by the best under the other form, and so on down to the worst. The superior character of the municipal undertakings over private undertakings in Great Britain is partly owing to their more recent construction, and the converse is true in the United States.

In Great Britain, but not in the United States, were

found systems of insurance, thrift funds, sick, death and accident benefits, both in municipal and private undertakings. The most extensive and elaborate of these is that of the South Metropolitan Company, connected with its system of profit sharing and compulsory investment of profits in the company's stocks. This system is ingeniously contrived to destroy the gas workers' union by subjecting its employees to the conspiracy laws, and to enable the company to " contract out " from the Workmen's Compensation laws. The municipal gas-works of Glasgow has copied the system so far as it relates to profit sharing and conspiracy, but not to workmen's compensation. All other municipal and private establishments pay accident benefits as required by this national legislation.

CHAPTER XIII

THE MILWAUKEE BUREAU OF ECONOMY AND EFFICIENCY[1]

[It is significant that the first official attempt on the part of an American municipality to install a complete system of business administration was made by the socialists of Milwaukee during their brief control of the city council and mayor's department in 1910 to 1912. The plan was ambitious and comprehensive. It had to overcome all of the obstacles and rule-of-thumb traditions of subordinate employees that have blocked this kind of work in every city where it has been attempted. It required at least a year for the socialists themselves to learn the "team work" necessary to get results. Finally, when the installation of the system seemed to lag unaccountably, they created a "put-over" committee selected from the common council and composed of a machinist, a paper-hanger and a die-sinker. This committee divided up its work, took hold of each executive department and put through the installation until stopped by the elections. The following report, written at the end of the socialist administration in April, 1912, sketches in brief the work as it stood at that time. The non-partisan administration that followed discontinued the staff of the Bureau of Economy and Efficiency, but afterwards created a Bureau of Municipal Research, similar to the "mayor's eye" referred to below. Most of the work of the former Bureau has been retained, and the new Bureau is continuing its unfinished work. A Citizens' Bureau supported by private contributors, as suggested below, is also in process of organization, to aid and criticise the municipal administration.

That a group of trade unionists and socialists, without experience in business management, and handicapped by their belligerent notions of "class struggle," should have set themselves to the

[1] Published as Bulletin No. 19, Milwaukee, Wis., April 15, 1912, under the title "Eighteen Months' Work of the Milwaukee Bureau of Economy and Efficiency."

serious study and vigorous support of this dry programme of modern business, goes far to justify the demand of labor for at least an equal share with business in the control of government. The Voters' League, a non-socialist organization, amidst condemnation of certain other practices, had the following to say to the voters of Milwaukee at the time of the election:

"The Bureau of Economy and Efficiency, inaugurated by the present administration has, we believe, justified its establishment, and is deserving of commendation.

"Its principal investigations and recommendations have been (1) the consolidation of the fire and police alarm telegraph systems, adopted by the council (23 to 9) against the opposition of the respective chiefs, (2) the consolidation of the plumbing and house drain inspectors, adopted by unanimous vote of the council, (3) a complete new system of accounting for the water department now being installed, (4) utilization of by-products at the garbage incinerator, (5) reorganization of garbage collection systems, (6) cost unit systems for the incinerator, garbage and ash collections, street sprinkling, oiling and flushing, and the inspection of plumbing and house drains, and (7) a general reorganization of the health department based on special reports of six principal subdivisions.

"The bureau's report on utilization of steam now going to waste at the incinerator is not in the nature of a reported discovery, but is the result of a study of methods taken up where the designers of the incinerator left off.

"Other recommendations ready for action by the council include a general city organization plan with complete accounting and cost unit systems. Special reports are completed on the subjects of water wastes, electrolysis of water mains, efficiency of pumping stations and operation of the high service water system. The bureau has also been engaged in arriving at the actual cost of delivering water, and so-called social studies have been made of the following subjects: housing conditions, legal aid to the poor, garnishment of wages, employment bureaus, workmen's accidents and women's wages.

"If capably managed, the bureau should continue to prove a valuable agency in promoting efficiency and economy in municipal business."]

In April, 1912, the Bureau of Economy and Efficiency completes eighteen months of work, beginning October, 1910. The first three months were occupied mainly with planning the work, engaging the staff, and enlisting the coöperation of outside agencies. The bulk of the detail work was done during the summer of 1911, when a large force of temporary assistants was secured, and the work of installing the new systems was well under way in the fall. At the present time certain parts of the work have been completed and installed, parts are in different stages of investigation and installation, while other parts necessary to a complete system have not yet been undertaken. The incoming of a new administration makes it advisable to prepare this report upon the plans and work of the bureau.

The Bureau of Economy and Efficiency is doing for the city of Milwaukee what is being done for great corporations by " organization " and " efficiency " experts. Cities, like corporations, have grown up piecemeal, by adding new departments or positions as needed or acquired. Two of the consulting experts of the bureau, to whom most of its preliminary work has been submitted, are Major Charles Hine, formerly organization expert of the Harriman Railroad Lines, and Mr. Harrington Emerson, Consulting Efficiency Engineer, of New York. Major Hine's problem has been that of bringing several lines or railways, formerly independent, into a single effective system. Mr. Emerson is called in by many great corporations for similar work and for working out the details of organization. Their problem is like that which the Milwaukee bureau found in the Public Works Department, where some twenty different subordinate heads reported directly to the

Commissioner, taking up all of his time with details. Both in private corporations and municipal corporations, the officials are compelled to attend to their immediate daily work of administration just as it has been handed down to them, and they have little or no time to make a thorough study of the system which buries them. For this reason it has been found necessary to bring in outside experts who are not tied down by details, but who are familiar with successful practice elsewhere and can, with the coöperation of the officials, systematize their work.

The first thing done by the Bureau was to secure a staff of consulting experts for each kind of work that had to be taken up. These men have been invaluable, and have gladly assisted, at little or no compensation compared with the payments they have received from private corporations or other municipalities. Without them it would have been impossible to find and select an expert staff of men for the bureau, each fitted for the special kind of work required. These consulting experts have criticised and passed upon all of the pieces of work before they were installed or published. Backed by this criticism and approval, the directors of the bureau could confidently recommend and publish the findings of the staff. Besides Major Hine, and Mr. Emerson already mentioned, Dean F. E. Turneaure, of the College of Engineering, the University of Wisconsin, has aided on all engineering work and the selection of all engineering experts.

Dean Russell of the Agricultural College and Experiment Station has practically guided the work on Health and Sanitation, and through him the services of Professor W. T. Sedgwick, head of the Department of Public Health and Biology of the Massachusetts Institute of Technology were secured. Dean Russell was made chairman of the Milwaukee Milk Committee, which was created to have special supervision over that branch of health work, and which approved of the milk report before its adoption by the bureau. It was under these auspices that Dr. S. M. Gunn, Professor of Public Health at the Massachusetts Institute of Technology, made and installed a plan of reorganization of the Health Department that has attracted wide comment and approval of sanitarians.

Dean Louis E. Reber, of the Extension Division of the University of Wisconsin, and formerly Dean of the College of Engineering, Pennsylvania State College, has aided on special problems, like the refuse incinerator.

In the accounting and cost-keeping divisions of the bureau's work, Professor S. W. Gilman of the University of Wisconsin has been depended upon for a large amount of detailed consultation with the staff and final approval of their work.

The Chicago Bureau of Public Efficiency contributed to the early organization of the Milwaukee Bureau through their chief experts, Mr. Peter White and Mr. H. R. Sands. These gentlemen had been with the New York Bureau of Municipal Research, the pioneer in this line of work, for several years, and their familiarity with municipal accounts and organization made them especially valuable in enabling the Milwaukee staff to begin right and to get early results.

In the second year of its work the bureau undertook the study and reorganization of the Tax Commissioner's office in coöperation with the Commissioner and under the guidance of T. S. Adams, member of the Wisconsin State Tax Commission.

The social survey of the bureau could not have been carried on except for the aid given by Mr. H. H. Jacobs of the University Settlement. Mr. Jacobs is distinguished among settlement workers in this country for his active share in most of the public movements of the city for the betterment of social, educational and industrial conditions.

The Milwaukee bureau is unique in that it is the first one of the kind to be supported mainly by the city government itself, and, secondarily, by private contributions. The New York Bureau of Municipal Research, now in its seventh year, is the pioneer bureau, and the men who got their training in its work have taken charge of similar work in Philadelphia, Cincinnati, Chicago, Memphis, St. Louis, and other places, as well as the work of President Taft's inquiry into economy and efficiency. Since the Milwaukee work was started St. Louis has begun the same work in the Comptroller's office, and the State of Wisconsin has created a Board of Public Affairs, which is doing the same for the state government.

Other bureaus were started as private associations to investigate municipal departments, to criticise, to propose improvements, and to inform the public on the actual conditions. But as soon as the importance of their work came to be realized and favored by the administration, they were taken over, to a greater or less extent, by the city department. This transfer is especially notable in New York, where an existing department, the " Commissioner of Accounts," usually known as " the Mayor's eye," but not used for a great many years, has now practically become the municipal section of a Bureau of Economy and Efficiency. The present city comptroller and certain of the several borough departments have also taken over the experts and methods of the New York bureau. In various ways, usually piecemeal, different cities have taken up this kind of work, and the inquiries received by the Milwaukee bureau for men and methods, from widely separate cities, show an awakening on the subject throughout the country.

When the Milwaukee bureau was started it was impossible to secure experts who had previous experience in this work for municipalities. The New York bureau has been drained of its men as fast as they were trained, and the salaries paid in these different cities were far ahead of anything that could be paid in Milwaukee. Added to this was the temporary and uncertain character of the work which made it impossible to offer positions of more than a few months' duration. Judging from the experience of other cities there was an estimate made in April, 1910, that $50,000 was as little as could be counted upon to get results worth while within two years. The bureaus in New York and Chicago had expended $30,000 to $100,000 a year, and during the first two or three years had scarcely reached more than below the surface of the work requiring to be done. The Milwaukee administration was able at that time to appropriate only $5000 from the contingent fund for the purpose. They secured the statistician of the State Railroad Commission to start the work on that account; but he made only one visit to Milwaukee and then accepted an important position with the city of Chicago as expert on gas and telephone costs.

The following September, upon the assurance of

B. M. Rastall, at that time in charge of the business courses in the Extension Division of the University, that he would supervise the work, I offered to take charge on the understanding that the Council would appropriate an additional $20,000 in the budget of 1911. Mr. Rastall at that time was considering the acceptance of a similar position with a private association in Boston, but he agreed, under an arrangement with the Extension Division, to give part time to the Milwaukee work for one year. In view of the fact that experts could not be secured from other bureaus I considered that it would be possible to carry on the work by part-time arrangements with the accounting and engineering experts of the University, the State Railroad and Tax Commissions and such private associations and individuals as might take a public interest in such constructive investigations. Meanwhile the office staff could be gotten together, and special pieces of work could be done by experts brought in temporarily.

All of the planning and details of this scheme were worked out successfully by Mr. Rastall, aided by the consulting experts. During the fifteen months from October, 1910, to December, 1911, over eighty different individuals were on the pay roll, their services ranging from a few days to fifteen months or more, but the work was so planned that they fitted in at the proper places, and the most important parts of the work were brought to a head and ready for installation before the year ended. Additional pieces of work, limited mainly to the Public Works and Health Departments, were taken up when it seemed assured that the bureau would be continued during 1912, but the greater part of the work remaining to be done consists of the installation of systems already recommended and of assisting officials to become familiar with the forms and procedure. A memorandum is given below of the several lines of work undertaken, and their present status.

Scope of the Bureau's Work

The name, "Bureau of Economy and Efficiency," was adopted some time after the work was begun, in order to indicate the kind of work and to designate the staff employed. The bureau was created by a resolution adopted in June, 1910. This resolution authorized the committee to investigate the system of accounts of all departments and powers granted to the City of Milwaukee, and to submit for adoption "a complete system of uniform accounts, vouchers and other forms that may be necessary or convenient for carrying out such systems, and recommendations for rendering more efficient and economical the administration of the city."

This resolution was adopted with a view to carrying out certain suggestions which I had submitted in April at the request of Mr. Berger and Mayor Seidel for a municipal survey similar to the Pittsburgh Survey. The plan of the Pittsburgh Survey, however, was modified by placing foremost the establishment of a cost-keeping and efficiency system for city departments, with bulletins of comparative costs to be published monthly. Subordinate to this was placed what the bureau afterwards designated as "the social survey." The subjects suggested for this social survey were cost of living, legal aid, hospitals and dispensaries, unemployment, poor relief, immigrants, industrial hygiene, industrial education, housing and sanitation, working women and children. It was suggested that much of this work could be done through the coöperation of other organizations and state and national governments. When it came to working out the details of the social survey with Mr. Rastall, it was decided to restrict it closely to a study of the efficiency of city departments, as stated in the following extract from the first bulletin of the bureau on "Plan and Methods," published in May, 1911:

The social survey is not an exhaustive investigation intended to expose conditions or to furnish material for social philosophy, but a means of measuring the efficiency or discovering the inefficiency of city government. It is based on the principle that the municipal government is a social corporation, conducted for the health, welfare and prosperity of its inhabitants. Consequently, the measure of its efficiency is the extent to which it makes its resources go in promoting health, welfare and prosperity. These are its dividends. . . . The social investigation discovers actual conditions, the efficiency investigation determines means and measures for dealing with them.

It was decided that the social survey should be financed outside of the appropriation from city funds, and that the latter should be expended under the direction of Mr. Rastall and devoted to the "efficiency survey." This was described in the bulletin on "Plan and Methods," as follows:

The efficiency survey is a thorough study of the work performed by departments for the city, to be followed by a reorganization of procedure along lines of the greatest economy and efficiency.

In line with this arrangement, Mr. Rastall took charge of the efficiency survey, and I made arrangements with other agencies for the social survey. With the help of Mr. Jacobs, private associations and individuals were solicited for funds and volunteer investigators. Among those who coöperated in this way, on different subjects of investigation, were the State Anti-Tuberculosis Association on the enforcement of the Housing Laws and ordinances by state and local authorities, on the registration of tuberculosis by the Health Department, and on the improvement of milk inspection; the State Bureau of Labor and Industrial Statistics on Housing Laws, Infant Mortality, Garnishment of Wages, and the Newsboys of Milwaukee; the Wisconsin Consumers' League on Women's Wages; the Playground and Recreation Association of America, the Milwaukee Child Welfare Commission and the Milwaukee Board of Education on the Survey of Public Recreation and Amusements and a constructive programme on recreation prepared by Mr. Rowland Haynes of the Playground Association; the Wisconsin Legislative Committee for Workmen's Compensation, on a study of accidents to workmen in Milwaukee; the University Settlement fellows and residents, on Free Legal Aid, Free Employment, Workmen's Accidents, Infant Mortality, Milk Supply and Milk Inspection. These were aided by other private contributions and by personal services furnished by the College of Agriculture, for the study of the Milk Supply and Milk Inspection, and by the services of university students and fellows, and other volunteer investigators.

The bulk of the work in the social survey turned on the work of the Health Department, and this made it possible finally for the efficiency survey, under the direction of Dr. S. M. Gunn, to take it over and to formulate a complete scheme of records and organization for that department. This has been partly installed, especially in the sections on tuberculosis, infant mortality and housing, under the guidance of citizens' semi-official committees on Tuberculosis, Child Welfare, Milk Supply and Housing. Other parts of the social survey furnished a basis for the coöperation of city and county with the state in the reorganization of the free employment office; for the regulation of newsboys and other street trades carried on by boys under sixteen; and for placing the responsibility for enforcing the laws on housing solely on the city departments, instead of leaving it to the divided authority of state and city. Parts of the originally proposed social survey which have not been taken up by the bureau are cost of living, hospitals and dispensaries, unemployment, poor relief, immigrants, industrial hygiene. The recommendations on free legal aid have not been adopted.

Efficiency Survey

After the bureau had been organized it was learned that there was pending before the railroad Commission a petition of citizens for the reduction of water rates. In view of this case it was decided to place foremost in the work of the bureau a complete investigation of the Water-works Department, which should include the preparation of non-legal parts of the city's case. The Common Council incorporated in the budget for 1911 two appropriations of $5000 each for the rate case and an efficiency, or " water waste," survey, to be conducted jointly by the City Attorney, the Commissioner of Public Works and the bureau. The first hearing on the case was set for September, 1911, and the preliminary work was practically completed by that time.

However, on account of several postponements of the hearings, the argument and brief remain to be finished after the hearings are completed. The water waste survey included also the preparation of a report on electrolysis for the use of the City Attorney.

Legal Digest and Organization Charts. — Soon after its organization the directors of the bureau, in consultation with the city officials, outlined a preliminary survey of all departments, and a plan of organization for the Public Works and Health Departments. The preliminary survey included a legal digest of the city charter, laws and ordinances, in order to show the powers and responsibilities of each city officer or employee and the legal procedure required of each. This digest is the foundation of all subsequent work and has been completed for each department of the city.

While the legal digest was in preparation, the bureau made a preliminary study of the actual organization of the departments, and this was put in the form of charts showing for all officers and employees their lines of responsibility and authority. This preliminary study included the actual duties performed, as well as enough of the business practice and accounting procedure of the city to furnish a working basis for future detailed work. The use made of these preliminary surveys is described in Bulletin No. 1, "Plan and Methods," pages 8 to 12.

Water Department. — Following the preliminary surveys a detailed study was made of the organization of the Water Department, its business practice, accounts and records, covering every phase of its work from the intake to the collection of consumers' bills. During the summer of 1911, on the basis of these studies, a complete revision of the organization, business practice, accounts and records was made and approved by the Railroad Commission, and ordered installed, January 1, 1912. The City Council provided temporarily for a chief accountant to supervise the installation. The reorganization will require changes in the laws and ordinances, especially in the matter of consolidating the Treasurer's and Water Registrar's Departments. The office of Superintendent of Water-works has been created. The cost bulletin has been audited by the Commission, and is ready for publication. A bulletin on the old and new organization is partly prepared but not yet written up for publication.

The Water Waste Survey, including the report on electrolysis and the study of the efficiency of the present system and plans for future growth, has been completed and the recommendations are being carried out. (See Bulletins Nos. 11, 14 and 16.) The survey was necessarily limited to a small section of the system, but it showed a probable loss of 23 per cent of the water pumped through underground waste, misuse and illegal use, and large savings which might be made. The waste survey, including inspection of sprinkler systems, is continued by a specially organized force under a chief engineer, reporting to the Superintendent of Water-works. The electrolysis report at this time is in the hands of the City Attorney.

The actual savings which will result from these preliminary surveys and the reorganization of the department depend, of course, on the extent and rapidity with which the recommendations are carried out. The cost bulletin, audited by the Railroad Commission, will furnish an exact measure of the amount of saving, and the citizens of Milwaukee will have the same opportunity of knowing exactly how their Water Department is conducted in all its details that a board of directors of a private corporation now has under the modern system of cost keeping.

Refuse Incinerator. — Following a complete study of the garbage incinerator, covering all features of administration, operation and accounts, and a special engineering study, a report was prepared and published as Bulletin No. 5. The recommendations include utilization of by-products, especially steam and clinker, and savings in operation estimated at $24,000 a year. The cost bulletin is ready for interpretation and publication.

Collection of Garbage and Ashes. — Following a preliminary study of the collection and hauling of garbage, ashes and other refuse, a set of forms and records was prepared and installed for securing information on actual costs. Based on these monthly reports of costs, a plan of reorganization and redistricting the city was prepared, reducing the force of collectors, improving the service, and saving about $10,000 a year. The city has been redistricted, new wagons have been ordered and the system of garbage collection is in process of installation. Final action on the report of ash collections has not been taken.

Bureau of Sewers. — Complete reorganization has been effected, system installed, special clerk detailed, and cost reports can be made after April 1.

Street Sprinkling, Flushing and Oiling, Sidewalk Repair. — A thorough study was made, and cost records were set up, furnishing a simplified method of determining unit costs upon which to figure assessments.

These have been installed, and are now being coördinated with the forms used for the tax rolls.

Street Construction. — A preliminary plan for reorganization and accounts for street repairs have been made and transmitted. An accounting system for this bureau is ready for installation. The filing system is completed and has been reviewed and transmitted.

House Drain and Plumbing Inspection. — A complete report, with plans for consolidation, forms and accounts, was published as Bulletin No. 10. The system was installed in November, 1911, and the cost figures of the first month show a reduction of costs per man per inspection to 31.2 c. compared with 61. c. the previous month. The total savings amount to about $6000 a year.

Fire and Police Alarm Telegraph. — A report on the advisability of consolidating the two systems showed that this could be done so far as construction and maintenance were concerned, but that the operation should be under the control of the two departments. The consolidation has been effected, and the forms for the office accounting system have been printed and are being installed. The saving that results from consolidation is estimated at $5620 a year.

Bridges and Public Buildings. — Preliminary studies were made of the operation, management and accounts of buildings, city hall power plant, bridges, natatoria and bathing beaches. The natatoria report is completed and transmitted, but not installed. The report on city hall power plant has been adopted and the schedule of accounts is being installed. Reports on costs of operation can be made after May 1.

Ward Labor Efficiency. — As the various studies were

being made the question of the efficiency of ward labor has come up, and valuable information has been collected for use in a more complete study of employment and individual efficiency, not yet undertaken.

City Engineer's Office. — Office and filing systems completed and transmitted. Forms are being printed. The accounting system has been planned and is ready for transmissal and installation.

Purchasing Department. — During the progress of the work in different departments, preliminary notes have been made on purchase methods, including standards, specifications, stock inspection, testing of purchases, and a comparative study has been made of purchase methods of private corporations. A number of purchasing agents of large Milwaukee corporations have agreed to serve as an advisory committee to the bureau as soon as it is in position to take up the detailed study of this department.

Harmonizing of Cost Systems and Comptroller's Accounts. — During the time when the bureau was devising cost systems for various departments, Mr. Leslie S. Everts, the deputy comptroller, was engaged in the complete reorganization of the Comptroller's office. That work has been completed and Mr. Everts has become associated with the bureau and is now engaged in the work of coördinating the two systems according to the plans that were agreed upon when the work was started. This check is vital to the whole system, and will require a considerable amount of detailed work in order to perfect it.

Tax Forms for Assessment Records. — Beginning in January, 1912, a complete reorganization of forms and records of the Tax Department was commenced, and these are ready for the printer. This reorganization contemplates a large reduction of clerical work, a consolidation of all assessments and the installation of tabulating machines. The forms of bills and personal property are nearly completed. This work will require installation and supervision until December. A study of the equalization of assessments of land values is being made under the direction of Mr. Adams of the State Tax Commission, and will be completed before the spring assessment. A preliminary study of the equalization of assessments for buildings and machinery has been made, but the detailed work is postponed until after this year's assessment has been completed.

Health Department. — The preliminary work of the Health Department consisted mainly of the social survey work. This was followed by a complete plan of reorganization and forms and records. The tuberculosis work has been completed and installed, under the direction of a semi-official commission representing different agencies interested in that work.[1] The Child Welfare work was similarly placed under a commission upon plans of operation prepared and installed by Mr. Wilbur F. Phillips. In both of these divisions a permanent secretary was provided, either through city funds or private contributions, the staff of the bureau assisting by way of the preliminary work and supervision.

The bureau has completed its study of the reorganization of the Health Department, as well as the preparation of all forms and records, and these are now being installed under the supervision of Mr. Leuning, chief of the Division of Education and Publications, who had coöperated with Dr. Gunn in their preparation.

[1] Afterwards incorporated as a division of the Health Department.

There remain to be completed the general accounts of the Health Department and their coördination with the Comptroller's office. The bureau's recommendations involve a considerable increase in the annual expense of this department, amounting to $32,920, before it can be said that the department will be able to provide adequate inspection, control of communicable diseases, and records. The sanitary inspection force has been increased in accordance with recommendations, and the city has been redistricted. Sergeants recommended for sanitary inspection districts have not been appointed. An ordinance placing out-door nuisance inspection in the hands of the police is at present in the Council. The milk inspection force has been increased. The divisions of milk and meat inspection have not yet been combined. The Division of Education and Publications has been organized and is operating on the basis recommended in the report. There has been no change as yet in the organization of the health laboratory.

Summary

The following is a summary of the work as it stands in April, 1912 :

A. Supervision of Systems Already Installed

Water Department, Bureau of Sewers, House Drain and Plumbing, Assessment Section, Incinerator, Garbage Collection, Bridges and Public Buildings.

B. Installation and Supervision of Systems Already Designed

Ash Collection, Natatoria, Fire and Police Alarm Telegraph, Health Department forms and reorganization, City Engineer's office and accounting systems, Street Construction accounting system.

C. Completion of Studies Partially Finished

Completeness of Collections and Personal Efficiency in the Water Department, Street Sanitation, Reorganization of Ward Crews, including Labor Efficiency and Accounting System; Street Construction Reorganization, Tax and Assessment, General Accounting System of Department of Public Works.

D. New Studies not yet begun Necessary to Complete the Programme Mapped out for the Bureau

Engineering study of street construction, purchases, engineering study of transportation of street and other refuse, engineering study of fire and police alarm telegraph, Health Department accounting system, coördination of records in offices of Comptroller, Clerk, Treasurer, with those of the departments.

E. Bulletins

The following bulletins have been issued: 1. Plan and Methods in Municipal Efficiency. B. M. Rastall. 2. Alarm Telegraph Systems. J. E. Trelevan. 3. Garnishment of Wages. W. M. Price. (Published by Wisconsin Bureau of Labor.) 4. Women's Wages and Proposed Minimum Wage Law. Ruby Stewart and Katherine Lenroot. (Published by Wisconsin Consumers' League.) 5. The Refuse Incinerator. M. Cerf, L. E. Reber, E. B. Norris, S. A. Greeley. 6. Citizens' Free Employment Bureau. Fred A. King. 7. Free Legal Aid. Fred A. King. 8. The Newsboys of Milwaukee. Alexander Fleisher. (Published by Industrial Commission.) 9. Review of the Bureau's Work, and Guide to Exhibit. 10. Plumbing and House Drain Inspection. F. H. Elwell. 11. Water-works Efficiency — 1. Water Waste Survey. Ray Palmer, W. R. Brown. 12. Garbage Collection. Robert E. Goodell. 13. Health Department — 1. Milk Supply. S. M. Gunn. 14. Water-works Efficiency — 2. Present Capacity and Future Requirements. F. E. Turneaure. 15. Health Department — 2. Education and Publications. S. M. Gunn, F. M. Luening. 16. Water-works Efficiency — 3. Operating Efficiency. Ray Palmer. 17. Recreation Survey. Rowland Haynes. 18. Health Department — 3. Communicable Diseases. S. M. Gunn. 19. Eighteen Months' Work. J. R. Commons.

Bulletins completed, ready for editing: Electrolysis of Water Pipes, Sanitary Inspection, Reorganization of Health Department, Ash and Garbage Collection, Sewers.

Bulletins in preparation: Filing System, City Engineer; General Plan, City Organization.

Manuscripts in office which can be used for bulletins if desired: High Level Pumping Station, Meats and Food Inspection, Reorganization of Public Structures.

Suggested bulletins: Budget Making, The Water Rate Case, Organization of the Water Department.

Cost Bulletins: Monthly statement of Water Department costs for January, published. Incinerator costs, house drain and plumbing inspection costs can be obtained. Sewer costs, costs of bridges and public buildings, City Engineer's office, can be obtained about May 1, 1912.

Permanent Organization

Since the bureau is only a temporary arrangement for investigation and recommendation, the matter of installing its recommendations when adopted and making them of permanent value to the city has received considerable attention.

The first step taken in this direction was the reorganization of the Municipal Reference Department on a permanent basis, independent of changing administrations, by placing it with the Board of Trustees of the Public Library. It is now maintained as a branch library at the City Hall. In this respect the example of the State Legislative Reference Department is followed, which is under the State Free Library Commission. Such a department is not merely a library — it is an agent for the investigation of laws and ordinances in all other states and countries in comparison with those at home, including the practical working of such laws and ordinances, and the drafting of effective and scientific ordinances, as well as aiding all the city departments in their administration. It fills the place of the statistical and research bureaus which have been the most important departments of European city governments, especially of Germany, in bringing those cities up to their high level of efficiency.

For Milwaukee it was considered that as fast as the bureau's investigations and recommendations had been completed and installed, the material and records should be turned over to the Reference Librarian for permanent possession, and that perhaps the bulletins, including the monthly cost bulletins, could be supervised and published from that office.

Another method of providing for permanent record and uniformity is that of State Supervision of Accounts. This is possible under the public utility law of the state in so far as the Water-works Department is concerned. The bureau's entire system of forms and procedure has been approved by the State Railroad Commission, with modifications preserving uniformity with their accounts for other cities, and the installation is in progress under the Commission's supervision. The great advantage of this method is that it secures the aid of an outside body of experts in a continuous audit and inspection of the accounts and procedure, with authority to require compliance with its orders. A similar arrangement is possible for all other city departments under the supervision of the State Tax Commission, authorized by law, Chapter 523, adopted by the legislature of 1911. In this case, however, the city is required to take the initiative and to request the assistance of the Tax Commission, meeting the actual expenses from city funds. A resolution under the provisions of this law has been introduced in the Common Council, but has not been acted upon.

State supervision is necessarily limited to audit and inspection of work actually done, and cannot take the place of active work on the part of the city itself. The experience of the New York bureau offers a model of what might be done in Milwaukee. That bureau found ready at hand the Department of Commissioner of Accounts, responsible solely to the Mayor. The department has been, as the bureau states in its latest report, " a handicap to civic progress," but, after its reorganization in 1909, it had become " a potent agent for efficiency and honesty." The department now has a large staff carrying on the work which the bureau has inaugurated for all city departments. Practically the same result would be accomplished in Milwaukee by erecting the present temporary bureau into a permanent department of the city government, reporting directly to the Mayor, and coöperating with the various departments, with the state commissions, and with private organizations of citizens.

A citizens' organization, like the New York bureau, might also be established, with funds secured from private sources adequate to keep competent experts continually in contact with the work done by the city. Such a bureau would act as a critic where the city departments were inefficient, and would sustain and support officials who were efficient. The New York bureau has accomplished remarkable results in this way.

Other plans of organization might be suggested more practical for Milwaukee than the New York example. The studies which the bureau has made of labor efficiency have so far been incidental to the work of reorganization.

Such studies properly belong to the City Service Commission, and are being taken up by the State Commission and the Chicago Civil Service Commission. They furnish a basis for the classification of salaries and for promotions and dismissals. A permanent organization of a Bureau of Efficiency would provide for coöperation in this matter with the City Service Commission.

The real test of work of this kind is economy where waste is found, in order to get efficiency where false economy is found. The conditions in Milwaukee are similar to those found by other bureaus in other cities, and in private corporations. They are mainly due to the fact that the business of the city has grown faster than its business methods. Forms of organization, procedure, and records which were satisfactory on a small scale, are not sufficient to conduct the business of a huge corporation. Most of all, what is needed is a simple system that will show to the citizens exactly what each department is costing and what it is doing. No corporation, public or private, can be economical and efficient without this kind of accurate information for its directors and stockholders. This is the work that a Bureau of Economy and Efficiency can perform.

CHAPTER XIV

AMERICAN SHOEMAKERS, 1648–1895 [1]

THE boot and shoe makers, either as shoemakers or "cordwainers," have been the earliest and the most strenuous of American industrialists in their economic struggles. A highly skilled and intelligent class of tradesmen, widely scattered, easily menaced by commercial and industrial changes, they have resorted with determination at each new menace to the refuge of protective organizations. Of the seventeen trials for conspiracy prior to 1842 the shoemakers occasioned nine. Taking the struggles of this harassed trade, it is possible to trace industrial stages by American documents from the guild to the factory. Organizations whose records give us this picture of industrial evolution under American conditions are the "Company of Shoomakers," Boston, 1648; the "Society of the Master Cordwainers," Philadelphia, 1789; the "Federal Society of Journeymen Cordwainers," Philadelphia, 1794; the "United Beneficial Society of Journeymen Cordwainers," Philadelphia, 1835; the Knights of St. Crispin, 1868; the Boot and Shoe Workers' Union, 1895. Each of these organizations stands for a definite stage in industrial evolution, from the primitive itinerant cobbler to the modern factory; each

[1] *Quarterly Journal of Economics*, Nov., 1909. References are to reprints in " Documentary History of American Industrial Society," edited by Commons, Phillips, Gilmore, Sumner and Andrews, and published by A. H. Clarke Co., Cleveland, O.

INDUSTRIAL STAGES, CLASSES AND ORGANIZATIONS OF AMERICAN SHOEMAKERS

	1 EXTENT OF MARKET	2 KIND OF BARGAIN	3 CAPITAL OWNERSHIP — CUSTOMER, MERCHANT, EMPLOYER, LABORER	4 INDUSTRIAL CLASSES			5 KIND OF WORK	6 COMPETITIVE MENACE	7 PROTECTIVE ORGANIZATIONS	8 CASE
1	Itinerant	Wages	*Customer-Employer* Material, Household, Board and Lodging / *Journeyman* Hand tools	Farm family, Skilled helper			Skilled supervision	Family workers	None	Itinerant individuals 1648
2	Personal	Custom order	*Merchant-Master-Journeyman* Material, Hand tools, Home shop	Merchant-Master-Journeyman			"Bespoke"	"Bad Ware"	Craft guild	Boston "Company of Shoemakers" 1648
3	Local	Retail	*Merchant-Master* Material, Finished stock, Short credits, Sales shop / *Journeyman* Hand tools, Home shop	Merchant-Master-Journeyman			"Shop"	"Market" work, "Advertisers", Auctions	Retail Merchants' Association	Philadelphia "Society of the Master Cordwainers" 1789
4	Waterways	Wholesale order	*Merchant-Master* Material, Finished stock, Long credits, Store-room / *Journeyman* Hand tools, Home shop	Merchant-Master	Journeyman		"Order"	"Scabs", Interstate producers	Journeymen's Society, Masters' Society	Philadelphia "Federal Society of Journeymen Cordwainers." 1794–1806
5	Highways	Wholesale speculative	*Merchant-Capitalist* Material, Finished stock, Bank credits, Warehouse, "Manufactory" / *Contractor* Work shop / *Journeyman* Hand tools	Merchant-Capitalist	Contractor	Journeyman	Team work	Prison, Sweatshop, "Foreigner", "Speeding up"	Journeymen's Society, Manufacturers'[1] Society, Employers' Association	Philadelphia "United Beneficial Society of Journeymen Cordwainers" 1835
6	Rail	Wholesale speculative	*Merchant-Jobber* Material, Finished stock, Bank credits, Warehouse, "Manufactory" / *Contract Manufacturer* Work shop / *Journeyman* Footpower machines	Merchant-Jobber	"Manufacturer"	Journeyman	Team work	Green hands, Chinese, Women, Children, Prisoners, Foreigners	Trade Union, Employers' Association, Manufacturers' Association[1]	"Knights of St. Crispin" 1868–1872
7	World	Factory order	*Manufacturer* Material, Stock, Credits, Power machinery, Factory / *Laborer* None	Manufacturer	Wage-earners		Piece work	Child labor, Long hours, Immigrants, Foreign products	Industrial Union, Employers' Association, Manufacturers' Association[1]	"Boot and Shoe Workers' Union." 1895

represents an internal contention over the distribution of wealth provoked by external conditions of marketing or production; each was productive of written documents preserving to us the types of social organization that struggled for adaptation to the evolving economic series.

I

"The Company of Shoomakers," Boston, 1648

Probably the first American guild was that of the " shoomakers of Boston," and its charter of incorporation, granted by the Colony of the Massachusetts Bay, on October 18, 1648, is the only complete American charter of its kind, of which I have knowledge.[1] The coopers were granted a similar charter on the same date. The act recited that on petition of the " shoomakers " and on account of the complaints of the " damage " which the country sustained " by occasion of bad ware made by some of that trade," they should meet and elect a master, two wardens, four or six associates, a " clarke," a sealer, a searcher, and a beadle, who should govern the trade. The "commission " was to continue in force for three years.

A contemporary reference to this incorporation of shoemakers is that of Edward Johnson, in his " Wonder-Working Providence of Sion's Savior in New England," 1651. Speaking of the material progress of the colony and the rapid division of labor, he says,[2] " All other trades have here fallen into their ranks and places, to their great advantage; especially Coopers and Sho-

---

[1] See Appendix to this chapter.

[2] Collections of the Massachusetts Historical Society, Vol. III, 2d Series, p. 13 (Boston, 1826).

makers, who had either of them a Corporation granted, inriching themselves by their trades very much."

In the charter of the Boston guild, the main object of the shoemakers was the suppression of inferior workmen, who damaged the country by " occasion of bad ware." The officers were given authority to examine the shoemakers, and to secure from 'the courts of the colony an order suppressing any one whom they did not approve " to be a sufficient workman." They were also given authority to regulate the work of those who were approved, and thus to " change and reforme " the trade and " all the affayres thereunto belonging." And they were erected into a branch of government with power to annex " reasonable pennalties " and to " levie the same by distresse."

At the same time it is evident that the colonial authorities took pains to protect the inhabitants from abuse of these powers by placing their determination " in cases of difficultie " in the hands of the judges of the county, and by allowing appeals to the county court. The two substantial reservations which the colony withholds from the company are the " inhancinge the prices of shooes, bootes, or wages," and the refusal to make shoes for inhabitants " of their owne leather for the use of themselves and families," if required by the latter.

From these reservations we are able to infer the industrial stage which the industry had reached at the time of incorporation.[1] It was the transition from the stage of the itinerant shoemaker, working up the

---

[1] See Bücher, "Die Entstehung der Volkswirtschaft." Citations are from Wickett's translation, "Industrial Evolution" (New York, 1901). Also Sombart, "Der Moderne Kapitalismus," Vol. I, pp. 93–94.

raw material belonging to his customer in the home of
the latter, to the stage of the settled shoemaker, working up his own raw material in his own shop to the
order of his customer. The reservation for the protection of inhabitants is suggestive of statutes of the
fifteenth and sixteenth centuries imposing penalties on
guild members who refused to work in the house of their
customer.[1] The fact that the colony, while granting
power to reform the trade, nevertheless thought it
necessary to require the shoemaker to continue to
work up the leather owned by his customer, although
conceding that he need not go to the house of the customer, indicates the source of the abuses from which
the shoemakers were endeavoring to rid themselves.
The itinerant was likely to be poorly trained, and he
could escape supervision by his fellow craftsmen. He
was dependent on his customer who owned not only
the raw material, but also the work-place, the lodging,
and the food supplies of the shoemaker, leaving to the
latter only the mere hand tools. He worked under
the disadvantage of a new work-place for each new
order, without the conveniences and equipment necessary for speedy and efficient work. He had to seek
the customer, and consequently was at a disadvantage
in driving a bargain. This made him, however, a serious
menace to the better trained shoemaker, working in
his own shop and on his own material, but waiting for
the customer to come.

The Boston guild represented the union in one person
of the later separated classes of merchant, master, and
journeyman. Each of these classes has a different
function. The merchant-function controls the kind

[1] Bücher, p. 169.

and quality of the work, and its remuneration comes from ability to drive the bargain with the customer in the process of adjusting price to quality. The master-function, on the other hand, controls the work-place and the tools and equipment, and passes along to the journeyman the orders received from the merchant. Its remuneration comes from management of capital and labor. The journeyman-function, finally, is remunerated according to skill and quality of work, speed of output and the amount and regularity of employment.[1]

Thus, from the standpoint of each of the functions that later were separated, did this primitive guild in self-interest set itself against the " bad ware " of the preceding itinerant stage. From the merchant stand-point the exclusion of bad ware removed a menace to remunerative prices for good ware. From the master standpoint the exclusion of the itinerant transferred the ownership of the workshop and the medium of wage payments from the consumer to the producer. From the journeyman standpoint, this exclusion of the itin-erant eliminated the truck-payment of wages in the form of board and lodging by substituting piece wages for a finished product. And this control of the finished product through all the stages of production gave a double advantage to the craftsman. It transferred to him the unskilled parts of the work hitherto done by the customer's family, thus enabling him at one and the same stroke both to increase the amount of his work and to utilize the bargaining leverage of his skill to get skilled wages for unskilled work.

[1] The table at the beginning of this chapter, showing industrial stages, classes, and organizations, should be consulted in reading this and the following analysis.

By this analysis we can see that when the three functions of merchant, master and journeyman were united in the same person, the merchant-function epitomized the other two. It is the function by which the costs of production are shifted over to the consumer. The master looks to the merchant for his profits on raw material, workshop, tools and wages, and the journeyman looks to him for the fund that will pay his wages.

Now, there is a prime consideration in the craft-guild stage that enhances the power of the merchant to shift his costs to the consumer. This is the fact that his market is a personal one, and the consumer gives his order before the goods are made. On the other hand, the bargaining power of the merchant is menaced by the incapacity of customers accurately to judge of the quality of goods, as against their capacity clearly to distinguish prices. Therefore, it is enough for the purposes of a protective organization in the custom-order stage of the industry, to direct attention solely to the quality of the product rather than the price or the wage, and to seek only to exclude bad ware and the makers of bad ware. Thus the Boston shoemakers and coopers, though enlisting the colonial courts only in the laudable purpose of redressing " the damag which the country sustaynes by occasion of bad ware," succeeded thereby in " inriching themselves by their trades very much." In this they differed from later organizations, based on the separation of classes, to whom competition appeared as a menace primarily to prices and wages, and only secondarily to quality.

II

The Society of Master Cordwainers, 1789, and the Federal Society of Journeymen Cordwainers, 1794, Philadelphia

The separation of classes first appears in the case of the cordwainers of Philadelphia, a century and a half later. Here appeared the first persistent discord that broke the primitive American harmony of capital and labor. So intense were the passions aroused, and so widespread was the popular irritation, that they have left their permanent record in one hundred and fifty-nine pages of " The Trial of the Boot and Shoemakers of Philadelphia, on an indictment for a combination and conspiracy to raise their wages." [1] Here we have a fairly full record of the first American association of employers and the first trade union. They were the " Society of the Master Cordwainers of the City of Philadelphia," 1789, and the " Federal Society of Journeymen Cordwainers " of the same city, organized in 1794.

Other journeymen may have had organizations prior to that time. Mr. Ethelbert Stewart [2] has, indeed, unearthed records showing that the printers in New York as early as 1776, and in Philadelphia as early as 1786, were organized for the purpose of supporting their demands by means of strikes. But these were temporary organizations, falling apart after a brief strike; whereas the cordwainers of Philadelphia in 1799 conducted a strike and lockout of nine or ten

---

[1] Doc. Hist., Vol. III, pp. 59–248.
[2] *Bulletin of U. S. Bureau of Labor*, No. 61, p. 860.

weeks. To them goes the distinction of continuing their organization for at least twelve years, and aggressively driving their demands at the end of that period to the extent that the public took notice and the employers sought refuge behind the arm of the law. And it is to this junction of popular excitement and judicial interposition that we owe the record which exhibits this earliest struggle of capital and labor on American soil.

The indictment charged the journeymen with conspiring not to work except at prices and rates in excess of those " which were then used and accustomed to be paid and allowed to them "; with endeavoring " by threats, menaces and other unlawful means " to prevent others from working at less than these excessive prices; and with adopting " unlawful and arbitrary by-laws, rules and orders " and agreeing not to work for any master who should employ any workman violating such rules, and agreeing " by threats and menaces and other injuries " to prevent any workman from working for such a master.

The conspiracy and strike occurred in November, 1805, and the matter came to trial in the Mayor's court in March, 1806. The court permitted the witnesses to recite the entire history of this and the preceding strikes, as well as the history of the preceding combinations both of journeymen and employers. Consequently we are able to trace from the year 1789 to the year 1806 the development of the boot and shoe industry in Philadelphia, along with the accompanying separation of the interests of the journeymen from those of the masters.

I do not find any record of a guild organization like

that in Boston, but there had been a " charitable society " to which both employers and journeymen belonged, and this was still in existence in 1805.[1] It was the masters who first formed themselves, in April, 1789, into a separate organization. Their early constitution was laid before the court, showing the purpose of their organization to be that of " taking into consideration the many inconveniences which they labour under, for want of proper regulations among them, and to provide remedies for the same." [2] They were to " consult together for the general good of the trade, and determine upon the most eligible means to prevent irregularities in the same." They were to hold four general meetings each year, and they had a committee of seven " to meet together as often as they think necessary." The society terminated in 1790, after the fifth quarterly meeting.

Apparently the masters had at that time just two kinds of " inconveniences " : the competition of cheap grades of goods offered for sale at the " public market," and the competition of masters who offered bargain prices by public advertisement. This is shown by their qualifications for membership. " No person shall be elected a member of this society who offers for sale any boots, shoes, etc., in the public market of this city, or advertises the prices of his work, in any of the public papers or hand-bills, so long as he continues in these practices."

Evidently this society of masters was not organized as an employers' association, for nothing is said of wages or labor. It was organized by the masters merely in their function of retail merchant. The

[1] Doc. Hist., Vol. III, p. 99.   [2] Ibid., p. 128.

attorneys for the journeymen tried to make out that
when the latter organized separately in 1794 they did
so in self-defence, as against the masters' association,
and they contended that in the masters' constitution
were to be found " ample powers " not only to regulate
prices, but also " to form a league to reduce the wages
of their journeymen." [1] And, although they admitted
that the association had terminated in 1790, yet they
held " it was a Phœnix that rose from its ashes." [2]
But it was brought out clearly in evidence that the
subsequent resurrections in 1799 and 1805 were provoked by the journeymen's aggressive society and
were but temporary organizations. The Phœnix that
kept on repeatedly rising was not the one that had
disappeared. In 1789 it had been an organization
of masters in their function of retail merchant. In
its later stages it was an organization of masters in
their function of employer. The distinction, fundamental in economics, caused a re-alignment in *personnel*,
as will be shown presently. The early organization
regulated prices and followed the vertical cleavage
between producer and consumer. The later organization regulated wages and followed the horizontal cleavage between employer and laborer. In the early
organization the journeyman's interest was the same as
the master's. In the later ones the journeyman's
interest was hostile to both consumer and master.

The foregoing considerations, as well as the transition
to later stages, will become more apparent if we stop
for a moment to examine the economic conditions that
determine the forms of organization. These conditions are found, not so much in the technical " instru-

[1] *Ibid.*, p. 166.   [2] *Ibid.*, pp. 129, 174.

ments of production," as in the development of new markets. The economic development of the market proceeded as follows : The cordwainer of the Boston guild made all his boots and shoes to the order of his customer, at his home shop. His market was a custom-order market, composed of his neighbors. His product, in the terminology of 1806, was a " bespoke " product. He was in his own person master, custom-merchant, and journeyman.

Next, some of the master cordwainers begin to stock up with standard sizes and shapes, for sale to sojourners and visitors at their shops. They cater to a wider market, requiring an investment of capital, not only in raw material, but also in finished products and per- onal credits. They give out the material to journey-men to be made up at their homes and brought back to the shop. In addition to " bespoke work," the journeyman now makes " shop work " and the master becomes retail merchant and employer. This was the stage of the industry in Philadelphia in 1789 — the retail-shop stage.

Next, some of the masters seek an outside or foreign market. They carry their samples to distant mer-chants and take " orders " for goods to be afterwards made and delivered. They now become wholesale merchant-employers, carrying a larger amount of capital invested in material, products and longer credits, and hiring a larger number of journeymen. In addition to " bespoke " and " shop " work the journeyman now makes " order work " for the same employer. This is the wholesale-order stage of the industry.

This was the stage in Philadelphia in 1806. At

that time we find the journeyman engaged on one kind and quality of work, with the same tools and workshops, but with four different destinations for his product. Each destination was a different market, with a different level of competition, leading ultimately, after a struggle, to differences in quality. The terms employed at the time recapitulate the evolution of the industry. " Bespoke work," recalls the primitive custom market of the Boston guild, now differentiated as the market offered by the well-to-do for the highest quality of work at the highest level of competition. " Shop work " indicates the retail market of less particular customers at a wider but lower level of competition and quality. " Order work " indicates a wholesale market made possible by improved means of transportation, but on a lower level of strenuous competition and indifferent quality projected from other centres of manufacture. " Market work " — *i.e.* cheap work sold in the public market — indicates the poorest class of customers, and consequently the lowest level of competition, undermining especially the shop-work level, and, to a lesser degree, the order-work level, but scarcely touching the " bespoke " level.

It was the widening out of these markets with their lower levels of competition and quality, but without any changes in the instruments of production, that destroyed the primitive identity of master and journeyman cordwainers and split their community of interest into the modern alignment of employers' association and trade union. The struggle occurred, not as a result of changes in tools or methods of production, but directly as a result of changes in markets. It was a struggle on the part of the merchant-employer to require the same *minimum quality* of work for each of the markets, but lower rates of wages on work destined for the wider and lower markets. It was a struggle on the part of the journeymen to require the same *minimum wage* on work destined for each market, but with the option of a higher wage for a higher market. The conflict came over the wage and quality of work destined for the widest, lowest and newest market. This will appear from the evidence brought out at the trial.

In the Boston guild it does not appear that there were any journeymen. Each " master " was at first a traveller, going to the homes of his customers and doing the skilled part of the journeyman's work. Next he was the all-round journeyman, not only " his own master " but, more important, his own merchant. The harmony of capital and labor was the identity of the human person. The market was direct, the orders were " bespoke."

Even in Philadelphia, in 1789, when the masters had added " shop work " and had separated themselves out as an association of retail merchants, the interests of the journeymen coincided with theirs. The journeymen were even more distressed by " market work " than were the masters. At the " market " there was no provision for holding back goods for a stated price. Everything had to be sold at once and for cash. Goods were not carried in stock. Consequently, the prices paid were exceedingly low. Job Harrison, the " scab," testified that, whereas he was regularly paid 9s. for making a pair of shoes, he could get only 3s. to 3s. 6d. on " market work." If he should quit his job by join-

ing the " turn-out " under orders from the society, he
would be " driven to market work," at which he could
not get half a living.[1] So also declared Andrew Dun-
lap and James Cummings, members of the society
who had resorted to " market work " during the turn-
out.[2] The journeymen's society, in its contest with
the masters, permitted its members to send their product to the public market, or to work for merchants
who supplied that market. The society members
pieced out their strike benefits and what they could
get by " cobbling," with what they could get at " market
work." [3] " You were at liberty to make market work,
or any other work you could get, except of master workmen? " " Yes," was the answer of Job Harrison.[4]
This was evidently a war measure, and not an indication
that the journeymen were less hostile than the retail
merchant towards the public market.

The two other kinds of work that prevailed in 1789
were " shop " work and " bespoke " work. The prices
paid to the journeymen for these two kinds of work
were originally the same. If they differed in quality,
the difference was paid for at a specific price for extra
work, as when Job Harrison got six pence extra a pair
if he would " side line " his shoes with silk.[5] But the
payment for extras was the same for shop work as it
was for " bespoke " work. The same workman made
both, and made them in the same way, with the same
tools. One of the grievances of the journeymen was
the innovation attempted in 1798 by one of the employers to reduce the price of shop work. " I made

[1] Doc. Hist., Vol. III, pp. 74, 83.
[2] Ibid., pp. 91, 96.   [3] Ibid., pp. 83, 91; 93, 96.
[4] Ibid., p. 88.   [5] Ibid., p. 94.

some work for Mr. Ryan," said John Hayes, " and he made a similar ɪeduction upon me, because they were to go into the shop, when he used before to give the same price for shop goods as he did for bespoke work." [1] The society demanded similar pay foɪ similar work, whether shop or bespoke. " None are to work under the price," said Keegan, a member of the committee that met the employers; " a good workman may get more." [2]

Thus the journeymen were at one with the masters in their opposition to " market work." For ɪhe journeyman it was a menace to his wages on shop work. For the master it was a menace to his business as a retail storekeeper.

It was the third, or " export " stage of the market, with its wholesale " order " work, that separated the interests of the journeyman from those of the master. Here the retail merchant adds wholesale orders to his business. We find John Bedford describing the way in which he branched out : [3]

Some time afterward [1799], my little capital being laid out in stock, and no way of mending it at home, an idea struck me of going to the southward, and endeavor to force a sale. I went to Charleston at the risque of my life, for the vessel in which I went had like to have been lost at sea. I put my articles at an extremely low price, by which I had but little profit, in order to induce people to deal with me. I got two customers at Charleston; from there I went to Norfolk, Petersburg, Richmond and Alexandria. . . . I returned with two or three small orders . . . business became a little brisk and the journeymen turned out again; on which account I was forced to raise the price of the work I had stipulated to perform.

[1] Doc. Hist., Vol. III, p. 121. [2] Ibid., p. 120.
[3] Ibid., pp. 100–101.

He goes on to specify the loss of four customers and " the sale of 4000 dollars' " worth per year.

Six years later Wm. Montgomery was doing an " export " business. He said : [1]

I had at that time [1805], order work from St. Thomas's, New Orleans and Charleston, to the amount of 2000 dollars, but I could not afford to give the rise of wages, without a loss in executing those orders.

Also Lewis Ryan : [2]

. . . Barnes and Snyder called on me [1805], and asked if I would give the new prices ?   I answered yes ; but as I had determined to relinquish order-work, it should be to the best workmen, and that only for bespoke work.

On the other hand, employers who were not branching out for export work were willing to pay the wages demanded and unwilling to join the employers' association. Wm. Young [3] had belonged to the masters' association in 1789, when it was only a retail merchants' association, and in 1805 he was still doing only bespoke and shop work.

Two of the journeymen waited on me together, [he said] ; they informed me that they felt themselves aggrieved, and had determined to ask higher prices ; a list of which they showed me. I told them I had been in the habit of giving those prices three months before. Q. Did the master workmen call on you ? A. Yes : I told them I could not retract with propriety, as I had been a long time giving the very wages for which the journeymen turned out. . . . The gentlemen, when they called upon me, tried to make some influence upon me to discharge my workmen : I told them I could not do it with propriety.

Likewise, the journeymen who did only bespoke and shop work, were not inclined to stand by the union for

[1] *Ibid.*, p. 105.   [2] *Ibid.*, p. 106.   [3] *Ibid.*, pp. 25–126.

the increase in prices. Job Harrison said,[1] "If shoes were raised to 9s. I should not be benefitted, for I had that price already, but you know it cannot be given only on customers' work." Afterwards he was asked:

Did I understand you to be satisfied all this time with the wages you had been accustomed to receive from Mr. Bedford, and yet they compelled you to turn out? *A*. I had as much as any man, and I could not expect more: but they did not compel me to turn out, any other way than by making a *scab* of me. . . . At length I received a note from Mr. Bedford, informing me that if I did not turn in to work I should hereafter have no more than common wages.[2]

The same was true of inferior workmen who could not command the wages demanded. These were doubtless kept on "order" work, and when the union demanded that the price on that work should be brought up to the same level as shop and bespoke work, they secretly worked "under wages." The union had a committee, "to hunt up cases of the kind," and to demand of employers that such men be discharged.[3]

Thus, as intimated above, the organization of the masters according to their employer-function, as compared with their former organization according to their merchant-function, caused a re-alignment of *personnel*. Both the employer and the workman on high-class custom-work "scabbed" on their respective class organizations struggling to control wholesale-order work.

The several steps in this alignment of interests will appear in the history of the journeymen's society. The first society of the journeymen was organized in 1792, two years after the masters' society had dissolved.

[1] Doc. Hist., Vol. III, p. 82.   [2] *Ibid.*, p. 84.
[3] *Ibid.*, p. 92.

This was apparently a secret society. At any rate it did not submit a scale of prices to the employers, and did not call a strike, but merely contented itself with a "solemn" oath taken by each member to the effect, "I will support such and such wages, to the utmost of my power, etc." But a number of the journeymen secretly violated their pledge. "I know a number," testified Samuel Logan, at that time a journeyman, but now a master, "to work under wages they had solemnly promised to support. . . . I therefore requested a repeal of this affirmation, which broke up the society." [1] The society dissolved in 1792, the year of its organization.

This society, however, must have had some effect on the price of shoes, for the price which had originally been 4s. 6d.[2] had been raised to 6s. before 1794.

It was in 1794 that the permanent society was organized, which continued until the time of the prosecution in 1806.[3] It secured in that year, and again in 1796, an increase in the price of shoes, first, to something under $1.00, then to $1.00 a pair.[4] These increases affected, however, only shop and bespoke work, so that after 1796 the "settled price" was 7s. 6d.; but Job Harrison, by making a lighter shoe with silk lining "so as to come nearer to the London dress-shoes," was paid 9s. a pair.[5] At the other and lowest extreme, only "five eleven penny bits" were paid for "order work." These prices prevailed until 1806. The bespoke and shop work was said to be sold to customers at $2.75 a pair, but the order work was sold to retailers at $1.80 a pair.[6] Thus it was that for

[1] *Ibid.*, p. 93.
[2] *Ibid.*, p. 118.
[3] *Ibid.*, pp. 174, 217–218.
[4] *Ibid.*, pp. 72, 93.
[5] *Ibid.*, pp. 74, 86.
[6] *Ibid.*, p. 86.

nominally the same quality of shoe the journeymen's society was able almost to double their wages on the custom and retail work, but had brought about an increase of only a few cents on the wholesale-order work. In other words, the employer as retail merchant gave to his employees an advance out of the advanced retail price of his goods, but as wholesale merchant he was not able to give a similar advance. Naturally the better class of workmen gravitated towards the custom and retail work, and the inferior workmen towards the wholesale work, so that what was originally the same quality of work, and nominally remained the same, became eventually different in quality.

This variation of price and quality is also observed in the price of boots. These had been advanced in price to the journeymen from $1.40 per pair in 1792, to $2.75 per pair in 1796. But the workmen conceded that they should make order work at $2.50 [1] " in order to encourage the exportation trade." [2] This was taken advantage of at the time of the cholera epidemic in 1798, when the journeymen were paid only $2.25.[3] After the journeymen returned to the city they organized their second strike, in 1798, for an increase. This was immediately granted by the employers, but in the following year, 1799, the employers effected an organization and ordered a return to the former wage. This caused the obstinate strike and lockout of nine or ten weeks, ending in a compromise. Again in 1804 there was another brief strike, at which the journeymen won, and the employers agreed to pay $2.75. But after Christmas, when the work became slack, the price of

[1] Doc. Hist., Vol. III, p. 121.   [2] Ibid., p. 124.
[3] Ibid., p. 121.

order work was reduced to $2.50.[1] This led to the obstinate strike of 1805, in which the journeymen demanded a flat increase all round to $3.00 on both wholesale and retail work. But the employers had perfected their organization, and their list of prices made no mention of order work. The workmen lost the strike and were compelled to accept the employers' list. Consequently in 1806, as compared with 1789, the price paid to the journeyman on retail and custom work had advanced from $1.40 to $2.75, while the price on wholesale work of the same quality, after futile efforts of the journeymen to equalize it, was left open to individual bargains.[2] Exactly as in the case of shoes, the differentiation in prices led to a differentiation in quality. The tendency of custom and retail work was towards improved quality, executed by superior workmen. The tendency of the wholesale work was towards inferior quality in the hands of inferior workmen. " At that time [prior to 1792], I believe we did not understand extra work in them, such as they do now," testified James Keegan.[3] " I never do order-work, I am always paid the full wages."

Notice now the characteristic features of the retail and wholesale-order stages of the industry. The master workman at the retail stage has added a stock of finished goods to his business of custom work. This requires a shop on a business street accessible to the general public, with correspondingly high rents. It involves also a certain amount of capital tied up in short

[1] *Ibid.*, p. 123.

[2] I am including here only the ordinary "long boots" and "cossacks." The society in 1805 also demanded an increase on the fancy kinds of work recently introduced. Doc. Hist., Vol. III, pp. 104, 107.

[3] *Ibid.*, p. 118.

credits and accounts with customers. In his shop he has a stock of raw material, besides finished and partly finished goods. The merchant-function has thus become paramount, and has drawn with it the master-function. The two functions have equipped themselves with capital — merchant's capital in the form of finished stock, retail store, and short credits; employer's capital in the form of raw material undergoing manufacture by workmen under instructions. The journeymen are left with only their hand tools and their home workshop.

Thus the retail market has separated the laborer from the merchant. Labor's outlook now is solely for wages. The merchant's outlook is for quality and prices. But the separation is not antagonism. The employer-function is as yet at a minimum. Profit is not dependent on reducing wages so much as increasing prices. Indeed, the journeymen are able almost to double their wages without a strike, and the merchants pass the increase along to the customers.

But it is different when the merchant reaches out for wholesale orders. Now he adds heavy expenses for solicitation and transportation. He adds a storeroom and a larger stock of goods. He holds the stock a longer time and he gives long and perilous credits. At the same time he meets competitors from other centres of manufacture, and cannot pass along his increased expenses. Consequently the wage-bargain assumes importance, and the employer-function comes to the front. Wages are reduced by the merchant as employer on work destined for the wholesale market. The conflict of capital and labor begins.

Before we can fully appreciate the significance and

the economic interpretation of these revolutionizing facts, we shall need to consider the next succeeding stage, that of the merchant-capitalist.

III

The United Beneficial Society of Journeymen Cordwainers, Philadelphia, 1835

The organizations of masters and journeymen of 1805 continued more or less until 1835. Then a new and more revolutionary stage of the industry is ushered in. This time it is the merchant-capitalist, who subdues both the master and the journeyman through his control of the new widespread market of the South and West. We read of his coming in the address " to the Journeymen Cordwainers of the City and County of Philadelphia," issued by the two hundred members of the " United Beneficial Society of Journeymen Cordwainers." [1] This organization took the lead in bringing together the several trade societies of Philadelphia into the Trades' Union, and in conducting the first great general ten-hour strike in this country. The reasons for their aggressiveness may be inferred from their " Address." They recite that the wages of $2.75 formerly paid for boots have fallen to 1.12\frac{1}{2}$; that their earnings of nine to ten dollars a week have fallen to four to six dollars; that, in order to earn such wages they must work, in many instances, fourteen hours a day; and that other skilled tradesmen are earning eight to twelve dollars a week, often " only working ten hours a day." This depression, they explain, has occurred since " a few years ago." It began with an

[1] *Pennsylvanian*, April 4, 1835; Doc. Hist., Vol. VI, pp. 21–27.

" unfortunate " coöperative experiment of the journey-men in " opening shops for the manufacture of cheap goods " for the purpose of winning a strike. It was intensified by the appearance of the merchant-capitalist. We are told that

"The cunning men of the East" have come to our city, and having capital themselves, or joining with those who have had, have embarked in our business, and realized large fortunes, by reducing our wages, making large quantities of work and selling at reduced price, while those who had served their time at the trade, and had an anxious desire to foster and cherish its interests, have had to abandon the business, or enter into the system of manu-facturing largely [*i.e.* on a large scale] in order to save themselves from bankruptcy.

Then they explain how this has come about " with-out any positive reduction of our wages."

The answer is plain and simple — by making cheap work, triple the quantity has to be made to obtain a living; this produces, at dull seasons, a surplus of work in the market; and these *large* manufacturers, taking advantage of the times, have compelled their journeymen to make the work so far superior to the manner in which it was originally made for the wages given, that it is now brought into competition with first-rate work. This again lessens the quantity of first-rate work made, and the journeymen, for-merly working for employers who gave them $2.75 for each pair of boots made, are forced to seek employment of the very men who had ruined their business.

The dubious position of the employers also, at this stage of the industry, is shown by the action of " a large adjourned meeting of the ladies'-shoe dealers and manufacturers." They unanimously adopted a pre-amble and resolution presented by a committee ap-pointed at a previous meeting reciting that,

Whereas, the laboring portion of this community have made a general strike for what they consider their just rights, knowing that if they were longer to permit the growing encroachments of capital upon labor, they would soon be unable to make any resistance . . . we feel a desire to aid and encourage them in their effort to obtain an adequate compensation for their labor. . . . Knowing that the pittance hitherto earned by them is entirely insufficient for their support, we do hereby agree to and comply with their demands generally, and pledge ourselves to do all in our power to support and sustain them. . . . Believing also that a trifling advance in the price of shoes would scarcely be felt by general society . . . we will agree to be governed hereafter by a list of prices for our work, which will render our business uniform and permanent.[1]

Nine months later these employers were forced by the exactions of the union and their inability to control the merchant-capitalist to take the other side of the question, organizing as an employers' association and making a determined fight against the union.[2]

At this stage of the industry we have reached the market afforded by highway and canal, as well as ocean and river. The banking system has expanded, enabling the capitalist to convert customers' credits into bank credits and to stock up a surplus of goods in advance of actual orders. The market becomes speculative, and the warehouse of the wholesale-merchant-master takes the place of the store-room of the retail capitalist. The former master becomes the small manufacturer or contractor, selling his product to the wholesale-manufacturer, the merchant-capitalist. The latter has a wide range of option in his purchase of goods, and consequently in his ability to compel masters and journeymen to compete severely against each other.

---

[1] *Pennsylvanian*, June 15, 1835; Doc. Hist., Vol. VI, pp. 27–28.
[2] *Pennsylvanian*, March 28, 1836; Doc. Hist., Vol. VI, pp. 32–35.

He can have his shoes made in distant localities.   The cordwainers relate [1] that

there are many employers of this city who have made off of the labor of journeymen a liberal fortune, and now refuse to accede to the justice of our demands, and in order to evade the same they are preparing materials (in this city) in order to send them into the towns of the Eastern states (where living and labor are cheaper and workmanship not so good) to get the same made into shoes, then to be brought here and sold for Philadelphia manufacture.

The merchant-capitalist can also discover new fields for the manufacture of cheap work, and for the first time we read of the competition of convict labor.   The cordwainers publish an advertisement,[2] warning their members against a firm who " are now getting work manufactured by convicts in the Eastern Penitentiary at less than one-half what our bill of rates call for. . . ." And one of their resolutions asserts that " shoemaking is found to be the most convenient and most lucrative employment of convicts, consequently almost *one-half* of the convicts in our different penitentiaries are taught shoemaking." [3]

The merchant-capitalist has also the option of all the different methods of manufacture and shop organization.   He can employ journeymen at his warehouse as cutters, fitters and pattern makers; he can employ journeymen at their homes to take out material and bring back finished work; but, more characteristic of his methods, he can employ small contractors, the specialized successors of the master cordwainer, who in turn employ one to a dozen journeymen, and by division

[1] *Pennsylvanian*, June 20, 1835;   Doc. Hist., Vol. VI, pp. 29–30.

[2] *Pennsylvanian*, Sept. 5, 1835.

[3] *Pennsylvanian*, Oct. 1, 1835.

of labor and " team work " introduce the sweating system.[1]

Through these different methods of manufacture we are able to see how it is that the merchant-capitalist intensifies and even creates the antagonism of " capital and labor." He does this by forcing the separation of functions and classes a step further than it had been forced in the wholesale-order stage. First, he takes away from the retail merchant his wholesale-order business. He buys and sells in large quantities; he assembles the cheap products of prison labor, distant localities, and sweat-shops; he informs himself of markets, and beats down the charges for transportation. Thus he takes to himself the wholesale business and leaves to the merchant the retail trade.

Second, he drives off from the retail merchant his employer-function. The retail merchant can no longer afford to employ journeymen on " shop " work, because he can purchase more cheaply of the merchant-capitalist. A few years ago, say the cordwainers in their " address," " such an article as boots was then unknown in the Market street shops : the manufacturing of that article being confined exclusively to those, who having served an apprenticeship to the business, knew best its value." [2]

Thus the merchant-capitalist strips the former mer-

---

[1] The term "manufactory," as distinguished from "factory," occurs in the merchant-capitalist stage to indicate the combined warehouse and place of employment where material is prepared to be taken out by journeymen or contractors. It is the "inside shop" of the ready-made clothing trade, the contractor's shops being known as "outside shops." See Commons, "Trade Unionism and Labor Problems," p. 316 (1905), article on "sweating system."

[2] *Pennsylvanian*, April 4, 1835; Doc. Hist., Vol. VI, p. 22.

chant-master both of his market and his journeymen. The wholesale market he takes to himself; the journeymen he hands over to a specialist in wage-bargaining. This specialist is no longer known as " master," — he takes the name of " boss," [1] or employer. He is partly a workman, having come up through the trade, like the master, and continuing to work alongside his men. He is an employer without capital, for he rents his workshop, and the merchant-capitalist owns the raw material and the journeymen own the tools. His profits are not those of the capitalist, neither do they proceed from his ability as a merchant, since the contract-prices he gets are dictated by the merchant-capitalist. His profits come solely out of wages and work. He organizes his workmen in teams, with the work subdivided in order to lessen dependence on skill and to increase speed of output. He plays the less skilled against the more skilled, the speedy against the slow, and reduces wages while enhancing exertion. His profits are " sweated " out of labor, his shop is the " sweatshop," he the " sweater."

Thus the merchant-capitalist, with his widespread, wholesale-speculative market, completes the separation and specializes the functions of the former homogeneous craftsman. The merchant-function, which was the first to split off from the others, is now itself separated into three parts, — custom merchant, retail merchant, wholesale merchant, — corresponding to the three levels of market competition. The journeyman-function is

[1] The first use that I have found of the Dutch word "bos," meaning manager of a group of workmen, is in the organ of the New York Trades Union, *The Man*, May 30, 1834; Doc. Hist., Vol. VI, p. 92. It was spelled with one "s," though the obstinacy of the printer of the " Documentary History " finally succeeded in using two in the reprint.

now segregated on two levels of competition, the highest level of custom work and the lowest level menaced by prison and sweatshop work. The employer-function, the last to split off, makes its first appearance as a separate factor on the lowest level of market competition. Evidently the wide extension of the market in the hands of the merchant-capitalist is a cataclysm in the position of the journeyman. By a desperate effort of organization he struggles to raise himself back to his original level. His merchant-employers at first sympathize with him, and endeavor to pass over to their customers his just demand for a higher wage. But they soon are crushed between the level of prices and the level of wages. From the position of a merchants' association striving to hold up prices, they shift to that of an employers' association endeavoring to keep down wages. The result of these struggles of protective organizations will appear when we analyze more closely the economic forces under which they operate. These forces turn on the nature of the bargain, the period and risk of investment and the level of the competitive menace.

1. *The Nature of the Bargain*

We have to do with two classes of bargains, the wage-bargain and the price-bargain. Each is affected by the increasing distance of the ultimate purchaser, the actual consumer, from the worker, the manual producer. In the primitive " bespoke," or custom-order stage, the market is direct and immediate. The producer is the seller to the consumer. The work is priced by means of a separate bargain for each article. The price-bargain is made before the work is done. The customer pays according to the quality, and if he desires an improved quality, he stands the increased price; or, if the producers are able to exclude an inferior quality, he pays the price of the quality supplied. Hence an increase of wages is shifted directly to the purchaser. The wage-bargain and price-bargain are identical.

In the retail-shop stage, the producer is removed one step from the ultimate purchaser. The merchant intervenes as a price-bargainer. This bargain is made after the work is done. The purchasers are now separated into two classes, those who are particular about quality and adhere to the custom-order bargain, and those who are particular about price and pass on to the " shop " bargain. To the latter is transferred a certain advantage, and the merchant is less able to shift upon them an increase in wages. The wage-bargain is made for a stock of shoes rather than an individual purchaser, and the goods are to be sold with reference to price rather than quality.

In the wholesale-order stage the market is removed a second step. There are two price-bargains that intervene between the worker and the market, one between the wholesaler and retailer and one between retailer and consumer. The wholesale price-bargain is indeed made before the work is done, and to that extent the wages, if previously known, can be shifted. But the retailer, as shown above, is himself restricted in his ability to shift an increase upon the purchasers, and he is more concerned than they as to price because his profit turns thereon, while he is concerned with quality only indirectly as their representative and not directly as the actual user. Consequently, the wholesale merchant is less able than the retail merchant to shift his wages. Of course, if an increase in wages is demanded after the orders are taken, he is compelled at once to make a fight against the workers. It was the opportunity offered by the wholesale-order stage to take this unfair advantage of the employer that provoked the first bitter struggle of capital and labor in 1806.

The wholesale-speculative stage of 1835 intrudes yet another step on the road from producer to market. The employer is now separated out from both the merchant and the worker, and, besides the wage-bargain, we have three price-bargains, — the employer-capitalist, capitalist-retailer and retailer-consumer. The second bargain, that of capitalist-retailer, is made after the work is done, and it is this that constitutes its speculative character. It transfers the advantage of position to the retailer, just as shop work had transferred the advantage to the consumer. Consequently, the employer, or " contractor," the sweatshop " boss," is now introduced as a specialist in driving the wage-bargain, with reference to the increased obstacles in the way of shifting wages along to the ultimate purchaser.

Thus it is that the ever-widening market from the custom-order stage, through the retail-shop and wholesale-order to the wholesale-speculative stage, removes the journeyman more and more from his market, diverts attention to price rather than quality and shifts the advantage in the series of bargains from the journeymen to the consumers and their intermediaries.

2. The Period and Risk of Investment

Throughout the four stages here described there have been no changes in the tools of production. The factory system with its " fixed capital " has not yet appeared, and the only capital invested is " circulating capital " in the form of raw material, finished stock and bills receivable. Upon this circulating capital the owner incurs the threefold expense of interest, risk and necessary profit. The amount of capital, per unit of product, remains the same, but the period during which it is locked up is lengthened in proportion as the market area is extended. In the custom-order stage this period is at its minimum; in the retail-shop stage the period is lengthened; in the wholesale-order stage, on account of long credits, the period is at its maximum; in the wholesale-speculative stage the average period is perhaps reduced, but this is more than offset by the increase in the rate of risk. This increase of expense for " waiting " and risk, owing to the lengthening of the period of investment, must either be added to the price paid by the consumer or deducted from the wage paid to the producer. But since the position of purchasers in the price-bargains is improved with the progress of the stages, the increased expense on account of circulating capital must be met by deductions from the rates of wages. This might not have been necessary if fixed capital had been introduced, bringing with it a greater speed of output at the old amount of earnings. But, in lieu of this cheapening by improved tools of production, the only way of meeting the increased expense of waiting is by reducing the rate of pay on each unit of product. The wholesale market is a market for " future goods," the custom-order market is a market for " present goods." The premium on " future goods " appears, therefore, as a reduction below the wages paid at the same time on " present goods." Shop work, order work and speculative work must be manufactured at a lower wage-cost than bespoke work of the same kind and quality.

3. *The Level of the Competitive Menace*

Defining the " marginal producer " as the one with the lowest standards of living and cost and quality of work, he is the producer whose competition tends to drag down the level of others toward his own. It is not necessary that he be able actually to supply the entire market or even the greater part of it. His effect on others depends on the extent to which he can be used as a club to intimidate others against standing out for their side of the bargain. He is a menace rather than an actual competitor. Now, the extension of the market for the sale of goods is accompanied by an extension of the field for the production of goods. This extension brings into the competitive area new competitors who are essentially a series of lower marginal producers. The capitalist who can reach out for these low-level producers can use them at will to break down the spirit of resistance of the high-level producers. In the custom-order stage there was but one competitive menace, the shoemaker who made " bad ware." In the retail-shop stage there is added the " advertiser," the " public market " and the auction system. In the wholesale-order stage there is added the foreign producer and in the wholesale-speculative stage the labor of convicts and sweatshops. Thus, the extension of the field of production increases the variety and discovers lower levels of marginal producers, and the merchant-capitalist emerges as the generalissimo, menacing in turn every part of the field from his strategic centre.

4. *Protective Organizations*

We have already seen the cumulative effect in 1806 and 1835, of these three sets of circumstances in dragging down the entire body of workmen. We now proceed to notice the resistance of protective organizations and their ultimate effect in bringing about a segregation of work and workers on non-competing levels.

This may be seen by following again the movement of wages in Philadelphia from 1789 to 1835, on the different classes of work. Prior to 1792, on common boots, the journeyman's wages were $1.40 a pair on both bespoke and shop work. In the course of fifteen years the price advanced to $2.75, and this price was paid for both bespoke and shop work, but a concession of 25 cents was made on wholesale-order work, bringing that price to $2.50. In 1835 the price had fallen to $1.12½ for wholesale work, while retail work had dropped out or had come down to the same price as wholesale work, leaving custom work at a higher figure. In the course of this movement, the better class of workmen restricted themselves as much as possible to custom work, and the quality of this kind of work was improved. On the other hand, the wholesale-order and wholesale-speculative work tended throughout to fall into the hands of inferior workmen, and this brought about an inferiority in quality. These inferior goods, made by inferior workmen, became more and more a menace to the superior goods and the superior journeymen, both on account of the lower levels of the marginal producers and on account of the smaller demand relatively for the production of superior goods.

Herein was the necessity of protective organizations. In order that these organizations might succeed, it was just as necessary to set up protection against inferior goods as against low wages. In the guild stage of the industry, when the three functions of journeyman, master and workman were united in one person, the protection sought was against the " bad ware " made by some of the trade. By " suppressing " those who made bad ware, the customers would be compelled to turn to those who were " sufficient " workmen and made good ware. Since the bargain was a separate one for each article, so that the price could be adjusted to the quality before the work was done, nothing more was needed on the part of the guild members for the purpose of " inriching themselves by their trades very much."

But in the later stages of the industry, the merchant-function, and afterwards the employer-function, were separated from the journeyman-function. It is the special function of the merchant to watch over and guard the quality of the work, because his bargain with the consumer is an adjustment of the price to the quality demanded. The journeyman's function is simply that of making the kind and quality of goods ordered by the merchant. The merchant, in his function as employer, gives these orders to the journeyman, and consequently, when the employer-function is separated from the journeyman-function, the employer, as the representative of the merchant, attends to the quality of the work. In this way the journeyman has lost control over quality, and is forced to adapt his quality to his price, instead of demanding a price suited to his quality. So, when he forms his protective organization, his attention is directed mainly to the compensation side of the bargain. In proportion as the quality of his work depends on his rate of pay, he indirectly controls the quality, but the primary purpose of his organization is to control the rate of pay. This he does, first, by demanding the same minimum rate of pay for all market destinations of the same kind of work. It was this demand that forced the alignment of classes, and drove the sympathetic merchant over into the hostile employers' association. The employer could yield if he confined himself to the narrow field of the " bespoke " market, but not if he was menaced by the wider field of the wholesale market. On this account it was possible in the retail-shop stage for the interests of employer and workmen to be harmonious. But the employer could not yield in the merchant-capitalist stage, on that part of the field menaced by prison and sweatshop labor. Consequently, the outcome of the strikes of 1835 was the differentiation of the market into two non-competing levels, the higher level of custom and high-grade shop work, controlled more or less by the cordwainers' societies for the next twenty-five years [1] and the lower level of inferior work controlled by prison and sweatshop competition.[2]

[1] Freedley, E. T., "Philadelphia and its Manufactories," p. 187, says in 1858: "Making men's wear and making women's wear are distinct branches. . . . The Men's men and Women's men, as the workmen are distinguished, have separate organizations, and neither know nor mingle with each other."

[2] "In addition to these there are a large number whose operations, though in the aggregate important, cannot easily be ascertained. They are known by a term more expressive than euphonious, 'garret bosses' who employ from one to twelve men each; and having but little capital, make boots and shoes in their own rooms, and sell them to jobbers and

IV

Knights of St. Crispin, 1868

We come now to an entirely different step in the progress of industrial stages. Hitherto, the only change requiring notice has been that produced by the extension of the market and the accompanying credit system. These changes were solely external. The next change is internal. Prior to 1837 there had been scarcely a hundred inventions affecting the tools used by the cordwainer. All of these may be described as " devices " rather than machines. Even as late as 1851 all of the labor in the manufacture of shoes was hand labor. In 1852, the sewing machine was adapted to the making of uppers, but this did not affect the journeyman cordwainer, because the sewing of uppers had been the work of women. Even the flood of inventions that came into use during the decade of the 'fifties were aids to the journeyman rather than substitutes for his skill. Indeed, some of them probably operated to transfer the work of women to men, for they required greater physical strength and endurance in order to develop their full capacity. Whether operated by foot power or merely facilitating the work of his hands, they were essentially shop tools and not factory machines. Such were the tin patterns for cutting, the stripper and sole-cutter, adjustable lasts, levellers, skivers, and the machines for heel making, lasting and sandpapering. Quite different were the pegging machine, introduced in 1857, and especially the McKay sole-sewing machine, introduced in 1862. These

retailers in small quantities at low rates for cash. One retailer, who sells $20,000 worth per annum, buys three-fourths of his stock from these makers." Freedley, p. 188.

usurped not only the highest skill of the workman, but also his superior physique. The McKay machine did in one hour what the journeyman did in eighty. These machines were quickly followed by others, either machines newly invented or old ones newly adapted, but all of them belted up to steam. The factory system, aided by the enormous demand of government for its armies, came suddenly forth, though it required another fifteen years to reach perfection. It was at the middle of this transition period, 1868 to 1872, that the Knights of St. Crispin appeared, and flourished beyond anything theretofore known in the history of American organized labor. Its membership mounted to 40,000 or 50,000, whereas the next largest unions of the time claimed only 10,000 to 12,000. It disappeared as suddenly as it had arisen, a tumultuous, helpless protest against the abuse of machinery. For it was not the machine itself that the Crispins were organized to resist, but the substitution of " green hands " for journeymen in the operation of the machines. There was but one law which they bound themselves by constitutions, rituals, oaths and secret confederacy to enforce and to support each other in enforcing: refusal to teach green hands except by consent of the organization. This at least was the object of the national organization. When local unions once were established, they took into their own hands the cure of other ills, and their strikes and lockouts were as various as the variety of shops and factories in which they were employed. The Knights of St. Crispin were face to face with survivals from all of the preceding stages of industrial evolution, as well as the lusty beginnings of the succeeding stage. They were employed in custom shops, in retail and wholesale-order shops, in the shops of the merchant-capitalist and his contractors, in the factories of the manufacturer-capitalist. A comparison of the objects of their strikes reveals the overlapping of stages. All of their strikes turned directly or indirectly on two issues, resistance to wage reductions and refusal to teach " green hands." The wage strikes took place mainly in the shops of the merchant-capitalist, the " green hand " strikes in the factories.[1] The merchant-capitalist was forced by the competition of the manufacturer, either to become a manufacturer himself (or to purchase from the manufacturer), or to cut the wages of his journeymen and the prices paid to his contractors. Neither the journeyman's devices nor his foot power machines yielded a sufficient increase of output to offset his wage reductions. His aggravation was the more intense in that the wage reductions occurred only on shop work and not on custom work. The anomaly of different prices for the same grade of work, which had showed itself with the extension of markets, was now still more exaggerated and more often experienced under the competition of factory products. Even prison labor and Chinese labor were not cheap enough to enable the merchant-capitalist to compete with the product of green hands and steam power.

The factory succeeded also in producing a quality of work equal or even superior to that produced by the journeyman. Consequently its levelling agencies reached upwards to all but the topmost of the non-

[1] For the detailed study upon which this brief summary of the Knights of St. Crispin is based, I am indebted to Mr. D. D. Lescohier, member of my research group. See *Bulletin* No. 355 of the University of Wisconsin, Economics and Political Science Series, Vol. VII, No. 1.

competing levels on which the journeymen had succeeded in placing themselves, and brought them down
eventually to its own factory level. The Grand Lodge
of the Knights of St. Crispin was the protest of workmen whose skill of work, quality of product and protective unions had for a generation preceding saved
for themselves the higher levels of the merchant-capitalist system against the underwash of prison and sweat-
shop competition. It was their protest against the new
menace of cheap labor and green hands utilized by the
owners of steam power and machinery.

It is not my purpose here to describe the familiar
factory system. Its place in the evolution of industrial
stages is summarized in the appended table. Suffice
it to note that in the shoe industry the factory system
was established in substantially its present form in
the early part of the 'eighties; that detailed piece-
work has taken the place of team-work and hand-work;
that the last vestige of property-right has left the worker;
that the present form of labor organization, the Boot and
Shoe Workers' Union, has endeavored, since 1895, to
bring together all classes of employees, men and women,
in a single industrial union rather than a partial trade
union; and that the two classes of protective organizations have asserted their political power for protection
against low levels of competition, the merchant-manu-
facturer against free trade in foreign products, the wage-
earner against foreign immigrants, prison labor, child
labor and long hours of labor.

V

Industrial Evolution in Europe and America. Organization and Legislation for Protection.

The foregoing sketch of industrial evolution in America brings into prominence the part played by the ever-widening area of competition, and the effort of protective organizations to ward off the peculiar competitive menace of each stage of development. From this standpoint the sketch may be compared with the investigations of Marx, Schmoller and Bücher. Karl Marx was the first to challenge the world with a keen analysis of economic evolution, but his standpoint is that of the mode of production and not the extension of the market. His two assumptions of a given " use value " and a given " average social labor " serve to obliterate, the one the part played by the price-bargain, the other the part played by the wage-bargain. With these assumptions out of the way he is able to concern himself with the production of " surplus value " by his theory of the working day and the cost of living. But these are secondary factors, results, not causes. The primary factors are on the side of the market where competition is carried on at different levels. Instead of " exploitation," growing out of the nature of production, our industrial evolution shows certain evils of competition imposed by an " unfair " menace. Instead, therefore, of an idealistic remedy sought for in common ownership, the practical remedy always actually sought out has been the elimination of the competitive menace through a protective organization or protective legislation.

Schmoller and Bücher have both avoided the narrow abstractions of Marx, because they have traced out the actual development of industry through access to a wealth of historical material not available to their predecessor. Schmoller, with his ever-widening area of village, town, territory and state under a single political control leading to extension of markets,[1] and Bücher with his ever-widening area of the markets leading to political extension,[2] have cultivated the field where the true explanation of industrial evolution shall be found. But there are certain considerations in European history which have obliterated or confused the pure economic facts. Industrial evolution, considered as a mere economic process, had to work its way up through superimposed racial, military, tribal, feudal, ecclesiastical and guild regulations and restrictions. These have been especially disturbing to Schmoller, but have been delightfully brushed aside by Bücher.[3] At the same time, in both cases they have operated to cover up certain significant stages and factors. For example, the retail-shop and the wholesale-order stages of the American shoe industry are not as strikingly apparent in the European process, probably because the powerful guild regulations served to maintain a uniform price for custom work, retail work and wholesale-order work.[4] But the guilds were unable to cope with the cut prices of wholesale-speculative work. Consequently, Schmoller and Bücher pass over with slight emphasis from the primitive guild stage of Boston, 1648, to the

[1] Schmoller, "Grundriss," etc., Vol. I, p. 254 ff.

[2] *Ibid.*, p. 89 ff., 135 ff.

[3] *E.g.* their controversy over the influence of heredity in "Jahrbuch f. Gesetzgebung," Vol. XVII, p. 303; Vol. XVIII, p. 318.

[4] Sombart, "Der Moderne Kapitalismus," Vol. I, p. 95.

merchant-capitalist stage of 1835.   But it is not enough to say that the retail-merchant and wholesale-order stages were only " transitional," for they bring to light the fundamental economic forces at work.   They reveal the segregation of the merchant-function and the joint effort of both employer and journeyman to extend markets.   They modify materially Bücher's modified theory of exploitation through intermediary merchants, by concentrating attention on the competitive menace and the function of protection.   It is this bald simplicity of American individualism, without much covering of races, armies, guilds or prelates, that permits us to trace out all of the economic sutures in their evolution from infancy to manhood.

The menace of competition may conveniently be described as internal and external.   The former arises within the area of the existing market, the latter proceeds from cheap producers abroad.   With the ever-widening area of political control these external menaces become internal, and it is this moving frontier that determines the scope and character of protective organization and protective legislation.

Throughout the course of industrial evolution the part played by the merchant stands out as the determining factor.   The key to the situation is at all times the price-bargain.   It is the merchant who controls both capital and labor.   If the merchant has a market, he can secure capital.   Even the modern " manufacturer " is first of all the merchant.   The "conflict of capital and labor " is a conflict of market and labor, of merchant and wage-earner, of prices and wages. With the extension of the market the merchant-function is the first to separate, unless prevented by guild or other regulations, and with each further extension the separation is greater. Just as the first " masters' society " of 1789 was really a retail merchants' association, so the modern " manufacturers' association " is a price-regarding association. Capital follows the merchant, and the manufacturers' protective organization is an organization to protect prices. When the extension of the market provokes the conflict of prices and wages, the wage-earners resort to independent protective policies. Then the manufacturer turns, for the time, from the market and faces the workman. His " employers' association " is wholly different in method, object and social significance, and usually in *personnel* from his " manufacturers' association." [1]

The conflict is ultimately one between the interests of the consumer and the interests of the producer. Wherever the consumer as such is in control, he favors the marginal producer, for through him he wields the club that threatens the other producers. Consequently, the producers resort either to private organizations equipped with coercive weapons to suppress their menacing competitor, or else they seek to persuade or compel the government to suppress him. In this way the contest of classes or interests enters the field of politics, and the laws of the land, and even the very framework of government, are the outcome of a struggle both to extend markets and to ward off their menace.

[1] The merchant and employer functions appear throughout different industrial stages and industries under different names, as follows:

Merchant		Employer	
	Master workman		Master workman
	Retail master		Contractor
	Wholesale manufacturer		Manufacturer
	Merchant-capitalist		
	Manufacturer		

In the early stages the agricultural, as distinguished from the " industrial " interests, are in control, and they stand to the shoemakers as consumers. Consequently, if the industrial interests secure protection, they must do it by carving out a jurisdiction of their own, enfranchised with political immunities and self-governing organizations. In this struggle did the guilds of Europe rid themselves of feudal agriculture. But in colonial America only the soft petition of the Boston shoemakers and coopers in 1648 shows the high-water mark of the guild. Here protection was grudgingly granted against the internal menace of bad ware and itinerant cobblers. In later times, a manufacturing colony, like Pennsylvania, enacted protective tariffs against external menace, and in 1787 the commercial and manufacturing interests, now reaching out for wholesale trade, secured in the Federal Constitution the political instrument of their mercantile aspirations. Forthwith, as we have seen, the shoemakers of Philadelphia experienced the stimulus of this extension of markets and entered the wholesale-order stage of their industry. At once what had been an external menace now became internal on this wider and lower level of competition, resulting in the separation and struggle of classes. The wage-class began its long contest for the political immunity of a private organization to suppress the " scab " in his many forms of non-unionist, sweat-shop worker, green hand, Chinaman and immigrant. But, prior to the merchant-capitalist stage, this separation of labor from merchant was sporadic and reconcilable. The employer, as such, with his specialized wage-bargain, had only occasionally appeared. Merchant and journeyman were at one in their effort to protect the price-bargain. Together they joined in their century-long effort, ever more and more successful, to use the federal constitution for the suppression of the cheap ware of the foreign producer. But after the merchant-capitalist period, the slogan of the protective tariff became protection for labor, where formerly it had been protection for capital. Eventually, with the further separation of labor under its own leaders, protection took the additional form of suppressing the Chinaman and the alien contract-laborer. Turning to the state governments, labor has summoned its political strength for the suppression of the internal menace of long hours, prison labor, child and woman labor. And finally, where neither politics nor organizations suffice to limit the menace of competition, both " manufacturers " and workmen in the shoe trade strive to raise themselves above its level by cultivating the good will of the consumers, the former by his trade mark, the latter by the union label.

Thus have American shoemakers epitomized American industrial history. Common to all industries is the historical extension of markets. Variations of form, factors and rates of progress change the picture, but not the vital force. The shoemakers have pioneered and left legible records. Their career is " interpretative," if not typical.

APPENDIX

"COMPANY OF SHOOMAKERS," BOSTON, 1648[1]

Vppon the petition of the shoomakers of Boston, & in consideration of of the complaynts which haue bin made of the damag which the country sustaynes by occasion of bad ware made by some of that trade, for redresse hereof, its ordred, & the Court doth hereby graunt libtie & powre vnto Richard Webb, James Euerill, Robt Turner, Edmund Jackson, & the rest of the shoomakers inhabiting & howskeepers in Boston, or the greatest number of them, vppō due notice giuen to the rest, to assemble & meete together in Boston, at such time & times as they shall appoynt, who beinge so assembled, they, or the greater number of them, shall haue powre to chuse a master, & two wardens, with fowre or six associats, a clarke, a sealer, a searcher, & a beadle, with such other officers as they shall find nessessarie; & these officers & ministers, as afforesd, every yeare or oftener, in case of death or departure out of this jurisdiction, or remoueall for default, &c., which officers & ministers shall each of them take an oath sutable to theire places before the Gounor or some of the magists, the same beinge pscribed or allowed by this Court; & the sd shoomakers beinge so assembled as before, or at any other meettinge or assembly to be appoynted from time to time by the master & wardens, or master or wardens with two of the associats, shall haue power to make orders for the well gouerninge of theire company, in the mannaginge of their trade & all the affayres therevnto belonging, & to change & reforme the same as occasion shall require & to añex reasonable pennalties for the breach of the same; provided, that none of theire sd orders, nor any alteration therein, shalbe of force before they shalbe pvsed & allowed of by the Court of that county, or by the Court of Assistants. And for the better executing such orders, the sd master & wardens, or any two of them with 4 or 6 associats, or any three of them, shall haue power to heare & determine all offences agaynst any of theire sd orders, & may inflict the pennalties pscribed as afforesd, & assesse fines to the vallew of forty shillings or vnder for one offence, & the clarke shall giue warrent in writinge to the beadle

---

[1] "The Records of the Colony of the Massachusetts Bay in New England," Vol. III, p. 132.

to leuie the same, who shall haue power therevppon to leuie the
same by distresse, as is vsed in other cases; & all the sd fines &
forfeitures shalbe imployd to the benefit of the sd company of
shoomakers in generall, & to no other vse. And vppon the com-
playnt of the sd master & wardens, or theire atturny or advocate,
in the County Court, of any pson or psons who shall vse the art
or trade of a shoomaker, or any pt thereof, not beinge approued
of by the officers of ye sd shomakers to be a sufficient workman,
the sd Court shall haue power to send for such psons, & suppresse
them; provided also, that the prioritie of theire graunt shall not
giue them precedency of other companies that may be graunted;
but that poynt to be determined by this Court when there shalbe
occasiō thereof; provided also, that no vnlawfull combination
be made at any time by the sd company of shoomakers for inhancinge the prices of shooes, bootes, or wages, whereby either or
owne people may suffer; provided also, that in cases of dificultie,
the sd officers & associats doe not pceede to determine the cause
but by the advice of the judges of that county; provided, that no
shoomaker shall refuse to make shooes for any inhabitant, at reasonable rates, of theire owne leather, for the vse of themselues &
families, only if they be required therevnto; provided, lastly, that
if any pson shall find himselfe greiued by such excessiue fines or
other illegall pceedinges of the sd officers, he may complayne
thereof at the next Court of that county, who may heare & determine the cause. This commission to continue & be of force for
three yeares, & no longer, vnles the Court shall see cause to continue the same.

The same comīssion, verbatim, with the same libtie & power
for the same ends, vpon the like grounds is giuen vnto Thomas
Venner, John Millum, Samuel Bidfeild, James Mattocks, Wm.
Cutter, Bartholomew Barlow, & the rest of the coops of Boston &
Charlestowne, for the pventing abuses in theire trade. To con-
tinue only for three yars, as the former, mutatis mutandis.

CHAPTER XV

BEGINNING in 1892 as a convention of delegates from ten local unions of lumber handlers from Ashland to Buffalo, under the name of the " National 'Longshoremen's Association of the United States "; changing its name to " International " in 1895 to take in Canada; changing again in 1902 to "International 'Longshoremen, Marine and Transport Workers' Association," — this organization now includes forty different occupations, and claims 100,000 members, of whom one-half are on the Great Lakes. As stated in its Directory, it

embraces in its membership and grants charters to Loaders and Unloaders of all Vessels and Ships; Marine and Warehouse Package Freight Handlers; Grain Elevator Employees; Dock and Marine Engineers; Dock Hoisters, Firemen and Marine Repairmen; Marine Firemen, Oilers and Water Tenders; Licensed Pilots and Tugmen; Tug Firemen and Linemen; Marine Divers, Helpers, Tenders and Steam Pump Operators; Steam Shovel and Dredge Engineers; Drill Boat Workers; Dredge Firemen and Laborers on Dredge Scows; Marine Pile Drivers; Lumber Inspectors, Tallymen and Lumber Handlers; Top Dockmen; Cotton and Tobacco Screwmen; General Cargo Dock Laborers; Pool Deck Hands and Fishermen, — along the Great Lakes, Rivers, and Sea-coasts in the United States, Canada, Central and South America and new United States possessions.

At one time the organization claimed railway freight handlers, sawmill workers, and all men employed in lumber yards; but it has receded from these claims.

[1] *Quarterly Journal of Economics*, November, 1905.

On the other hand, it is now organizing the pilots and mates on the lake steamers, and has demanded the revocation of the charter of the Seamen's Union.[1]   The wages and salaries of its members range from those of laborers at 22 cents an hour to those of divers at $10 or $15 and, in some instances, $25 a day, and tug-boat captains at $165 a month and board.   In thus reaching out for all employees engaged in water transportation, the Directory says:

The business of handling transporta ion is now unified.   It presents a distinct branch of commerce to which has been applied all the known scientific principles of the organization of capital and labor.

I

An account of the lumber handling " locals " will give a clew to the other locals.   They are the oldest, those at Bay City and Saginaw running back to 1870, and the one at Chicago to 1877.   The Chicago and Detroit locals have furnished the president, D. C. Keefe, and the secretary, H. C. Barter, whose experience and policies have guided the International throughout its history.   The aim of the lumber locals from the beginning has been to become coöperative contractors.   In their first preamble they say, —

Having proved through experience that the system of loading and unloading boats by individual jobbers is one that robs our labor of its wages, we have determined to use every legitimate means in our power to suppress it, and to give every man an equal opportunity to secure work and receive the profits of his labor.

[1] Disallowed by the American Federation of Labor.   The organization has now gone back to its earlier name, "International 'Longshoremen's Association."   The general scheme of organization remains, except as indicated in footnotes (1913).

And the " Rules for Locals " declare [1] " all Locals are requested to endeavor to abolish the stevedore system by taking the work themselves directly." This object has been kept in the front at all times, and is the key to an understanding of much that the union has done and is trying to do. In 1905 the president of the union addressed the convention of Lake Carriers on this subject, as follows : [2]

A year ago we urged your coöperation to assist us in bringing about the abolition of the stevedore system in connection with the handling of grain at Chicago, in which I am pleased to say that our efforts were quite successful, and since then the grain has been handled to the entire satisfaction of all concerned. To my mind there can be no suitable apology offered for the further continuation of the obnoxious practice anywhere. We stand ready and willing to furnish a guarantee that we will do all the work that properly belongs to our organization to the entire satisfaction of the Lake Carriers and employers generally. . . . The system is a reflection on the intelligence of the American worker, maintained by the employer, where the employee is compelled to pay tribute to a drone for the privilege of working. We again pray your honorable body to unite with us in bringing about the complete abolition of this unjust system.

The stevedore was usually a labor contractor without capital. He furnished the men for loading or unloading the boats on contracts made with the captains or owners. At the Gulf ports the stevedores have formed associations for regulating charges ; but on the Lakes they were usually competitors. Often they were saloon-keepers and ward politicians, or partners of such ; and the conditions on which they hired men included patronage of the saloon and political errands. The men " bunked "

[1] Sec. II.
[2] *Proceedings, Fourteenth Annual Convention*, p. 34.

in the saloon in order to be ready when a boat arrived, and they received their pay in the saloon.

The coöperative system, however, is not practicable as a substitute for the stevedore, except on a piece-work basis. For example, in the loading of lumber on the upper lakes the conditions vary greatly. In some cases lumber is run down through chutes; and, where it is taken from the docks, it is brought from different parts, so that it is impossible to agree in advance upon a rate per thousand feet. At 50 cents per hour in wages the cost to the owner varies from 23 cents to 90 cents per thousand feet. But the unloading of lumber is uniform. A man in the boat passes the lumber to a man opposite on the dock, and it is piled one tier in depth. The prices paid by the vessel owner have always been made on a piece-rate, both to the stevedore when he hired the men by the hour and to the union when it took the contract. In the latter case the local union makes a contract for the season with the vessel owner, or the owners' or dealers' association, containing a scale of prices, beginning, say, " white pine, 1 inch, 1¼ inch, and 1½ inch, No. 3 and better, 10 feet and over, at 33 cents per M.," and so on for different sizes and grades. To do the work, the union distributes its members in gangs. The Cleveland local, No. 3, with 200 members, has 8 gangs of 25 men each. The Buffalo local has 36 men in a gang. One, two, or even three gangs may work on a boat, according to its size. Each gang has a stevedore or boss, or, in a German local, a *Gangführer*, who is elected by the union at the same time and for the same period as the other officers. This boss works with the men, if necessary; but, since the gang works in pairs and he is the odd man, his actual work consists in placing the men and overseeing the work. In any dealings between the captain or lumber dealer and the union, only the business agent or the gang boss has the right to speak. If any other member takes part, he is reported by the agent or boss at the next meeting of the union, and, if found guilty, is punished as the union sees fit. If he creates disturbances at the union office or at work, he may be suspended eight days, and on third offence expelled.[1] The business agent (*Geschäftsführer*) has charge of all the bosses and the gangs. The bosses take their orders from him. He makes a report at union headquarters two or three times a day of the boats to be unloaded, and especially sees to it that each gang gets its turn. If this equalizing of work cannot be done from week to week, it is evened up towards the close of the season, so that one man's earnings are very nearly the same as those of all other men in the union. In fact, the Cleveland union of Germans, on yearly earnings of $487, has come within 75 cents of bringing the members out equal. Other locals earning from $500 per member at Chicago to $750 at Tonawanda[2] have not been able to equalize so exactly. The business agent is fined and even ousted, if he does not keep the turns equalized.

The members of the gang are required to obey the gang boss and to be industrious and punctual, and they cannot leave the job until it is finished. If disobedient, the gang boss can lay them off. If they have a grievance, they must wait and bring it up in union meeting; and the gang boss can be fined or suspended if he is to blame. After the ship is unloaded, the boss collects the amount

[1] *Constitution*, Local No. 3, Cleveland, p. 13.
[2] Raised to $1100 in 1912.

due from the captain, but he must take with him one member of the gang as a witness. He has the right to inspect the original bill of lading in order to verify the amount. He takes this to the union headquarters, and divides it equally with all the members of the gang. His own share is exactly the same as that of the other men in his gang, with 10 cents added for each boat to pay book-keeping expenses. Finally, he makes a report at the union meeting of the work done and the amounts received and distributed.

This is the method followed by all of the lumber un-loading locals except those at Chicago, Milwaukee and Michigan City. At these ports the gang bosses are selected by the captain or dealer. The latter method is the one also followed by the ore unloaders and the coal loaders, even though they are paid by the ton. For a single year the ore shovellers at Cleveland tried the plan of electing their gang bosses, but their experience was discouraging. Factions were formed within the union, popular favorites and skilful wire-pullers secured elec-tion for themselves and their friends or relatives, and the union was weakened by dissensions. Since that trial the superintendent selects a gang boss from among the members of each gang, and the union, as well as the su-perintendent, is much better satisfied with the selections. But the union assigns the members to the respective gangs.

Local No. 205, ore shovellers, for example, of 200 mem-bers, is divided into eight gangs, of which two are Irish, one is German, one is Polish, one is Croatian, and three are mixed. But each gang is again divided into three sections of eight members each; and the sections of the mixed gangs are also based on race lines, one gang, for example, being composed of one Polish section, one German section, and one Irish section. Some sections have Irish and Germans together, but otherwise the races are usually separated. Each section works in one hatch of the boat, where they load the buckets by shovel, which then are hoisted by the engineer, or operator. A boat with nine hatches will have three gangs at work, the boss of each gang belonging to the nationality of the gang, except in the case of mixed gangs, where he is usually an Irishman. The gang boss has the same duties and is governed by the union in the same manner as when elected. The union can even secure his dismissal, but this must be done by lodging a grievance under the arbitration agreement with the association of carriers or dock managers, as the case may be. He is a member of the gang, and receives exactly the same share of the gang's earnings as the others. But he does not work in the hold. He watches the machinery, to see that it is in working order and that repairs are promptly made. He watches the gang, to see that no one is shirking; and he has authority to lay off a member, subject to appeal to the union. The union generally has also its business agent to preserve the equality of turns among the gangs, to inspect bills of lading and to verify the amounts due for unloading. Since the operating companies are large concerns and have the contracts for unloading many vessels, pay day is arranged once a week instead of collecting the amount due on each boat when it is finished, as is done by the lumber locals. Both the business agent and the gang bosses keep these accounts for their men.

Before the union was organized, the gangs were hired and made up by foremen to whom their earnings were paid and by whom they were distributed to the men, usually in a saloon kept by a friend or brother. Any complaint or grievance was followed by dismissal. No record could be kept of the amount of work done, except when the ore was loaded in cars and the weight was kindly furnished by the railroad yardman. It was, of course, suspected that the foreman pocketed a share of the proceeds. Now the men receive their pay in envelopes at the companies' offices, and the business agent is at hand to verify all accounts and take up all complaints or discrepancies with the superintendent. The foreman has disappeared, and in his place is the coöperative gang boss, sharing equally with his fellows. This change alone, apart from the increase in tonnage rates, has added materially to the earnings of the shovellers.

As already stated, the coöperative plan is impracticable where the men are paid by the hour, and the progress of improvement in hoisting machinery has substituted hourly wages for tonnage rates. Within the past five years automatic " grab buckets," or " clam shells," have been introduced, and are operated by the hoisting engineer. The shoveller is not needed except to clean out the corners after the boat is practically unloaded. The ore is even pulled from the sides up to the hatches, where the buckets can reach it, by means of road shovels or great iron hoes operated by men in the hold with cables from a steam or electric winch. The men working in the holds with this automatic machinery get 28 cents an hour but it is stipulated that they shall be paid during the time the machinery is working in the boat. This gives them two to four hours' full pay before the buckets get down deep enough for the road shovel or the hoe to begin. Already six of the eight gangs in Local No. 205

have been put on the automatic machines, leaving but two gangs on the tonnage or coöperative basis. On these machines their earnings are much less. At 14 cents a ton for shovelling they earn 55 to 60 cents an hour, or about $600 a year, as against 28 cents an hour, or $500 a year, on the hourly basis. On the other hand, however, the hoisters operating the machines have had an increase, since they joined the union, from $60 or $65 a month of 84 hours per week, to $80 or $105 per month of 66 hours a week. The work of the shovellers is, of course, much harder than that of the laborers at the automatic buckets. On hot days they are naked to the waists. There is no period of waiting on full pay. But, notwithstanding the harder work, there is great dissatisfaction among the younger and stronger men if they are not permitted to work at shovelling on the old-style buckets at the higher earnings. The older and less active men seek the easier conditions with the lower earnings. There is also a wide difference among the nationalities. Very few American-born men are found in the holds. They have been promoted to hoisting. The supply is kept up by immigration. The Croatians are large and powerful mountaineers with magnificent arms and legs, who rejoice in the heavy work. At the other extreme are the Poles, a smaller and weaker race. The Germans are heavy workers, but they lack endurance, a weakness ascribed by the Irish to their diet. The Irish, being more Americanized than others, do not work as hard as they did. Yet all get the same pay on the same boat, sharing equally the tonnage receipts. The only criterion is willingness. The gang leaves to the older men the lighter work, such as signalling to the hoister; and the younger men do the heaviest work, such as running up the pile of ore and heaving and pulling the heavy buckets in place. It is an interesting fact that, in all instances, this sytem of gang piece-work which, in the clothing, machinery and other trades, has developed into a sweating system, and is therefore vigorously opposed, is looked upon by the 'longshoremen with the greatest favor. Instead of stirring up jealousy and factions, it joins the union together in feelings of friendship and mutual aid, and is being extended wherever the union can do so. Doubtless the secret of its success lies in the fact that the gangs do not compete with each other in making the contract prices whenever a boat comes to dock, but all are subject to the same uniform scale of prices made annually in advance by agreement.[1]

The coal handlers also are paid by the ton. The work is mainly trimming the cargo in the hold of the vessel after the railroad car has been dumped on board by the hoister. The superintendent appoints the gang boss. Since each gang of sixteen or twenty men is hired for the season for a single dock, the earnings as between the gangs cannot be equalized. On one of the docks in Cleveland in one year the men earned $1200, while on another only $600 were earned. However, as between members of the same gang, earnings are equal. An automatic trimmer has recently been introduced, displacing the gang, and operated with the aid of a few 'longshoremen at 33 cents an hour when actually at work. This has materially reduced their earnings.

Grain scoopers at Buffalo are paid by the thousand

[1] Ore shovelling and trimming, above described, are now (1913) lost arts, except for a few men at South Chicago. The boats are built with hopper bottoms, and the clam shells do the entire work, leaving no trimming to be done even by hand. With this change the union has also been eliminated.

bushels on the gang-sharing plan, the bosses being selected from the union by the superintendent. At Chicago the grain elevator employees, with automatic machinery, are on hourly wages or monthly salaries.

II

The 'Longshoremen's Association has entered into agreements annually with several associations of employers, especially the Lumber Carriers, the Lake Carriers, the Dock Managers, the Great Lakes Towing Company and the Great Lakes Tug and Dredge Owners' Protective Association. The agreements with the Lumber Carriers were the first in point of time. Local agreements had been made at early dates by local unions and local associations of dealers or carriers, but the unions favored dealing only with individuals. The lumber carriers had formed associations at several times since 1883, but those associations were short-lived. The present Lumber Carriers' Association of the Great Lakes has had a continuous existence only since the year 1900. The weakness of earlier associations may be judged from the appeal made by the executive committee of one, organized in 1898, to the convention of 'longshoremen at Sheboygan in July of that year.[1] The employers' committee, consisting of the president and the secretary of the association, in appearing before the convention, represented that the great interests, such as the railroads and railroad steamers, opposed to the 'longshoremen, were also attempting " to drive the lumber carriers to destruction by reducing the carrying charges below a point where they can live."

[1] *Proceedings, Seventh Annual Convention*, 1898, pp. 19, 20.

The committee continued:

Many of you remember the aid extended by your organization, by one of your local unions, in keeping the carrying rates at living prices on the Great Lakes. This was several years ago at Bay City, which then made the rates on lumber.

The committee then stated the existing situation and their proposed remedy, as follows:

The ship-owners or vesselmen, having carried lumber at a loss for the past two years, and witnessing the effect and success of your efforts and organization, decided last winter to follow your example, — organize for a living hire, and appeal to your body so closely identified with us for aid and assistance. At a meeting held in Detroit in February last the vessel-owners did succeed in effecting a voluntary association for the purpose of mantaining a uniform minimum rate which should cover the cost of transporting lumber and forest products. They succeeded in enlisting a large majority of all the vessels on the lakes. Unfortunately there were a few who did not come in. They threaten to disrupt our association, and we therefore, the Executive Committee of the Lumber Carriers' Association, come before your honorable body, asking and appealing for the coöperation which is necessary for our existence, for our success as well as yours. This assistance which we request is that you should either refuse to load boats not belonging to the association, or boats belonging to the association that cut rates, or impose a heavy fine, heavy enough to prevent such suicidal business or to drive them all into the association. This we recommend be done on the entire chain of lakes, or more especially the Lake Superior districts.

After promising the 'longshoremen an increase in wages if the Lumber Carriers' Association could be kept together during the season, the committe concluded:

Whatever action you may take, it should be taken as soon as possible, for the reason that members and non-members are cutting the rates, and we fear that, if some action is not taken promptly, it will become general and the association will go to pieces.

This appeal of the lumber carriers was not indorsed by the convention. "The delegates," said the secretary in his report the following year, " did not wish to decide the matter, because it included the fining of boats not enrolled in the association and referred it to the Locals."[1] Meanwhile the Lumber Carriers' Association disbanded, and was followed in 1900 by the present association, which then made an agreement with the union, and has done so each succeeding year. These agreements, which cover all the loading and unloading ports, contain no clause whatever relating to non-association boats. It is, indeed, on the side of the 'longshoremen, provided that the union shall furnish all the men to unload the boats. The employers are protected by a clause which reads, —

Failing to supply such men within twelve hours, said boat shall have the right to employ enough outside labor to unload said boats.

It is also agreed that, if a boat has been loaded by non-union men the unloading local shall charge 5 cents per M. extra.

This practice of fining a boat which has been loaded or unloaded by non-unionists has a bearing on the relations of the union to the Association of Lumber Carriers, as will appear when the practice is described. It has been in vogue since the beginning of the national organization, and, indeed, was the strongest weapon of mutual protection which brought the scattered locals together. The convention of 1893 adopted a resolution providing for the practice, and the constitution of the international association contains the following sections:[2]

[1] *Proceedings, Eighth Annual Convention,* 1899, p. 19.
[2] Art. XVI.

Penalties

SECTION 1. Whenever any vessel or barge loads or unloads with non-union men, then it shall be the duty of such Local where the loading or unloading was done to notify the General Secretary-Treasurer to enforce extra charge of ten cents per hour for loading lumber and five cents per thousand for unloading lumber, two cents per ton for unloading iron ore and coal, twenty-five cents per thousand bushels for elevating or trimming grain, two cents per ton for trimming ore and coal, and for boats which do not trim two cents per ton extra for unloading. Provided, further, that boats loading or unloading lumber shall be punished by enforcing grain, coal, or ore rates, and those loading ore, coal, or grain shall be punished by enforcing lumber rates, and where boats, after being fined, still refuse to employ union labor at the ports where loaded or unloaded, the Locals in ports for which said boats are destined are requested to double the fine for each succeeding offence, and it shall be the duty of the Locals to notify the General Secretary-Treasurer that the said fine has been enforced.

SECTION 2. It shall be the duty of the Local that has received such fine to give the captain of such vessel or barge a receipt for the same, with the seal of the Local attached.

SECTION 4. The President and Corresponding Secretary of all Locals shall notify, under seal of their respective Local, the Secretary-Treasurer of any boats that have violated the constitution of our association, and in case of error or misunderstanding the Local that orders the fine imposed shall reimburse the Local collecting the fine. When the boats are to be fined for violation, the order must be sent through the General Secretary-Treasurer to enforce the fine.

When a fine has been wrongfully imposed, the matter is brought by the secretary of the Lumber Carriers to the general secretary-treasurer of the 'longshoremen, and he refunds the amount and collects it from the offending local.

Since this practice of fining boats has long been

recognized and enforced as a penalty for hiring non-union 'longshoremen, it naturally also might be enforced as a penalty for refusing to join the Lumber Carriers' Association, as requested by that association in 1898. This has been done by some of the locals, though others charge the non-association boats the same prices as the association boats. The union refuses to make agreements with individual vessel-owners. Thus it has reversed the policy of earlier days, when the locals, in order to prevent the employers from organizing, preferred to deal only with individuals. By dealing with an association the competitive conditions are equalized at loading and unloading ports, and the Carriers' Association becomes responsible for violations by individual owners. The non-association owner, having no agreement, may be charged any price that the local wishes and can enforce. If he protests, the answer is that he can get the association price by joining the association. This opportunity to make extra earnings is enough of an inducement to the locals to lead them to put a higher price on non-association boats, without any request to do so from the association or its representatives. Such a request the present association has not made. It, of course, would consider its agreements violated if the union charged a non-association boat less than an association boat, and would have its remedy by an appeal to the international officers.

In addition to fines the local unions give priority in loading and unloading their boats to members of the association over non-members. Such preference is prohibited as between members, the Buffalo agreement providing that " boats shall be unloaded strictly according to priority of arrival at this port." Not protected by such a clause, the non-association boat in a busy season is at a disadvantage. In the agreement it is stipulated that a verified list of the members of the Lumber Carriers' Association in good standing, and the name of the vessel annexed, shall be sent by its secretary to each of the local unions on the chain of lakes, and each vessel carries a certificate showing that it is properly enrolled and in good standing.

Owing largely to this support by the union, the present Lumber Carriers' Association has been able to hold its members and to enforce its scale of freight rates. It includes 85 per cent of the lumber-carrying tonnage on the Lakes, the outside vessels being the older and smaller boats, doing but little of the business. The association is controlled by lumber dealers, who are also vessel-owners, though a number of them are solely carriers. By resolution adopted in 1903 the owners agree not to charter their boats through agents who do not belong to the association, and shippers agree not to allow charters to be made of any vessel whose owners are not members in good standing.

The association adopts a scale of freight rates to and from each port on the Lakes. These rates have been materially reduced in the past two years, notwithstanding the great increase in wages, the firemen and seamen having secured advances from $15 to $25 a month for deck hands, and the wheelsmen from $20 or $25 to $45. The recent advances in 'longshoremen's wages are not as great proportionally, since they have been organized much longer. Railroad competition has become a serious matter on account of better facilities and lower wages. The railroad car goes direct from the shipping yard into the receiving yard. The yard hands are paid

17 cents to 20 cents an hour, while the vessel-owner must pay 50 cents an hour to the loader and a piece-rate for unloading, at which the 'longshoreman earns 60 cents or more per hour.   In spite of their association the vessel-owners claim that the union " gets all the juice out of the orange."   The members of the union on their side realize that the lumber supply is falling off, and they are satisfied that top wages have been reached.

The Lake Carriers' Association includes the leading owners of the ore, coal and grain carrying vessels, the largest one being the Pittsburg Steamship Company, a branch of the United States Steel Corporation.   This association was inaugurated thirty years ago to oppose burdensome legislation at Washington, and has been the most important agency in securing aids to navigation on the Lakes.   Some fifteen years ago it broke up the sailors' union, and for a number of years was not confronted by any union of employees.   Since 1900, however, it has made agreements with two branches of 'longshoremen, the grain scoopers at Buffalo and the firemen on the boats; also with the lake seamen and its affiliated union of marine cooks and stewards; and, finally, with the Marine Engineers' Beneficial Association.   In this way all of its employees have been organized.   Even the remarkable spectacle was seen in 1904 of the captains and mates following the example of their crews, and organizing a Masters' and Pilots' Association which ordered a strike and tied up the shipping on the Lakes for nearly two months. The Lake Carriers at first tried to reach an understanding with this association, but felt compelled to resist the essential feature of an agreement, namely, that the owners should not deal individually with their own captains.   These, they insisted, are the executive personal representatives and vice-principals of the owners. On this ground they drew a distinction between a union of captains and a union of the crews. The latter are not hired and discharged by the owners, but by the owner's representative, the captain or mate. The masters and pilots were defeated in their strike; and many of them, as a condition of re-employment, signed contracts not again to join a marine labor organization. Commenting on this defeat, the president of the 'longshoremen's union, in his address at the convention of 1905, said : [1]

Had there been a federation of all the maritime organizations, working in harmony and union, the humiliating ending of the masters' and pilots' strike could not have happened. We had it in our power to win the battle for the masters and pilots, if given an opportunity to do so, but were not permitted by their officials, who were carried away by their own importance, believing that they were equal to the situation without the coöperation and assistance of any other organization, and that it would cast a reflection on them as professional men if they were to be identified with a common, every-day lot of workers like the I. L. M. and T. A.

Taking advantage of the defeat of the captains and mates, the 'longshoremen have proceeded to organize the pilots (that is, the mates), and to bring them in as another branch of their association. At the convention of 1905 these new pilots' local unions were represented by four delegates; and, while it is understood that under no circumstances would the Lake Carriers concede the organization of the masters, yet they seem to have conceded to the 'longshoremen the organization of the mates and pilots.[2]

[1] *Proceedings, Fourteenth Annual Convention*, 1905, pp. 36, 37.
[2] The Lake Carriers have practically eliminated all unions (1913).

The outcome of the masters' and pilots' organization is significant by way of contrast with that of a similar organization on the tug-boats. The Licensed Tug-men's Protective Association, organized in 1900, is composed of captains, mates and engineers. In 1902 this organization was involved in a contest with the Great Lakes Towing Company, known as " the trust," a member of the Lake Carriers' Association, and operating 90 tug-boats. After the strike had been in progress two months, the association asked for affiliation with the 'longshoremen; and charters where thereupon granted to each of the twenty-eight locals on condition that the 'longshoremen should not be asked to enter on a sympathetic strike. Conferences were arranged with the company through the good offices of the 'longshoremen and the Lake Carriers' Association, by which, in 1903, the Licensed Tug-men's Association secured the exclusive employment of its members and a scale of wages. Meanwhile the tug firemen and line-men had been organized by the 'longshoremen; and an agreement was also secured for them with the same company. These agreements were renewed in 1904 and 1905. Consequently, the 'longshoremen's union, through these two branches, controls the captains and all members of the crews operating nearly all of the tug-boats on the Lakes.

The Association of Dock Managers at Lake Erie ports represents the employers of much the largest proportion of 'longshoremen. They are the great railroad companies or their lessees, operating the docks for unloading iron ore and loading coal, including the United States Steel Corporation at Conneaut, M. A. Hanna & Co. at Cleveland and Ashtabula, and others. The association has been in existence since 1874, for the purpose of establishing uniform scales of charges for loading and unloading boats. When the ore shovellers and coal handlers were organized by the 'longshoremen in 1898, they secured agreements with individual managers; but, finally, in 1900 the Dock Managers' Association took up the problem of regulating wages as well as charges. At that time the 'longshoremen had organized all ports, except Toledo and Sandusky; the dock managers entered into an agreement providing for the exclusive employment of union men at these as well as other ports; and the union agreed to admit to membership all of the local men. In this agreement the 'longshoremen extended their jurisdiction to cover also the highly skilled hoisters and engineers, as well as the wholly unskilled dock laborers and all employees on the docks.

In contrast with the lumber carriers, the dock managers do not depend upon the union to maintain their organization. They had regulated charges for twenty-five years before the unions were strong enough to share with them. It is an interesting fact that the prices charged to vessel-owners for unloading iron ore are 2 or 3 cents a ton lower in 1905 than they were in earlier years, while the tonnage rates paid to 'longshoremen are 4 to 6 cents higher. Prior to 1899 the shovellers at Cleveland received 8 to 10 cents per ton, the rate standing at 9 cents in 1898. The first effect of the union is seen in the fluctuating piece-wages of 10 to $12\frac{1}{2}$ cents in 1899; and the final effect is seen in the uniform rate of 14 cents in 1900, reduced to 13 cents in 1901 and 1904, but restored to 14 cents in 1903 and 1905. The rate charged to the vessel-owner by the dock managers is 19 cents a ton, leaving a margin of only 5 cents to the dock manager against a margin of 10 or 12 cents in earlier years. This margin, it should be said, is no longer decisive; for it applies only to the old style of hoisting bucket paid for at tonnage rates, — a style which, as already shown, has been largely displaced, and will soon disappear under the competition of the great automatic buckets operated at day-wage rates. These revolutionizing improvements have been introduced during the period since the union began to secure advances in wages, so that, notwithstanding those advances, the cost of handling ore has been reduced. Further, as already stated, the advance in earnings, except for hoisters and engineers, has not been nearly so great on the new machinery coming into use as on the old machinery going out of use.[1]

III

Enough has been said to show that the 'longshoremen's association has grown up and extended its organization without any preconceived plan. This will be seen further in noticing the variety of relations existing between " locals " and " branches " and the international organization. The locals are usually very small in the number of members, since they are organized on craft lines; and there are some forty crafts or occupations within the organization. Seven of the crafts are spoken of as " branches." [2] The branch in some cases is admitted as a local, and in other cases it is an association of locals. Only locals as such are represented in the 'Longshoremen's Convention. Thus the International Brother-

[1] The new machinery is deunionized (1913). See note, p. 276.
[2] Five in 1913.

hood of Steam Shovel and Dredgemen is an organization which has been in existence several years, with headquarters at Chicago, with its general president and other general officers, its board of directors and its general executive board, with its twenty local " lodges " widely scattered (including one at Panama) and with its own official journal, *Steam Shovel and Dredge*. Yet this organization is known simply as " Local 460 " of the I. L. M. and T. A., with two votes in the last conventions. The same is true of the International Brotherhood of Steam Shovel, Dredge Firemen, Deck Hands, Oilers, Watchmen and Scowmen of America, known as " Local 470." [1] Likewise the Marine Firemen, Oilers and Water Tenders' Benevolent Association, with branch offices at seven ports on the Great Lakes and headquarters at Buffalo, is known as " Local 124," with six votes in the 'Longshoremen's Convention.[2]

On the other hand the Licensed Tug-men's Protective Association [3] is composed of twenty-eight locals, with separate charters from the 'Longshoremen's Association entitling each local to at least one vote in the convention, and an additional number if its membership exceeds one hundred. The Tug Firemen and Linemen have a representative for each of thirteen separate locals, and the Fishermen for twenty-two locals. Each has its " branch " organization with general officers, like the dredgemen.

These branches hold their own annual conventions, and conduct their business entirely separate from the 'Longshoremen's Convention. They select their conference committees to meet the employers and to make

---

[1] Now the International Dredge Workers' Association.
[2] Deserted to the Seamen (1913).   [3] Eliminated (1913).

agreements. It would seem on paper that they are important wheels in the 'longshoremen's union. As a matter of fact, however, their powers are no greater than those of any local union of ore handlers or grain scoopers. This is on account of the position that has gradually been conceded to the executive council of the international association, consisting of the president, secretary-treasurer and nine vice-presidents elected at the annual convention (biennial after 1905). All locals

have full power to regulate their own wages, whether by the hour, by the thousand or by the ton; but the association recommends that the locals whose interests are identical in the same locality establish a monthly correspondence, so that a more uniform scale of wages may be established.[1]

In this effort to secure uniformity the locals with identical interests, whether they are recognized as branches or not, send their delegates to the conferences with the associated employers. Such a delegate is not recognized unless he comes with credentials showing that he has full power to bind his local to whatever agreement is entered upon. The agreement takes precedence over all constitutions and by-laws, whether of locals, branches or the international organization. It cannot be reviewed by referendum or by convention. In fact, as viewed by their employers, " the only capital the union has is their reputation of fulfilling their contracts." They are in the peculiar position of making a contract to furnish all of the labor necessary to do certain work at certain wages or piece-prices, yet without subjecting themselves to a penalty for failure. Naturally, the employers look to the international officers to see that

[1] *Constitution*, Art. VI, Sec. 4.

the locals furnish the men. They, indeed, always reserve " the right to secure any other men who can perform the work in a satisfactory manner until such time as members of the I. L. M. and T. A. can be secured." [1] This reservation applies to two classes of cases, — inability of the local union to furnish men and a strike of the local union. Where the local cannot furnish men, it is the duty of its president or manager to notify the captain within twelve working hours of the time when the boat is placed at the dock.[2] The captain then employs outsiders if he can find them, but hoists a flag to indicate that a non-union man is at work. As soon as a member of the union appears, the non-unionist is laid off, the union man is employed and the flag is lowered.

The other case — a strike or refusal by a local to work on a vessel, — is considered a violation of the contract, and the vessel may be sent to another dock or port to be unloaded according to the agreement, and the men who refuse to work are discharged.[3] Resort to this clause has seldom been necessary, because the international officers have promptly furnished men, even going so far as to furnish men outside of their own organization to take the places of the strikers. The constitution of the international organization also provides for such contingencies, by giving adequate powers of control over the local unions. Locals are forbidden to take part in any sympathetic strike or any other strike, or to assist another local, without the consent of the executive council.[4]

[1] Dock Managers' Agreement, 1905, Sec. 3.
[2] Lumber Carriers' Agreement, Secs. 1 and 2.
[3] Dock Managers' Agreement, 1905, Sec. 12.
[4] *Constitution*, Art. XIII, Secs. 3, 4, 8.

The council has the power to fine a local $10 for the first offence, $25 for the second offence and to expel the local for the third offence.[1] With these powers the executive council, through the international president, has enforced all of the agreements so promptly and effectually that the employers, without exception, have only the strongest words of commendation for the record of the union in this respect.

Practically all of the very few strikes that have occurred in recent years have been those of new organizations not yet admitted to membership in the 'Longshoremen's Association. Indeed, the growth of the association, especially in the way of organizations other than 'longshoremen proper, has followed upon the defeat, or the prospect of defeat, of those organizations in strikes of their own initiation. This has already been shown in the case of the pilots. The same was true of the tug-men, whose strike in 1902 was lost, but who secured their agreement through joining the 'longshoremen's union. Without mentioning other instances, it is evident that the 'longshoremen show a reversal of the usual course of unionizing, in that with them the skilled and salaried employees have not led in organization, but have followed and relied upon the disrespected " dock-wolloper." It was the lumber handler, the ore shoveller, the coal handler, who led the way, and afterwards took in and gained for many skilled occupations favorable conditions and union recognition which they were unable to gain for themselves. In no case has this been done through a sympathetic strike or a violation of any agreement. The newly admitted organization has usually been required to wait until the existing agreements expired, and

[1] *Ibid.*, Art. XVII, Sec. 1.

then, in the conferences with employers on a renewal of agreements, it has been cared for the same as the others.

Naturally, with so many occupations and races there arises dissatisfaction with some of the agreements. But the members of the various branches have seen a few vivid lessons of the penalties inflicted when a branch or a local attempts to act alone. This was spectacularly true of the strike called by Local 124 in April, 1903, when that local was dissatisfied with an agreement just about to be made. Local 124 is known as the Marine Firemen, Oilers and Water-tenders,[1] employed on all the lake steamers, and had been a " branch " of the 'Longshoremen's Association for four years. Its officers, unable to carry their point, brought on the strike without the knowledge of the executive council. The latter declined to permit a sympathetic strike of other locals, although the work of all of their members was interrupted. The lake carriers filled the places of the firemen, and the other 'longshoremen continued to work with the non-unionists. After being defeated in a two months' strike, the firemen offered arbitration, which the lake carriers refused, but finally, through the representations of the 'longshoremen's officers, they made an agreement, and the firemen were granted the terms which two months before they had refused to accept. This salutary lesson, administered to a well-organized branch, whose members visit every port on the Lakes, has greatly strengthened the hold of the international officers on all the locals. The lesson is all the more impressive, for it has been accompanied in this case by an increase in wages from $25 or $30 a month to $45 to October 1, and $65 from that date to the close of navi-

[1] Deserted to the Seamen, then eliminated (1913).

gation. There has also been a lessening in the amount of work by increasing the number of men, so that one man fires four doors where he formerly fired six.

It is significant that this strong position of the international has been accomplished without the backing of a treasury. Other national and international unions have built up strike or " defence " funds, held by the general treasurer and available only for those local unions whose strikes have been sanctioned by the international officers. These funds are accumulated through a per capita tax on all members of local unions. But the per capita tax of the 'longshoremen is only 5 cents, as against 15, 25, and 40 cents a month in other organizations. This barely meets the expenses of the central organization. The executive council may, indeed, levy assessments on local unions; but this has never been done. On the other hand, the dues of the local unions are 50 cents a month, enabling them, after paying the per capita tax, to accumulate a good-sized treasury which may be used as they see fit, for strikes or for insurance benefits.

This extreme local autonomy in the constitution of the union, accompanied by unusual discipline and centralization in all dealings with employers, suggests the question whether, perhaps, this union is merely a " one-man " organization, depending for its unusual success on the personality of the able executive officers who happen to have been in charge during the period of its growth. Neither the organization nor its leaders are as yet old enough to answer this question.[1]

It will have been noted that all of the agreements of

[1] The history of the organization since 1906 shows that this surmise was correct. The membership fell to 13,700 in 1909 and has risen to

the 'longshoremen are strictly "closed-shop" agreements, stipulating the employment exclusively of union members. This is true not only of the dock workers, whose agreements are something more than scales of wages, — contracts to load or unload cargoes, and therefore necessarily exclusive; it is true also of all the crafts and occupations. The first agreement of the association, made in 1893 for the port of Chicago only, was silent on membership in the union; but in 1894 the union accepted a reduction of 20 per cent in wages, but extended the agreement to all ports on Lake Michigan and Lake Huron, and secured the exclusive employment of union men. Similar strategy has been shown at other times, as when in 1901, after substantial advances during the preceding years, a horizontal reduction in wages of $7\frac{1}{2}$ per cent was agreed upon with the Dock Managers, and continued for 1902, accompanied, however, by a reduction of working hours to 9 or 10 per day in some cases, and 11 per day in handling iron ore and coal. This reduction in hours has been maintained, but wages were advanced 8 per cent in 1903. They were reduced again $7\frac{1}{2}$ per cent in 1904, with various compensations in the conditions and hours of work, and restored in 1905 with the compensations retained. This adaptation of wages to industrial conditions indicates an unusual degree of discipline in the union and a willingness to avoid strikes; and this, naturally, wins the employers to the closed-shop agreements.

On the side of the dock laborers and 'longshoremen proper, the closed-shop agreements are looked upon

38,000 in 1913, although the increases are at the ocean ports instead of those on the Great Lakes. The former president of the organization became Commissioner-general of Immigration.

mainly as a protection against immigrants. The higher grades of skilled employees, such as hoisters and engineers, are filled, according to the agreements, by promotion from employees on the docks where the promotions are made. These promotions come almost solely to the English-speaking laborers, especially Irish and Germans, so that these races are gradually rising from the lower grades. But the 'longshoremen and dock laborers, from whom these promotions are made, are themselves recruited from foreign immigrants; and the pressure of immigration therefore bears directly upon them. Prior to the organization of the unions there was a rapid influx of these laborers. The boss or a friend would bring up a dozen men from a distance, and put them to work, while men who had been there for years were displaced. But with the closed-shop agreement these newcomers are not admitted unless the amount of work is greater than the number in the union can supply.

This supply is regulated automatically through the initiation fees. These are under the control solely of each local union. Beginning with fees of $5, the locals have raised the amount to $25 or $50, and even $100, according as the pressure for admission increased beyond the opportunity for steady employment of those already admitted. Again, when the pressure lightened or the work increased, the initiation fee was reduced; but the majority of the locals seem inclined to place it at $50. Since the wages earned are much higher than what the Poles, Croatians, Italians, Roumanians and similar races can earn outside, and since these races are notedly thrifty even on those lower wages, it has been found that $50 is just about the rate of tariff that equalizes supply and demand.

I have not mentioned the spread of the 'longshore-men's union to the Gulf and Atlantic and Pacific coasts. The original and characteristic features are found on the Great Lakes, especially the control by one organization of both ends of the vessel's trip, so that by their system of fines a weak union at one end can be promptly and effectually aided by a strong local at the other end. The salt-water locals have looked forward to a similar arrangement with the dock workers of other lands, and recently an affiliation was arranged with the International Transport Federation, headquarters, London. Thus it is something more than a dream that the oceans shall be governed like the lakes, and vessels loaded or unloaded by non-union men in any port of the world shall be punished when they touch a port across the ocean controlled by union men.[1]

[1] The dream did not materialize, but an agreement has been made with the Transatlantic Steamship Company at Boston, and all of the Pacific Coast, except San Francisco, is organized under the 'Longshoremen.

CHAPTER XVI

THE MUSICIANS OF ST. LOUIS AND NEW YORK [1]

IT has been a long struggle of the musicians to get themselves looked upon as workers instead of players. Even yet they are not taken as seriously as they wish, though they have practised trade-union methods these ten to twenty years. The contest was first internal; for they could but painfully give up the idea that they were artists, and neither players nor workers. Even conceding that, though artists, they worked hard for their living, the old-fashioned ones contended that they were at least a profession, and not a craft. This internal revolution is the first stage in their history. The second is their growth as a trade union into a more complete control of their business throughout the United States and Canada than that enjoyed by any other large union in the American Federation of Labor.

The former National League of Musicians represented the artistic and professional element. It was organized in 1886 by delegates from musical societies in New York, Boston, Philadelphia, Cincinnati and Milwaukee. Ten years thereafter it included 101 " locals." Some of these had been in existence several years, the one in New York dating from 1863. The National League had no effective control over the locals, and prescribed no rules binding upon them. Consequently they differed widely

[1] *Quarterly Journal of Economics*, May, 1906. The figures have been corrected for the year 1913.

in their policies and tactics. The older ones were incorporated under State charters, and held property. Each of them, like the trade unions which they shunned, set up a scale of minimum prices. Likewise they prohibited their members from playing with non-members. But their State charters made it precarious for them to expel a member who cut the prices or played with outsiders. They were, in fact, in a position similar to that of an association of physicians which adopts a schedule of recommended prices to be charged by its members. They lacked, however, that protection, through limitation of numbers, which comes to physicians and lawyers in the legal certificate of competency based on an apprenticeship of study and an examination.

The younger locals, especially those in the West, were less influenced by the professional element whose centre was in New York. They were organized after the example of the Knights of Labor or the trade unions of the American Federation of Labor. Although the National League had been invited year after year by the Knights and by the Federation to become affiliated, yet it always declined. Had the vote been taken by locals, the invitation would have been accepted; but, by a peculiar system of proxies assigned through a committee after the convention assembled, the vote of these smaller locals, which could not afford to send delegates, was cast by the older locals, and thus New York and Philadelphia were able to control the conventions. Meanwhile, the American Federation of Labor had chartered musicians' unions in several localities, with the object of forming them eventually into a national body. To prevent this dual organization, local officers of the National League at St. Louis, Cincinnati, Chicago and Indianapolis joined with the Federation of Labor in 1896 in calling a convention. The invitation was extended to locals of the League, as well as those organized by the Federation. The convention met at Indianapolis, the headquarters at that time of the American Federation of Labor, and included delegates from 19 locals of the League and 5 other locals chartered by the Federation. The fact that these 5 locals contained members suspended from the League, nearly disrupted the convention, since to admit such was inconsistent with the object of preventing a dual organization. But this difficulty was bridged by a formal reply from the Executive Council of the Federation, that national bodies once affiliated are guaranteed autonomy in regulating their membership, so that the proposed association would become the sole judge of the qualifications of union musicians throughout the country. With this assurance the American Federation of Musicians was organized, with a charter of affiliation from the American Federation of Labor. It elected as its president Owen Miller, of the St. Louis local, a former president of the National League and still in good standing.

The officers of the League would not be conciliated. At once they expelled every local that joined the new association. But their efforts were futile. Within five months 48 of their 101 locals went over, and in 1902 only 3 locals were left in the old organization. A decision handed down from a Missouri court reinstated the expelled locals and compelled a division of the funds. This was the final blow. The League held its last convention in 1902. " It started at the top, ignoring the rank and file, and finally came out at the bottom." The New York local, the Musicians' Mutual Protective Union, with

4000 members, held out for a year longer, but was compelled to yield and become "No. 310." In 1913, the new organization has 636 locals and 64,000 members. It has brought in practically all instrumental musicians in the United States and Canada, who play for a living, either as leaders or as members of orchestras and bands, including all travelling musicians, and excepting only those who are soloists or organists and those members of local companies who play only their own series of concerts. How this has come about will appear from the history of the St. Louis local, which led the movement of organization on trade-union lines, and furnished both the model constitution and by-laws which others have copied, as well as the national officer who has guided the Federation.

A musicians' union is similar to a stock exchange or a produce exchange, and its headquarters are a "pit" where buyers and sellers of instrumental music meet to make engagements. The buyers are "leaders" of orchestras, bands or concerts: the sellers are the musicians. The buyers are also contractors or agents, who represent, for the time being, the owners or managers of theatres, concert halls, summer gardens, restaurants, parades, pageants, and so on. But, like the broker on the exchange, they must be members of the union if they are to have the privileges of the floor. Like the broker, too, they are prohibited from buying musical talent of those who are not members. Thus the musicians' union, like the stock exchange, is "closed" on both sides, — members only can buy and sell, hence members only can be employers and employed. Every member is entitled to become a "leader," if he can find a client (that is, if he can find a proprietor or manager who will make a contract authorizing him to furnish musicians). Consequently, like the brokers, a member may be to-day a buyer, that is, an employer of his fellow-members, making a contract for their services, and to-morrow he may be a seller, that is, a wage-earner, contracting for his services with a fellow-member. Thus, the lines are not always closely drawn. Only a few of the members are known solely as leaders. They are the fortunates who have contracts with theatres and the like, or who make up orchestras designated and advertised under their own name as " director." In the St. Louis union of 975 members, only about 100 are employed steadily by these directors in theatres. The others are employed now by one leader, now by another, on short engagements and for special occasions. Yet those who are predominantly leaders are clearly set off from the others. They are a small minority, and the policy of the union is determined by the majority, whose interests are those of wage-earners. This will be seen at many points.

Formerly, the musicians met at saloons to make their engagements, each clique or grade of the local talent having its favorite " joint," whose proprietor collected his rent in the " drinks." The first step of the union was to rent its own headquarters. The next was to bring in all the local musicians. The two worked together, as will appear. In the matter of headquarters, unlike other unions, the musicians must have a room large enough for their daily gatherings. The New York union provides a floor where a thousand or more of its members can meet every day. The St. Louis local accommodates five hundred or more. To secure such a place with offices adjoining, the larger locals have found it necessary to buy or build a house. To do this, the older ones took out articles of incorporation under State laws, not as unions, but as benefit associations, enabling them to hold property not for profit. But these articles of incorporation prevented them from freely enforcing discipline by fines, expulsion and boycott. The younger locals, of which St. Louis is the type, avoided incorporation, but shrewdly resorted to the device of the stock exchange. The " New York Stock Exchange Building Company " is composed of the same members as the " New York Stock Exchange." But the former is incorporated, owns the building and leases it to the latter, which is unincorporated. The Aschenbroedel Club of St. Louis is an incorporated body, and the unincorporated Musicians' Mutual Benefit Association (" Local 2, St. Louis, American Federation of Musicians ") has a bylaw, adopted in 1894 :

Whereas the main object for the formation of the Aschenbroedel Club was to unite the professional musicians of St. Louis into a social body, with corporate powers, with a view of securing a suitable property for a home ; and

Whereas, in spite of all inducements offered, a large number of the professional musicians are still outside of the organization ; and

Whereas, the fact is that every professional musician in the city is reaping the benefit of this organization (and with the exception of those that are members) without assuming any of its responsibilities ; and

Whereas, believing that every professional musician ought by right to be a member of this organization, — therefore be it

Resolved, first, That in future all who are accepted members of the Musicians' Mutual Benefit Association shall also become members of the Aschenbroedel Club.

Second, That a violation of the rules and regulations of the Aschenbroedel Club shall be considered a like violation in the Musicians' Mutual Benefit Association, and punished accordingly by the proper authorities of the Musicians' Mutual Benefit Association.

Third, That the Musicians' Mutual Benefit Association shall in no sense be held responsible for any of the liabilities of the Aschenbroedel Club.[1]

The St. Louis Aschenbroedel Club has one set of officers chosen from the older, conservative and commercial-like men, and holds only an annual meeting. The Benefit Association, or union, has younger and more aggressive officers, and holds fortnightly or special meetings. The Aschenbroedel Club collects no dues or fees, but covers its expenses through a lease of its building and equipment to the union. It operates a bar and buffet, billiard tables, and so on. It never expels or disciplines a member, but, when one loses his membership in the union on account of an infraction of union discipline, his membership in the incorporated body is worthless.

This dual arrangement has allowed the union to slip through the meshes of the law by means of a frank and unusual plea. A member was expelled by the Benefit Association, or union, for violating a sympathetic strike order, forbidding him to ride on the cars of the street railway company during a strike of its employees. He secured a permanent injunction in a lower court restraining the officers from enforcing the order, on the ground

[1] The term "Aschenbroedel" is not the equivalent of "Cinderella." After the death of a beloved leader in New York, named Asche, a social club of musicians, desiring to honor his memory, but to avoid the epithet "ashes," added the suffix "broedel," signifying the rollicking character of their club. The term has spread to similar clubs throughout the United States. The New York club was the original musicians' club in America, organized in 1860. Unlike the St. Louis Aschenbroedel, its membership is limited to those who speak German, and it includes only about one-fifth of the members of the union. It owns a club-house valued at $250,000. The local union is separately incorporated. Other nationalities within the union have their own clubs.

that he had a property right in the sick and mortuary benefits of the association, and that the order of expulsion was not passed in the manner provided for amending its by-laws. The higher court reversed this judgment on the plea set up by the union [1] that its by-laws and regulations were contracts in restraint of trade; that it was a monopoly, in that a musician could not find employment without being a member of the association; that the plaintiff was aware of its illegal character when he joined, and had indeed joined for the purpose of profiting by such monopolistic regulations which he had faithfully observed; that the benefit sections of the by-laws were merely aids to enforce the restrictive sections, and could not be separated from them; and that for the court to sustain the injunction would be specifically to enforce a contract with a monopoly or association in restraint of trade. To support this plea, the union submitted its constitution and by-laws showing its scale of minimum prices, its prohibitions, and other compulsory conditions affecting membership, and the application for membership signed by the plaintiff. The court, in rendering its decision, said:

In the case at bar the by-laws impose on the members of the association a most slavish observance of the most stringent rules and regulations in restraint of trade. So strict and far-reaching are they that no musician in the city of St. Louis; and for that matter in any city of the country, can find employment as a musician unless he is a member of the association. Such a confederation and combination is a trust, pure and simple. . . . The plaintiff is in the attitude of asking the court to keep him where he says he has no right to be and to retain him in a position where he may aid in the support and maintenance of an illegal association,

[1] St. Louis Court of Appeals, 1901, Froelich *v.* Musicians' Mutual Benefit Association, *et al*. Brief of Appellant, Frank R. Ryan, attorney.

and where he may continue to support and keep up a monopoly of the services of musicians. Courts have never dealt with monopolies except to restrain or destroy them, and we decline to depart from this wholesome rule in this case and reverse the judgment with directions to the trial court to dissolve the injunction and to dismiss the plaintiff's bill. Decision unanimous. 93 Mo. App. 383.

The legal mind is perhaps profound where it seems comical. At any rate, the St. Louis local thus demonstrated that to enforce discipline it should avoid incorporation. The secretary has impressed the lesson on other locals, and has advised all that hold State charters to give them up or to use them for conducting the social and business functions of the organization, leaving the enforcement of prices and regulations to unincorporated associations which cannot be " haled into court every time they attempt to enforce the discipline of the American Federation of Musicians." [1]

Turn now to the New York local. Its members, operating under a State charter granted by special act in 1864, soon learned its limitations. They went again to the legislature, and secured in 1878 an amendment so extraordinary as scarcely to be explained on modern lines of legislation.[2] This amendment added to the other objects of the union " the establishment of a uniform rate of prices to be charged by members of said society, and the enforcement of good faith and fair dealing between its members." The amendment continues:

It shall be lawful for said society, from time to time, to fix and prescribe uniform rates of prices to be charged by members of said

[1] *International Musician*, June, 1904.
[2] Laws of 1878: "An act to amend chapter 168 of the laws of 1864, entitled 'An act to incorporate the Musical Mutual Protective Union,' passed April 11, 1864."

society for their professional services, and for that purpose from time to time to make and adopt such By-laws as it may approve. And any member of said society violating any such By-law may be expelled from said society (after being afforded an opportunity to be heard in his defence) in such manner as such society may, from time to time, prescribe by By-laws which it is hereby authorized to make.

By this remarkable act of legislation the New York musicians, twenty-five years before they joined the trade unions, sought legally to practise trade-union tactics. Yet, while the act grants certain powers assumed by trade unions, it fails, of course, to grant the most effective weapons of unions, the power to strike or boycott and the power to fine or expel a member for working with a non-member or working for an " unfair " employer. Nevertheless, the union adopts and enforces this class of by-laws, as well as by-laws enforcing the minimum prices. But the fact of incorporation gives to a fined or expelled member a standing in court, and this is seen in the cautious use of its discipline by the musicians' union. An act of incorporation is strictly construed by the courts. All powers not expressly granted by the legislature are withheld. But an unincorporated union enjoys all powers not expressly prohibited by the courts. In States other than New York, this principle would work against the incorporated union. But in New York, where the courts have permitted large powers to unincorporated unions, they have allowed the same powers to the incorporated musicians' union.[1] Consequently, the union has not seen fit to abandon its charter, but rather has recently gone to the farthest extreme of any American union in exposing itself to attack by investing its funds in a building for headquarters costing $250,000.

[1] Thomas v. Musicians' Protective Union, 121 New York, 46 (1890).

The St. Louis local worked out another legal device bearing on the " closed orchestra." This is the form of contract between managers, leaders and members. Formerly the leaders were in the position of independent employers without capital, who contracted with managers to furnish musicians. Now the leader is made the agent of the musicians whom he employs. He first enters into a contract with the manager to furnish musicians as his agent, either for the season or for a special occasion. The form covering a special occasion has a clause :

It is further agreed that if there are any bands or orchestras employed for this engagement who are unfair to the American Federation of Musicians, this contract shall be considered null and void, as far as the party of the first part (the leader) is concerned, but does not relieve party of the second part.

The leader then makes contracts with individual musicians, " subject to the rules and regulations of the Musicians' Mutual Benefit Association, Local No. 2, American Federation of Musicians, as prescribed in the Constitution, By-laws, and Price-list." These contracts are signed in duplicate, and a copy is filed with the recording secretary, on the pain of penalties of $25 to $100 for failure. By making the leader the agent of the manager instead of the principal to the contract, the manager is made responsible for the wages of the musicians, while, as agent of the musicians, the leader who fails to pay them can be prosecuted for embezzlement instead of sued for a debt, and at the same time their wages while in his hands are exempt from attachment for his debts. These contracts probably would be thrown out of court on the same ground that the foregoing injunction was dissolved, although they have never been tested. The union has a more expeditious remedy. It fines or expels the leader for violating the rules, and the St. Louis local has collected in this way at least one fine as high as $1000.

Evidently, it is through control of the leaders that the union is trying to control the trade. Partly on this account the union has failed as yet to introduce well-recognized agencies of other crafts composed solely of wage-earners. Few of the locals have a "business agent" or "walking delegate." Such an officer has not been needed for purposes of organization, since the trade has been fully organized in other ways. He would be needed only as a detective to prevent leaders and members from violating the rules, and especially from paying and accepting less than the minimum scale of prices. The usual method of cutting prices is for the members to pay back secretly to the leader a rebate on the published tariff. There are other forms of rebate easily prevented, such as accepting tickets as part payment, giving presents, allowing one's self to be fined or paying extortionate prices for articles. But these secret rebates are not discovered unless the parties have a "falling out" and one of them "turns union evidence." It was through such an exposure that the leader of the Metropolitan Opera in New York was fined $200 by the union. In lieu of a business agent, the unions have given much attention to perfecting their control of the leaders. These are required to be members of the union, and members are prohibited from playing for non-union leaders. This, of course, subjects the leader to discipline, but it injects a diversity of interests into the organization. The result is several more or less futile rules. The leader in St. Louis is expelled if he offers a member less than the schedule of rates, or if he threatens to blacklist a member, either for accepting other engagements or for reporting infractions of the rules. Again, the leaders, although a small minority, are likely to have undue influence through their power as employers. To reduce their power, nearly all of the unions prohibit a leader from taking a contract for a season engagement where he cannot personally be present. The value of this rule is seen by contrast in the case of Baltimore, where one leader has secured the contracts for all of the theatres. He thereby controls the best opportunities for employment of his fellow-members, and this enables him to control the meetings and to dictate the policy of the union. Consequently the scale of wages is lower and the conditions of employment inferior to those in other places, and Baltimore musicians are considered a menace in competition with Washington and Philadelphia musicians. In Brooklyn, too, a single leader controls all of the theatres, but this has not led to abuse, because the Brooklyn musicians are a small minority of the metropolitan union. The rule of several other unions, by preventing such a monopoly, preserves to the rank and file a stronger control. The Chicago local expelled a leader for taking the contracts for three theatre orchestras.

A local leader is not permitted to import or " colonize " musicians, even if they are members of other locals, without the consent of his local. The case is different with " travelling leaders." There are three well-known grades of travelling theatrical companies. New York is the centre where these are made up, though a few go out from Chicago. One grade is the opera, or minstrel show, with its own complete orchestra and leader, or the symphony company. Such a company is independent of local musicians, and, like the Boston Symphony Orchestra, is able to continue non-union. The next grade is the " skeleton " orchestra, composed of three or four musicians and the leader. These must be members in good standing, else they cannot secure local musicians in the places visited, to fill out their orchestra. Last is the theatrical company that carries only its leader, who must be a pianist, in case he cannot make up a local orchestra, and must be a member if he expects to employ local players. If the skeleton orchestra or single leaders remain in a place less than four weeks, they do not take out transfer cards from the local of their origin. If they stay longer, they must transfer their membership. Some of these leaders are not members of a local, and, in order to bring them in, the Federation at a recent convention provided a card of conditional membership issued by the national organization. When such a leader " locates," his card is converted into a local membership. If a leader holding such a card plays in a non-union house, his card is forfeited, and this prevents him from getting an orchestra in a union house. By means of these rules the Federation has effectually " unionized " the theatres and orchestras throughout the United States and Canada. There remain but few leaders, theatres and orchestras on the "unfair list," the Boston Symphony Orchestra being the only important one.

It will be seen that the musicians' union is not only a " closed shop " union: it is also a closed employers' association. The contractor, or leader, must be a member of the union. Consequently, unlike other crafts in the modern labor movement, the musicians retain the character of a guild with its masters and journeymen. This diversity of interest has led to considerable discussion and to the proposal that, imitating other unions, the leaders should be excluded, and that a member who takes a contract should be given an honorary discharge. The nearest that this proposal has come to be acted upon is at Cedar Rapids, where the local classifies the leaders and requires them to take out a leader's license, for which they pay $25. This arrangement is an innovation. In other places the leaders are on the same basis as other members, and any member can become a leader simply by getting a contract. The musicians point out that their leaders are on much more intimate terms with the rank and file than are the contractors in other trades. Their interests are the same. They require no capital beyond that of the others; they perform in company with their fellows; and they are continually reverting to ordinary membership. On the other hand, the ease with which a member becomes a leader causes a severe competition for leadership. In New York fifty musicians may be " pulling the wires " to get a theatrical leader's position away from him. Nearly all the grievances and discipline with which the union is occupied spring from this cut-throat competition. If the leaders were separated, if they formed their own contractors' association with their own rules and discipline, and if they then worked under a trade agreement with the union, the two together could rule out the unscrupulous leader, and the conditions would be bettered for both leaders and men. These views, however, are as yet held by but a few. To the historical student it is interesting to see in this belated organization the same forces at work which long since separated the guilds of other crafts into the trade union and the employers' association.[1]

[1] A similar development, completed in the year 1902, is described in the article, "The Teamsters of Chicago." See the author's "Trade Unionism and Labor Problems," pp. 36–65.

The American Federation of Musicians, as its name indicates, is a federation of local unions rather than a fully developed national union. While the national organization is supreme, yet the spirit of local autonomy is so strong that the delegates have withheld important powers conceded to other national trade unions. The Federation is prohibited from adopting a general benefit or insurance assessment. The revenues of the national are only two cents a month from each member, — a sum less than one-half the revenue of the 'longshoremen, and only one-twentieth of that of the moulders and one-sixtieth of the cigar-makers. The locals regulate their initiation fees, and a local with high fees assesses the difference on a member admitted by transfer from a local with low fees. That the power of the national organization is growing is seen in the recent rule that this assessment shall not exceed $25. This was directed against the New York local whose fees are $100, making the difference assessed to members coming from other locals as high as $75 to $95. This question of " universal membership " has agitated the conventions more than any other, and has led to the partial breaking down of local barriers already described. Remnants of the barriers are seen in the rule against " colonizing," by which a local prevents a local leader from bringing in members of other locals for permanent engagements and even for single engagements. Evidently, until universal membership is fully established, the closed shop remains a local monopoly.

Naturally, the local unions of musicians are jealous in admitting members, and the national organization has been compelled to legislate upon this subject. Each local is required to have an examination board to pass upon the eligibility of applicants, but any local rule prohibiting the admission of any competent musician is declared null and void,[1] and the applicant has an appeal to the national executive board. All new locals must hold their charters open for at least one month, and must invite all musicians within their jurisdiction, through the press or otherwise, to become members.[2] Only expelled or suspended members of the Federation are excluded, and these may be readmitted on appeal or by payment of a fine. Members are strictly forbidden to play with non-members, except in the cases already noted.[3]

These rules maintaining the closed shop have their significance in view of the wide recruiting area for the supply of musicians. The union necessarily can prescribe no term of apprenticeship. A musician's training begins in childhood, and requires many years of application. Teachers of music are found in every considerable locality, and those who are members of the union are as free as others to organize classes and solicit pupils. In fact, this is a source of income to many of them. Of the thousands who take up instrumental music, there are relatively few who come to look upon it as their vocation from which to earn their living. These must be admitted to the union, else their competition on the outside will menace the scale of prices. But there are others to whom music is only an avocation, at which they can pick up a few dollars outside their regular vocation. These, like the women who work at home for " pin money," are the more serious menace to those who depend on their skill for all their money. To bring them

---

[1] *Constitution*, Art. V, Sec. 20.
[2] *Ibid.*, Sec. 1.   [3] *Ibid.*, Sec. 16.

into the organization and to bind them to a minimum scale of prices is a decided protection to the professional element. Of the 64,000 members throughout the country, over one-half are working also at other occupations. One consequence of the musicians' affiliation with the trade unions, is their rule requiring such members to join also the local union of their regular craft, wherever such exists.[1] Thus the musicians offer the peculiar spectacle of a union largely composed of members of other unions and confronted by the problem of maintaining two minimum scales of wages. However, this applies mainly to smaller towns. In such a town, perhaps, only the leader may follow music for his livelihood, while all the other members follow other occupations as well. In such a town the initiation fee is usually $5, — the minimum prescribed by the national organization. In larger towns the highest is $25, excepting New York, Chicago and San Francisco, which in the past ten years have placed it at $100. These larger fees tend to exclude the incidental musician and to reserve the field for the strictly professional.

This competition of semi-musicians has led those who look upon themselves as artists to advocate, in times past, State regulation of the profession instead of trade-union regulation of the craft. They point out that State governments restrict the practice of some professions to those who have passed a prescribed examination, and that this restriction covers not only lawyers, physicians, dentists, pharmacists and teachers, but also veterinarians, architects, horse-shoers, bakers, and so on. In line with these precedents a bill was introduced in the Illinois legislature creating a " Commission of Music,"

[1] Standing Resolution 15.

to be composed of five members selected by the governor from ten persons nominated by the Illinois Music Teachers' Association, with power to grant licenses on examination to teachers of music. Its advocate contended that the low state of their art was due to the many self-styled artists, and that, like other professions, theirs would be improved and elevated by legal selection of the fit and exclusion of the unfit. In lieu of the enactment of such a law the musicians' union tries to reach a similar result through its " closed shop," its examination boards and its minimum wage. The restrictions which the professional musician advocates for the sake of his art, the trade-union musician enacts for the sake of his living. The latter frankly bases his policy on the commercialism which has gained control of the country, and which, on the one hand, sends its greatest of artists " out for the almighty dollar," and, on the other hand, " cheapens the wages of the ordinary musician by the same tactics that employers pursue with other hired help."

This effort to protect the minimum wage is seen in several of their regulations. One is the exclusion of " juvenile bands." A leader or teacher organizes his pupils and advertises them under a taking or deceptive name. Their parents provide uniforms and instruments, besides paying the teacher a small sum for tuition. After a few months the leader takes contracts, and his pupils play in public for " the experience." This form of child labor is prevented by the exclusion of " incompetent " musicians and of persons under sixteen years of age from membership in the union.

Another rule prohibits coöperative or " share plan " engagements, unless the same are " proven absolutely non-competitive." A coöperative band plays on a speculation for a manager, the pay of the members being a share of the receipts. If such a band comes in competition with a leader who pays the union scale, the latter may find it difficult to secure the contract. Non-competitive engagements, where such bands may play, are those for practice, or for educational purposes, or for raising funds to buy a uniform or for creating a class of engagements not in vogue heretofore.[1] In these the band assumes all responsibility, is not engaged and so does not compete with other bands.

The opposition of the musicians to army and marine bands has come vividly before the public more than any other policy of the organization. Enlisted musicians of the army and navy are not admitted to membership, and a member enlisting severs thereby his membership. No member is permitted to play a paid engagement with any enlisted man On noted occasions at Baltimore, Chicago and San Francisco union bands have withdrawn from pageants in which government bands took part. Repeated complaints against their competition have been made to the authorities at Washington, and in this even the National League of "artists" led the way twenty years ago. The enlisted men are equipped by the government, and are paid a salary somewhat less than the union scale. They are allowed to supplement their salaries by private engagements. In most cases their orders forbid accepting less than prevailing civilian rates, but the National League in 1888 compiled one hundred cases of violation of these orders. The situation illustrates the economist's " marginal man." In St. Louis, prior to 1886, there were five civilian bands and one Cavalry

[1] "Decisions of the President," *International Musician*, Feb., 1903, p. 2.

Depot band stationed at Jefferson Barracks. The five bands were at all times compelled to adjust their prices to what managers said they could get the army band for. The one band was a club used in turn on each of the others. Finally, the others adopted a joint defence, — a boycott. This was effective only where the manager needed more than one band or needed one band continuously. Last of all, the Federation appealed from the military and naval authorities to Congress, and now secured legislation to raise the pay of all members of enlisted bands and to prohibit them from playing at paid engagements while in the service of the government.

It is significant that the union's antagonism does not apply to navy yard bands. These are composed of local musicians who do not take contracts as a band, but go out as individuals. The antagonism applies only to enlisted musicians, and these, by their oath of service, are under control of the government rather than the union. They cannot be ordered on strike or boycott if their superior officer orders differently. They cannot be summoned to union meetings or examined and punished for cutting under the union prices. They menace the minimum wage because they menace the union discipline.

Immigration, too, is a menace that has troubled the musicians. Though themselves largely foreign-born, especially German, yet they have taken a stand against free immigration. Even the officers of the National League, in spite of their artists' pride, seriously contended before the immigration authorities that under the alien contract labor law musicians should be excluded, on the ground that they were laborers rather than artists, whom the law admits. The Federation, in line with its trade unionism, consistently urges Congress to class musicians as laborers, thereby bringing them under the alien contract labor law.[1] It declaims against " the wholesale importation of musicians " as " endangering the existence of musicians in this country, and depreciating their opportunities to earn a respectable livelihood as American citizens." [2] It decries the influx of foreign bands, adopting " some high-sounding royal or other foreign title," " picked up in the streets of large cities," managed by some shrewd American, " who lines his pockets by adopting the degrading padrone system of Europe, under which no self-respecting American citizen can exist," and proceeds to declare such aggregations " unfair " and to boycott managers who hire them. It welcomes " legitimate " foreign bands and orchestras making concert tours under fair conditions, "but will resist to the last these fraudulent aggregations."[3] The Federation sent a circular in their own languages to the musicians of Europe, warning them against speculators for the World's Fair at St. Louis and advising them that they would find the cost of living five times as great as in their own countries.[4] Finally, the constitution of the Federation requires all members to be citizens or to have " declared their intention," and to complete their naturalization " with due diligence." [5] Thus the closed shop and the boycott are the musicians' regulation of immigration.

Wages and Hours

There is hardly a craft whose earnings are more uncertain than those of the musician. The steadiest job

---

[1] Standing Resolution 10.   [2] *Ibid.,* 1.   [3] *Ibid.,* 15.
[4] *International Musician,* June, 1902, p. 9.
[5] *Constitution,* Art. V., Sec. 8.

is that in theatres for eight months and summer gardens for four months. In the St. Louis local of 975 members, only about 150 have these positions. There the union scale for theatres provides $23 per week, for not more than seven performances, up to $30 for not more than fourteen performances, to which is added one rehearsal a week. At these prices a musician playing every night in the year, with two matinées and a rehearsal each week, could earn, say, $1200. But such a feat is impossible. These men actually earn about $700 or $800 in eight months and $300 in the summer months, making $1000 or $1100 for the majority of theatrical positions. These, of course, are minimum rates of pay, as are all of the other scales; and there are certain ones, such as first violin, first cornet and so on, who receive more than the minimum. There are also " extras," so that a few may earn as much as $1200. When the St. Louis union was organized twenty years ago, there were three theatres paying the above rates. These were not changed, but the others were raised to the same level, bringing them up about 15 per cent. The best men have always received the higher rates of pay, in addition to more frequent employment. Their gain has come from regulating the hours, limiting the number of rehearsals, getting paid for extra rehearsals and extra performances and prompt payment of salaries in full.

The other eight hundred musicians in St. Louis must depend for their earnings upon all sorts of fleeting engagements. It is here that the union has mainly affected the rates of pay and the hours of work. The " price-list " covers them all with particularity and is amended whenever a gap appears. Formerly, at private parties, weddings, balls, entertainments and the like, the pay was $2 to $4 for the night. The concessionaire might keep the musicians till daylight, though but a few dancers held out. Now the player gets $4 till 2 A.M. and $1 an hour thereafter. Hence the dancers do not remain after 3 or 4 A.M. Parades were $3 for four hours. Now they are $4 for the first hour on Sundays and $3 on week-days, with $1 for each additional hour. All day to 7 P.M., or afternoon and evening to 11.30 o'clock, is $10. Funerals were $1.50. Now they are $3 or $4 " if to a cemetery," or $5 " with marching after leaving the cemetery." And so on for baseball, Fourth of July, corner-stone laying, flag-raising, dedications, saloon concerts and the hundred other occasions where the musician softens sorrow, fires patriotism or drowns bedlam.

Several kinds of calls formerly were not paid for at all, but now they have a scale of prices. Members are prohibited from donating their services unless the union as a whole votes to volunteer, as for some great public service, like the relief of the Johnstown sufferers. Thus church music was often furnished free as an advertisement for other work. Now a single service is $5, and three services the same day $10. Decoration Day and memorial services were free on account of sentiment. They are $4, with marching extra at $1 an hour. Serenades were free, and a leader could control the time of his men by calling them together when they had " a night off " to serenade a hoped-for patron. Now serenades are $3 the first hour, with extras for marching and overtime.

The cost of their uniforms is also a matter of wages. Each bandmaster or leader wishes his own uniform, sometimes fantastic and costly. This the musician is often compelled to buy, and so to own, say, four or five different uniforms. The St. Louis local led the way in establishing a regulation uniform, which members are required to wear. It costs about $18.50, can be made by one's own tailor, hence is always a fit, avoids contagion, provides a new suit for clear days and indoors and an old one for wet days and parades, and, not least important, enables the public to distinguish between union and non-union bands. A leader may furnish, if he likes, a distinctive suit for himself, or he may furnish only a one-inch band with his own lettering to be placed on the cap. When the Chicago local, in 1905, adopted the regulation uniform, they were checked by an injunction obtained by certain leaders. This, later, was withdrawn, and the union uniform is in line of general adoption.

Curiously, the musician's demands have not lessened his calls. Guests at cafés, restaurants and hotels were regaled by dirty gypsies or mandolin negroes or other itinerants. Now fifty musicians in St. Louis are regularly employed at $5 for a single day of seven hours, or $21 a week of seven days or a score of other price and time combinations. Trolley parties have appeared. Picture shows employ hundreds. Phonograph musicians in New York dispense harmony to the ends of the earth at $1.25 an hour. The taste of the community has improved, its wealth has grown, its accessibility has extended and the musician gets more pay and more work.

The foregoing prices and changed conditions pertain mainly to the St. Louis local. In New York the price-list is somewhat higher and has not been changed for forty years. The difficulty there has been in enforcing the scale. About 300 of the best men earn from $1500 to $2000 a year, getting steady employment at the minimum scale, while about one in fifty of all the members gets more than the minimum. But the majority earn less than $1000, and in some lines, like balls, the competition and evasion have been so great that the scale became a dead letter and had to be reduced.

Although the demand for musicians has increased, yet there is a rule of the national union which carries the suggestion that the doctrine of " making work " has a place in the craft. This law permits a local to specify the minimum number of men allowed to play in a theatre orchestra. The New York local places the minimum number of men to be employed in a theatre at six; St. Louis at seven. But these absurdly low figures give evidence rather of the musician's longing to produce artistic music than of his policy to make work. This is shown by the refusal of Henry Irving, on his first appearance in New York, to go on with the regular house orchestra of twelve men, when he had been accustomed in England to forty. He compromised on thirty-five. The union minimum of six or seven is but a feeble effort to counteract the managers' view that the American musician, like the American mechanic, should turn out more work than his European competitor. With the more recent increase in wages and business methods the union minimum is becoming the manager's maximum. For Henry Irving's artistic reaction in this matter, the union made him an honorary member.

Doubtless the idea of making work appeals to the locals and the members. The New York local fines a member for playing more than one instrument at a time at a single engagement, " this being against the interest of our fellow-members." For the same reason it denounces by resolution the " exactions of unscrupulous leaders who require bass drummers to play cymbals with drum while marching, and snare drummers to play bass drums with pedal attachments on single-night engagements." The musician, like the machinist, clings to the " one-man-one-machine " tradition of his craft. His arguments are right in esthetics, and may be right in economics, for he reasons that, if the ear of the American public were cultivated to good music, it would demand more of it.

CHAPTER XVII

" Pittsburgh the Powerful," " The Iron City," " The Workshop of the World " — situated on the Alleghany plateau at the headwaters of the Ohio, rich in mineral resources, easily accessible to markets, this district is beyond all others the strategic centre for the production of wealth.

" Pittsburgh Riots of 1877," " Homestead Strike of 1892," " Pittsburgh Millionnaire " — these tell of Pittsburgh's strategic position in another campaign — the world-wide struggle for the distribution of wealth.

Gigantic in its creation of wealth, titanic in its contests for the division of wealth, Pittsburgh looms up as the mighty storm mountain of Capital and Labor. Here our modern world achieves its grandest triumph and faces its gravest problem.

Andrew Carnegie has said that the iron and steel industry is either Prince or Pauper. Certainly, no staple manufactured article responds so violently to the prosperity and depression of the country as pig iron. So it is with all the industries of Pittsburgh that follow in the train of King Iron. When the Pittsburgh Survey began its work in September, 1907, the Prince was on

[1] *Charities and the Commons*, March, 1909, afterwards *The Survey*. In the collection of material and the preparation of this article I have had the assistance of William M. Leiserson and John A. Fitch, graduate students in the University of Wisconsin, and others, engaged on the "Pittsburgh Survey." The figures are for 1907–1908.

his throne — full years of prosperity and glorious op-
timism had been his. Long before September, 1908,
Carnegie's pauper walked the streets. From every type
and class of labor came the report of a year with only
half, or three-fourths or even one-third of the time
employed. Hardly another city in the country was hit
as hard or stunned as long by the panic as Pittsburgh.
The overwork of 1907 was the out-of-work of 1908.

First Prince, then Pauper; overwork, then under-
work; high wages, no wages; millionnaire, immigrant;
militant unions, masterful employers; marvellous business organization, amazing social disorganization. Such
are the contrasts of Pittsburgh the Powerful, the Workshop of the World.

Outwardly, western Pennsylvania is not inviting.
The surface is hilly, with narrow and precipitous valleys
and few flood plains. Not much of the land is suited
to cultivation, and its meagre agriculture is confined
to the uplands. But for heavy manufactures nature
has peculiarly exerted herself. Three great rivers and
three smaller ones afford transportation. The Allegheny comes down from New York, draining an area
of 11,500 square miles. From West Virginia comes the
Monongahela. At "The Point" of Pittsburgh these
two rivers mingle their waters to form the Ohio, and this
river carries the products of Pittsburgh to the West and
South. Within the district the larger rivers receive the
waters of smaller ones. The Monongahela receives the
Youghiogheny, the Allegheny is joined by the Kiskemine-
tas, and Beaver River flows into the Ohio.

Through the hills which line these rivers run enormous
veins of bituminous coal. Located near the surface,
the coal is easily mined, and, elevated above the rivers,

much of it comes down to Pittsburgh by gravity. There are twenty-nine billion tons of it, good for steam, gas or coke. Then there are vast stores of oil, natural gas, sand, shale, clay and stone, with which to give Pittsburgh and the tributary country the lead of the world in iron and steel, glass, electrical machinery, street cars, tin plate, air brakes and fire brick.

To the gifts of nature has been added the bounty of government. Besides Pittsburgh's share in tariff legislation, Congress has appropriated over $17,000,000 for river improvements. The Monongahela in its original condition was navigable for steamboats only at high stages. Now the river is navigable for its entire length in Pennsylvania; and in West Virginia steamboats can go up as far as Fairmont, fifty-two miles beyond the state line.

As the result of these improvements, freight rates have been reduced and manufactures stimulated. Coal formerly shipped by rail now goes by river at a cost in some cases reduced as much as eighty per cent. The work of the government on the other rivers and in Pittsburgh harbor proper has brought similar results. The Allegheny River and the Ohio about Pittsburgh formerly abounded in boulders, snags, bars and shoals. Most of these obstructions have been removed, and the government is continuing its work of making navigation easy.

The transportation system provided by nature and government is supplemented by a network of railroads. Five trunk-line systems have main lines, branches and leased lines to the number of twenty-two radiating from the city. Besides these, there are several connecting lines owned by the steel companies binding together the various parts of their plants.

Business enterprise, taking advantage of these resources, is able to turn out from the Pittsburgh District the greatest annual tonnage of any similar area in the world. The greater part of this tonnage, of course, arises from the heavy products of coal mines and steel mills. Coal mining has been marvellously perfected. Electricity applied to undercutting and hauling enables a single mine to turn out over 6000 tons of coal a day. On certain days the output of this mine has reached even 7000 tons. In the district 46,000,000 tons are produced yearly.

In the production of this enormous wealth thousands of workers have coöperated. According to the census, Pittsburgh had a population of 406,533. According to enthusiasts, the population is 2,500,000. Both figures are misleading. The first limits the city to its old political boundaries, not including Allegheny; the second extends it over a radius of seventy-five miles from the Court House, and includes a territory under the government of three states and a score or more of counties. It is difficult to define the limits, but the whole of Allegheny county is homogeneous in an economic and social sense and corresponds roughly to what is termed the Pittsburgh District. In 1907 this Greater Pittsburgh had a population of about 1,000,000, of whom the wage-earners were approximately 250,000 employed in 3000 establishments.

How do these wage-earners fare in the division of products derived from these magnificent resources? What is their share and how do they get it? These are questions which are fundamental to our inquiry. First, there is, everywhere, the great ocean of common labor, — unprivileged, competitive, equalized. Above this expanse, here and there for a time, appear the waves and wavelets of those whom skill, physique, talent, trade unionism or municipal favoritism lifts above the fluid mass. Restless, unstable, up, down, and on, like the ocean, so is the labor of Pittsburgh. From the employment bureau of a hugh machine works I learned that in the single year of continued prosperity, 1906, they hired 21,000 men and women to keep up a force of 10,000. If six months is the average stay of a workman at his job, I should speak not of the ocean but of the maelstrom. And this restless *go-and-come* is only slightly less with the skilled than with the unskilled, for the foreman of the tool room in the same establishment estimated that to keep up his force of the hundred highest grades of mechanical skill, he had hired a hundred men during the year. The superintendent of a mining property, lacking, however, the exact records of my machine-shop bureau, insisted on the amazing figure of 5000 hired during the year to maintain a force of 1000. The largest operator of the district thought this was too high, but said that 2000 hirings in a year for 1000 permanent positions was not an exaggerated index of labor's mobility in the Pittsburgh District.

What are we to infer? Seemingly the economist's hypothesis of the immobility of labor compared with the mobility of capital is almost reversed within the Pittsburgh District. The human stream from Europe and America whirls and eddies through the deep-cut valleys of the Monongahela, the Allegheny, the Ohio, like the converging rivers themselves. But the ponderous furnaces and mills remain fixed like the hills. Is it the climate, the fog and the smoke? Is it the difficulty of finding homes and the cost of housing and living? Yes, answers my employment bureau, which has made a careful study of its own peculiarly ill situation. Is it the defeat and exclusion of trade unionism, which in other places make for stability and the rights of priority for the man who has longest held the job? No, for neither the inflow nor outflow of organized mine-workers is appreciably less than that of unorganized machine-workers or steel workers. Is it low wages and long hours? No, answer the mine workers again. Is it specialization, speeding up, over-exertion? Yes, very largely. These are both cause and effect of excessive restlessness. By minute specialization of jobs, by army-like organization, by keeping together a staff of highly-paid regulars at the top, the industries of Pittsburgh are independent of the rank and file. Two-thirds of the steel workers are unskilled, and thousands are as dumb as horses in their ignorance of English, if we may judge by the kind of " gee," " whoa," and gestures that suffice for commands. Specialization, elimination of skill, payment by the piece or premium, speeding up, these are necessarily the aims and methods of Pittsburgh business, that turns out tons of shapes for the skilful workers of other cities to put into finished products. Without its marvellous framework of organization, elim-inating dependence on personality in the masses, and thereby rendering personality more indispensable in the captains, it would be impossible for Pittsburgh to convert its eddying stream of labor into the most productive labor power of modern industry. Enormous rewards for brains, overseers, managers, foremen, bosses, " pushers " and gang-leaders; remarkable pressure towards equality of wages among the restless, movable, competitive rank and file, — these are results in the distribution of wealth of Pittsburgh's supremacy in the production of wealth.

Day Labor. — When he is free to make his own bargain with the employer, and competition is unrestricted, the Pittsburgh laborer without skill or command of English gets in prosperous times $1.35 to $1.65 for a day of ten hours. Outside Pittsburgh, in the mills and yards, 16½ cents an hour seems to be the prevailing rate for the kind of work done by the Slav immigrant, but in Pittsburgh proper 15 cents is more generally paid for such labor. Jones and Laughlin, on the South Side, can hire Slavs at 15 cents when Homestead and the mill towns pay 16½ cents. The difference is due to the greater congestion of immigrants in Pittsburgh, the place of their first arrival, and to their preference for the city with its agencies for employment and its fellowship and support when looking for employment.

To the railroads and contractors goes the distinction of paying the lowest wages for day labor. Section hands, mostly Italians, in the Pittsburgh District, earn 13½ cents an hour. But the *padroni* on special contracts, seem to be able to get 16½ cents. I struck up a bargain with one of these enterprising wholesale dealers in humanity as he was leading his gang to the depot, whom he claimed to have sold at this rate of pay for work in Allegheny county. He offered to furnish me a hundred like them for a month, to lay natural gas pipe in Wisconsin at $2 a day, provided I paid their round-trip travelling expenses back as far as Chicago and gave him the exclusive contract, together with the sole privilege of running the commissary. Giving me his name and number in the telephone book, he referred me to the Standard Oil, for whom he claimed to be sending men to

Oklahoma for the same kind of work on the same terms, but with round-trip expenses back to Pittsburgh. Probably the railroad companies, at $1.35 a day, were paying the Italians as much or more than they netted out of their fellow-countryman, this Americanized *padrone*.

Eight to ten dollars for a week of sixty hours is thus the level toward which the wages of the unskilled gravitate, when competition is free and English unessential. A higher level is reached when trade unionism, mechanical skill, municipal politics or the English language, intervene.

The building laborers, for example, get two dollars for a day of eight hours. This is fifty to sixty per cent more by the hour than is paid for a similar zero degree of mechanical skill in other jobs. The hod-carrier, whose work is no more skilled but more risky, gets $37\frac{1}{2}$ cents, or $3 a day. The Building Laborers and Hod Carriers' Union is an effort of the American-born and English-speaking white and colored common laborers to protect themselves against the green Slav and Italian, but it is a weak organization, and only the aid of the skilled, organized trades in building construction preserves their short hours and high pay. Doubtless, also, the long slack period of building operations necessitates a higher rate, though the Italian on contract work is also idle in winter. Municipal and state politics shows its hand in the rate of $2 for eight hours for city work, the same rate as that of the building laborers.

In passing, it may be said that the English language is worth two cents an hour. The non-English worker who starts at $16\frac{1}{2}$ cents would start at $18\frac{1}{2}$ cents if he were sufficiently Anglicized for a job where English is needed. Additional fitness, adaptability, politics or trade unionism, without additional mechanical skill, brings him an additional two cents, eight cents or even ten cents an hour.

Transportation Work. — In the factories and on the railroads the Slav and the Italian fill the ranks of common labor; it is among the teamsters that the Negro finds his congenial job. The factory is too confined, the work too monotonous; but following his horses, he can see the sights and get paid for riding. Of 9000 teamsters in the district, more than one-half are Negroes. Their occupation requires no more skill than that of the ordinary common laborer. The usual wage is $10 a week for the driver of a single horse, and $12 for two horses. In the suburban towns, $14 is usually paid for driving a two-horse team. Thus the predominant rate is 18 to 20 cents an hour.

A teamster reaches his stable between 6 and 6.30 A.M. He quits at 5 in the afternoon. He must clean and take care of his horses. Usually he gets an hour for dinner. On the average he works ten hours a day; but this is not fixed. He must get through with his route. If he has very much overtime he usually receives his regular rate per hour for it. Sunday and holiday work are paid for at the same rate.

The express companies pay $55 and $60 a month. There are no fixed hours, and the men must work until all deliveries are made. They get every other Sunday off.

To cab drivers is paid $14 a week on carriages and $15 on hearses. They must clean their own carriages and work Sundays, holidays and any hour of the day or night without extra pay. In 1904 their wages were $9 and $10 a week. A strike in 1905 raised the wages to the present rates. The bosses signed an agreement which was renewed in 1906. The following year they refused to sign, but wages were not reduced. The steel companies pay their teamsters $2 a day of ten hours, with overtime and Sunday at the same rate.

Work for teamsters was plentiful up to November, 1907. In the city they did not have much overtime, but in the mills overtime added a considerable amount to the drivers' earnings. One man got nineteen and one-half days' pay in two weeks. He averaged right along about eighteen days at every fortnightly pay day.

Five years ago the team drivers organized a union. A year later the ice drivers were organized, and the cab drivers formed a union three or four months after them. The three locals at the height of their power numbered about 3000 men, but the recent period of unemployment has practically destroyed the organization.

A class of American workmen, akin to the teamsters in skill, but not in color, are the marine transport workers. The majority of them, deck hands and firemen, get $50 a month. The wages of mates are $70. Hours are twelve on the double crew boats and somewhat more than that on boats with single crews. Double crews are six hours on and six hours off. The men eat and live on the boats and work seven days in the week. The effect is demoralizing. They work for a " stake " and then " knock off " until their money is gone. Drunkenness is the evil among them. About five hundred river men, organized in a local branch of the International 'Longshoremen, Marine and Transport Workers' Association, called a strike in January, 1907, demanding $60 a month for firemen and deck hands and $80 for mates. The strike was lost, and, after two months, the men went back to work at the old rates.

So far I have been discussing the transportation men whose work is closely kin to primitive methods of haulage. These lead up to employments which have come in with mechanical horse power. A motorman or conductor can be broken in almost as fast as a teamster. Yet the wages of the street railway men are twenty to thirty per cent higher by the hour, and they work an hour or two less per day. They have more responsibility and are fitter and steadier men than the teamsters, and their organization, the Amalgamated Association of Street Railway Employees, is a strong one and makes annual agreements with the Pittsburgh Railways Company. The union has almost 2700 members, and includes, with exception of about 100 men, all the motormen and conductors working in Pittsburgh. At present, this is the third largest local union of street railway employees in the United States, and the wages it secures by joint agreement are the highest east of the Mississippi. Prior to the absorption of all the street railway lines by the Pittsburgh Railways Company and the adoption of the secret ballot in political elections, employment could be secured through political leaders. Now the men are hired as they come according to fitness. The agreement fixes the wages of first-year men at $24\frac{1}{2}$ cents, and the rate advances by stages until after three years it is $26\frac{1}{2}$ cents an hour. The same rates are paid to motormen and conductors. The present scale represents a reduction of one-half cent per hour from that of the preceding year, made by a board of arbitration in view of the loss in earnings since the panic. On April 1, 1907, the Pittsburgh Railways Company revised its schedules so as to shorten all the runs and equalize the work. The longest run is now ten hours and forty minutes. Formerly it was eleven hours. Nine or ten hours are now the day's work for most street railway employees. This represents a reduction of thirty to forty per cent in the hours of labor since 1902. Runs on the street cars are continuous; there is no time off for meals. Extra pay for Sunday, holidays or overtime is not allowed, but Sunday runs are somewhat shorter than week-day schedules. Most of the men get three days' rest per month.

To handle the enormous traffic of the Pittsburgh District, the various railways employ about 50,000 people. Of these the Pennsylvania lines have about 35,000. The men actually employed on the cars and engines are classed as switchmen (or yardmen) and roadmen. Yardmen do not go outside of the switching yards. They receive the trains, distribute them to the various tracks for unloading and make up trains to be given over to the road men. A switching crew is composed of one conductor or foreman, three brakemen or helpers, an engineer and a fireman. They work in two shifts of twelve hours each, one coming on, the other off, at 6.30 A.M.; but they are paid for eleven hours, the dinner hour being deducted. The conductor of a switching crew gets 35 cents an hour when he works on the day shift and 36 cents at night. The brakemen's rates are 30 and 31 cents an hour. On switching engines, to the engineer is paid 38.3 cents an hour and to the fireman 23.7 cents. Considering the requirements of the railway service, its severity and danger, as well as the wages and hours, the condition of the yardmen is similar to that of the roughers and catchers in the rolling mills. They are much the same kind of men, American born, of strong physique and endurance, working long hours at the hardest work.

In some of the steel mills which have their own switching yards, the night crew and the day crew change shifts every two weeks. This was before the enactment of the federal law. Once a month, therefore, these switchmen were confined to their engines or cars for a stretch of twenty-four hours. In the railroad yards, day crews usually get off every other Sunday. Night crews work one Sunday and have two off. Outside of emergencies the hours of yardmen are regular. Little overtime is made after twelve hours. In case of wrecks, however, crews are out as long as twenty-five, thirty and even forty-eight hours without rest.

Roadmen, on the other hand, regularly have much overtime. While the time tables are so arranged that the hours shall approximate twelve or thirteen per day, the congestion of freight often compels the men to work much longer. A man starting out with a freight train cannot tell when he will get back. He may have to lie waiting for hours at a siding. Some men have been out thirty, forty and even sixty hours at a stretch, prior to the operation of the federal law restricting the hours. During the winter months eighteen to twenty hours were the regular thing for freight crews. The time record of an engineer for two months in 1907 was: August, twenty-six days, 391 hours; September, twenty-five days, 386 hours; average fifteen hours a day. Twice during September he worked forty hours at one turn. He began Saturday noon and quit Monday morning.

Passenger crews have their schedules so arranged that on through passenger trains they make a trip of about seven and one-half hours out of Pittsburgh. They then take another train back to the city. Thus they work fifteen consecutive hours for which they get two days' pay. Fifteen round trips per month form their regular schedule. Local passenger runs are so arranged that the crews may be back in Pittsburgh in thirteen hours.

The pay for men on the road is fixed by a combination of hourly rate and mileage run. To a through-freight engineer is paid $42\frac{1}{2}$ cents an hour on an assumed run of 100 miles in ten hours. If he is out eleven or twelve hours, he gets no extra pay. But if he is out thirteen hours or more, he receives his hourly rate for the excess beyond twelve hours. Similarly, the local freight engineer gets 36 cents an hour, the firemen 23 and 28 cents according to the type of engine, the conductors $32\frac{1}{2}$ cents, brakemen 24 cents, flagmen 25 cents. Passenger crews earn higher rates.

Some of the railway brotherhoods have strong organizations in the district, but their insurance features and the difficulty of calling a strike on a railroad system serve to make the men conservative and to delay improvements in their condition. It required federal legislation to set a limit of sixteen to their consecutive hours of labor. The Switchmen's Union, affiliated with the American Federation of Labor, — as the railway brotherhoods are not, — has shown a more aggressive spirit, and has incurred the hostility of the railway managers who are inclined to favor the rival union, the Brotherhood of Railway Trainmen. This conflict of jurisdiction, especially in the switchyards, also stands in the way of improvement.

Indoor Labor. — What might be called the " indoor

trades " comprise such a variety of occupations that
there is no special significance in considering them together, except as a convenient group for purposes of
presentation. They range from the mercantile employees,
the press men and type setters of the printing plants,
the bakers and the brewers, to the larger and more
coherent occupations which are mechanical in an old
sturdy sense, machinists, foundrymen, blacksmiths and
the like.

At the farthest extreme from the railway worker is
the retail clerk. Formerly the clerks began at 6 or 7 in
the morning and quit at 9 or 10 at night. Then they
organized one of the strongest unions of their class in
the country, affiliated with the Knights of Labor.
Though the union has disappeared, the improved hours
and conditions remain. The stores, for the most part,
open at 8 and close at 5.30, except Saturday when they
close at 9. Legal holidays are generally observed. During the last year a movement toward the old conditions
has been noticeable. The stores were open on Labor
Day and, instead of closing at 5 during the summer
months, as was the custom, many kept open until 5.30.

Among the bakery workmen unionism also is weak,
hardly twenty per cent of them being organized. But
their conditions improved considerably during the recent
period of prosperity, a change due to the fact that the
supply of bakers was not up to the demand. The long
hours and Sunday work had kept boys out of the trade.
When the panic with its consequent unemployment came,
the men were not able to stave off a reduction of $2 a
week for all hands. Bakery workmen are divided into
three classes according to their work. A " first hand "
is one who tends the oven. " Second hands " work at

the bench and are sometimes called " bench hands." The " third hand " is the helper. Wages since the reduction are as follows : First hand, $16 a week ; second hand, $12 ; helper, $11. The hours of work for most bakers are not fixed. Ordinarily ten or eleven hours constitute a day's work, except on Friday when the usual time is thirteen hours. Work begins late in the afternoon and ends in the morning. The longer hours on Friday are due to the fact that no work is done on Saturday.

The printers of Pittsburgh are poorly organized, compared with those of other cities. They have about 400 members in the union, or less than half of the men working at the trade. Three newspapers, one of them German, and about half the job offices work under agreements with the Typographical Union. The minimum wage is $16 a week, in the union as well as in the non-union book and job offices. Union shops, however, work eight hours while the others have a nine-hour day. For night shifts the rate is $19 a week. Time and one-half time is paid for overtime and double time for Sunday and holiday work.

In the composing rooms of the daily newspapers all employees work on the hour basis, — 61 cents an hour being the rate on morning newspapers and 56 cents on evening papers. In the union shops the hours are seven a day; the other shops work eight hours. Proofreaders have an eight-hour day and receive $22 a week. Work for the Pittsburgh printers was very abundant up to a year ago. Job printers could earn annually from $800 to $1000 and morning newspaper men up to $1500.

Machinists, moulders, pattern-makers, boiler makers, and blacksmiths, are a large and important element in

Pittsburgh's industry. Probably 15,000 machinists are employed in the county. The highest skill is found among the 5000 who work in contract or jobbing shops. These are all-round mechanics; they may have a different kind of work to do each day and are able to work from blue prints. About one-fourth of them belong to the union. There are perhaps 10,000 more working in "specialized shops." Here a particular product is constantly duplicated, and each workman is confined to making just one part of a machine. These specialized shops are entirely unorganized. Such specialization in the machine industry has been one of the causes which has weakened the machinists' union throughout the country. Formerly the Pittsburgh branch controlled nearly all the machinists in the district. Then it was able to establish the nine-hour day (1890) several years before the general agitation for the nine-hour day began in other parts of the country. Now the union in Pittsburgh confines its efforts entirely to controlling the contract shops. Even in these it is being beaten.

Machinists had a minimum hourly rate of 30 cents up to 1907. To many, however, more than 40 cents was paid. On April 1 of that year the union called a strike for a 40-cent minimum, a fifty-hour week and an increase of ten per cent for those who were earning more than the new minimum. The strike was lost. The machinists' union lost in numbers and prestige, and the employers were able to make the open shop universal throughout the district. No trade agreements are now made; the fifty-four-hour week is the general rule, and there is no minimum wage. Employers pay what they consider the men worth. Rates run up to 45 and 50 cents an hour according to the skill of the machinist and the size of the tool which he operates. Few men now get less than 30 cents an hour, and most machinists are started at 32 or 33 cents. In the specialized shops an unskilled man starts at 18 to 22 cents and works up to 25 or 27 at piece or premium work for a ten-hour day.

About 4000 people are employed at moulding in the Pittsburgh District. Less than half of these are members of the International Moulders' Union. The six locals have together some 1900 members including 300 core makers. Three-fourths of the latter are organized. Of the skilled workers only about 300 are outside the unions, while in the malleable iron works, employing about 1000 men of less skill, there are no union men whatever.

To moulders was generally paid $3.50 per day of nine hours in 1906 and 1907. On March 1, 1908, employers forced a reduction of 25 cents a day, and the union was too weak to withstand it. In the malleable iron works moulders are paid by the piece. Rates are so arranged that men make about $3 in nine hours. The union is opposed to the piece-work system, but in these shops it cannot enforce the day system.

The higher wages of the pattern makers, — generally $4 per day, — may be explained by the fact that there are comparatively few engaged in the trade; only about 450 in the district; and the union' 's two-thirds of these.

The boiler makers might be classed among either the metal or the building trades. They work in shops, do outside work on buildings and work for the railroads. Less than half of the 1500 boiler makers in the district are organized. When employed outside they have the wages, hours and conditions general in the building trades. Their scale is $3.60 per day of eight hours, or 45 cents an hour. Inside men have the nine-hour day like the machinists and the moulders and their pay is about the same, — $3.15 a day or 35 cents an hour. In the railroad shops, boiler makers, like all other employees, have less favorable conditions. The hours are ten and wages $3.30 a day. Four or six hundred men who work in the steel mills repairing boilers and similar work are all non-union. They get $3 per day of ten hours.

The brewery workers are the only workmen whose entire industry is thoroughly organized, and this favored position they owe to the union label and the boycott. Every brewery in the Pittsburgh District works under a signed agreement with the Brewery Workers' Union and every agreement provides for the closed shop. In these breweries are employed about 1900 people. The union takes all employees in and about a brewery regardless of their occupation. This has brought it into conflict with the engineers' and coopers' unions, but in these jurisdictional disputes the brewery workmen have come out victorious.

The effect of the union is seen in the wages, hours and conditions of labor laid down in the agreements. For all men who work in the brewery proper eight hours constitute a day's work, and their wages range from $16 to $20 a week. All bottling house employees working for breweries get $2.50 per day of eight hours. Work is steady, and though it requires but half the time to learn the trade, the journeyman has an annual income equal to, if not greater than, that of the ordinary building trade mechanic.

Nine hours are required of brewery drivers and stablemen. Those working for wholesale liquor dealers have a ten-hour day. The wages of stable men are $15 a week; drivers receive from $16 to $21. Considering the reduction of hours, the union has, therefore, increased the wages of teamsters fifty to sixty per cent by the hour over those of unorganized teamsters. Further, engineers who in other places usually work twelve hours, have the eight-hour day in the breweries.

Building Trades. — Turning now to the building trades we find workmen who have put up their daily rates of wages higher than those of any others in the district. Three things helped them to do this: First the skill of the trades; second the union, and third the seasonal character of the work. Rates of wages are highest in those trades which have the longest periods of unemployment during the year and the longest period of apprenticeship.

The wages run from $42\frac{1}{2}$ cents an hour for the painters, up to 65 cents for the bricklayers. Most of the trades pay 50 cents an hour. Next in number come those in which the rate is $56\frac{1}{4}$ cents. All men who earn 45 cents an hour or more, with the exception of the roofers, have spent at least four years in learning their trade. The slate and tile roofers have an apprenticeship period of only three years. The steam fitters and the plumbers require five years, while the structural iron workers require eighteen months of actual work at the " construction of bridges, viaducts, building or other constructional work, either of wood or iron." The tile layers' apprenticeship period is only two years, but the apprentices are taken only from among the helpers, who may have worked a good many years at not much over half the journeymen's pay. Hoisting engineers get 50 cents an hour and have no specified apprenticeship rules.

·But the state requires these men to be licensed, and a license is issued only after an examination and two years' work around an engine.

The bricklayers get the highest wages per hour in the building trade, — 65 cents. But they have a longer period of unemployment than any other trade. Seldom do they work more than six or seven months; and their yearly earnings average not much over $800 a year.

Next to the bricklayers the plasterers lose the most time. They work perhaps seven or eight months in the year. Fifty-six and a quarter cents is their hourly rate, but the annual earnings of the ordinary plasterer are only about $700.

Whatever the rate per hour may be, it works out that the annual earnings in most of the building trades run from $700 to $800. In those trades which have a high daily wage and steady work the year round, such as the elevator constructors and electricians, there is a scarcity of workmen. The inside wiremen get four dollars per day of eight hours. The line men who are not connected with the building trades recently had their wages reduced 25 cents an hour. Their general rate is now $3 for a nine-hour day. Those working for the city get $90 a month and they work only eight hours a day.

All together about 15,000 workingmen are organized in the building trades unions. This represents perhaps seventy-five per cent of all the men working at these trades. In the individual unions, the proportion of organized to unorganized workmen varies greatly. The plumbers, bricklayers, elevator constructors and tile layers have over ninety per cent of their craftsmen in the unions. Other trades run from fifty per cent upward.

There is seldom much difference between the wages of

union and non-union mechanics. In most cases the union rate is also paid to non-union men. Where there is a difference the union rate is usually paid to some men, while to others less is paid. In a union shop there is usually a flat rate for all; for, although the union fixes only the minimum wage, employers are not inclined to go above that.

The hours of labor in all the building trades are eight per day. In most of the trades this was established during the years 1900–1902. The bricklayers and masons secured their eight-hour day in 1896 and the plumbers in 1898. Many of the trades now have a four-hour day on Saturday during the summer months.

Most of the building trade mechanics are well organized in trade unions, but some of their organizations seem to be losing ground. Within the last few years the employers in at least three trades have established the open shop, and in each case this has been followed by a reduction in wages. The Pittsburgh Local of the Bridge and Structural Iron Workers' Union has been almost disrupted in a struggle with the employers organized as the National Erectors' Association. The latter refused to pay the union scale of $56\frac{1}{4}$ cents an hour. They refuse to recognize the union and they pay 50 cents per hour to their skilled mechanics and less to the less skilled. Almost all master plasterers are now running open shops, and they have reduced wages from $4.50 to $4.20 a day. The carpenters' union is unable to maintain its scale of 50 cents an hour, and the master builders pay anywhere from $43\frac{3}{4}$ to 50 cents. In several other trades the employers and the union have been fighting over the closed shop and scales of wages. In this struggle the employers have been aided very much by the recent panic, which threw many men out of work and weakened the unions.

So long as the workmen's organizations were strong, they secured signed agreements from the employers. Now, however, most of the trades work without agreements, and the union officials claim to be opposed to agreements. It is noticeable, however, that unions without agreements are with difficulty maintaining their wage scales, while the plumbers and the elevator constructors, who have signed agreements, have been secure in their union wages even through the panic.

Mine Workers and Steel Workers. — Finally, we come to the two industries employing the largest number of men in Allegheny county, coal mines and steel mills. There are probably 20,000 mine workers in the county and 70,000 steel workers. In some cases, the mines are owned by the steel corporations. The nationalities of the two sets of men are quite similar, with their large proportion of unskilled and semi-skilled Slavs and their smaller proportion of skilled Americans and English-speaking nationalities. The hours of labor in the mines are eight per day without Sunday work, as against twelve in the mills with considerable Sunday work. The wages paid to the common laborer underground at the coal mines are $2.36 per day of eight hours, while the wages paid to the same class of Slavs at the Pittsburgh mills are $1.80 for twelve hours, and in the other mill towns $1.98 for twelve hours. Measured by the hour, to the Slavs employed by the same company are paid 90 to 100 per cent more as mine workers than as steel workers.

Again, the " loaders," who follow the undercutting machines in the mines, and who are practically common laborers paid by the ton instead of by the day, earn about $2.40 to $3 for eight hours, while the metal-wheelers and cinder-pitmen, doing similar heavy work in the mills and paid by the ton, earn $2.28 to $2.41 for twelve hours. The miner earns 30 to 37½ cents an hour and the steel worker 19 to 20.

When we come to the highest job, there is no position in the mine to be compared with the roller on a bar and guide mill or on a plate or structural mill. The bar and guide mill rollers earn $10 to $16 a day of twelve hours, and the plate and structural mill rollers earn $7 or $8 a day. But these men, though usually spoken of as work-men, are really foremen instead of workmen, because they oversee the work rather than do it, and the company hires and discharges the crew on their recommendation. The blooming-mill roller is different. He actually works the levers himself, and to him may be compared the electrical undercutter, who operates the machine that undercuts the coal. The undercutter earns $3.25 to $5 a day of eight hours, and the blooming-mill roller an average of $6.25 for twelve hours. The miner earns 40 to 65 cents an hour and the blooming-mill roller about 50.

In another respect, the mine-worker's position is superior. The houses in which he lives, many of them belonging to the company, are quite convenient, with open spaces, and the rentals paid are about $2 per room against $4 paid by the mill worker. Taking everything into account, — wages, hours, leisure, cost of living, conditions of work, — I should say that common laborers employed by the steel companies in their mines are fifty to ninety per cent better off than the same grade of laborers employed at their mills and furnaces; that semi-skilled laborers employed at piece rates are forty to fifty per cent better off in the mines; and that the highest paid laborers, the steel roller and the mine worker, are about on a footing.

In 1897 the conditions in the mines were similar to those in the mills. The day laborer received $1.35 to $1.50 for ten hours. It was in that year that the long strike of coal miners throughout the interstate field took place, with the result that for the past ten years wages, hours and conditions have been established by agreement between the United Mine Workers of America and the Coal Operators' Associations. Under these agreements, the conditions of the poorest paid laborers have been improved one hundred per cent, while their fellow workers in steel have improved perhaps twenty per cent.

The fate of unionism in the two industries is interesting and enlightening. Prior to the Homestead strike of 1892, the steel industry was dominated by the Amalgamated Association of Iron, Steel and Tin Workers. There were two defects in this organization. It included only the skilled or semi-skilled and high-priced workers, and it had no effective discipline over its local unions. The situation was such that the manufacturer was handicapped by arbitrary restrictions which the national officers of the union deprecated, but could not correct, while the common laborer was not benefited or was even deteriorated. For the sake of both the manufacturer and the laborer, the union, which had overreached itself and was headstrong in its power, had to be whipped and thrown out. Since that time the manufacturers have gone to as mad an extreme in bearing down on their employees as the employees had previously gone in throttling the employer.

Contrast this with the history of the mine workers, a body of men of the same general intelligence as the steel workers. With a national union able and willing to discipline its local unions, the leading coal operators assert that they can carry on their business to better advantage with the union than without. If there were no union, they would be menaced by petty strikes whenever a few hot-heads stirred up trouble, and at times when the operator might be tied up with contracts to deliver coal. But under the annual agreements with the union, the operators are safe in making long contracts, and they can conduct their business on even a closer calculation for labor than for materials whose prices and supplies fluctuate. Furthermore, this union, taking into its membership the entire body of workers, has been a greater benefit to the mass of unskilled labor than to the few who are highly skilled.

CHAPTER XVIII

TARIFF AND LABOR[1]

FOR nearly seventy years the effective arguments that have sustained the protective tariff have been the home market for farmers and a high standard of living for wage-earners. The first depends on the second, for without a purchasing power of American labor greater than that of foreign labor the home market is not much better than the foreign market. The standard of living is the really enduring justification of the protective tariff. The tariff prevents the competition of foreign low-standard labor and draws a protective circle within which American labor may gradually work out its own higher standards.

It is an important fact that the principal leaders and advocates who framed the pauper labor argument two or three generations ago, and who won its acceptance by the country, did not believe that the tariff alone would bring about a high standard of living. They looked upon the tariff merely as defensive. It needed to be supplemented by positive efforts, by voluntary organizations, by legislation, within this country. In fact, the tariff was to them simply the means by which these domestic efforts could be guaranteed a free field for successful experiment and adoption. Matthew Carey, from 1820 to 1840, did more than any other American

[1] *Annals of American Academy of Political and Social Science*, September, 1908, pp. 209–213.

to establish the tariff on a protective basis in the interests of labor. His indefatigable investigations furnished the arguments for petitions which manufacturers sent to Congress; for reports of Congressional committees; for speeches of Congressmen; and he, more than any one else, changed the tariff argument from protection of capital to protection of labor. Yet Matthew Carey, although an employer, was prominent in the labor agitation of the 'thirties and in his support of the labor organizations of that period. He aided and defended their strikes and brought down upon himself the blows of the free-trade organs, which rightly identified his protectionism with his trade-unionism.

Following him came Horace Greeley, who did for the people what Carey had done for the politicians. He converted them to protection by the home-market and the standard-of-living arguments. Yet there was no man of national fame in his day who did as much effective work for trade-unionism and even socialism as Horace Greeley. He endorsed the industrial congresses to which delegates came from the labor unions, the land reformers, from the Fourierite, and other socialistic societies. He opened the *Tribune* to these radicals and avowed himself for socialism at the time when he was also powerfully supporting protection. Indeed, he claimed that protection was necessary to enable socialism to work itself out to a successful issue free from the destructive competition of pauper labor.

When we come to the period after the war, Congressman Kelley, of Pennsylvania, so persistent and able a champion of protection as to be known to the nation as "pig-iron Kelley," often asserted, as I have been told by his daughter, Mrs. Florence Kelley, that the work of his generation must be to establish American industry, the work of the next generation would be to diffuse its benefits.

It is this hope of Congressman Kelley which I believe points toward the duty of the present day in the revision of the tariff. The socialism of Horace Greeley has long since been proved visionary. The trade-unionism of Carey and Greeley has been proved ineffective in the very industries where the tariff is most protective. In Greeley's and Kelley's time the iron and steel industry seemed to be firmly established on a system of joint trade agreements of capital and labor, but, since the Homestead strike, the once powerful trade union of that industry has dwindled to a remnant. The hours of labor for men on shifts have been increased almost uniformly to twelve per day; night work and Sunday work have been extended wherever possible; twenty-four hours' consecutive work on alternate Sundays in order to change the night and day shifts has become necessary for many employees; while speeding up to the limit of endurance and cutting piece rates with increase of speed have been reduced to a science. The glass industry, too, is marked by the decline of unionism in certain branches, and even with the aid of unionism it is notorious for the exploitation of child labor. In the textile industry child and woman labor, long hours and interstate competition, have defied the loudest agitation and have kept the wages and conditions at a point actually inferior in places to those of its free-trade competitor, England. In other protected industries unionism is making a retreating fight, and I do not see how it is possible in those which have reached the stage of a trust for unionism to recover its ground. Labor cannot concentrate as capital does. It is among the industries and laborers not directly protected by the tariff, like the building trades, the railroads, the 'longshoremen of the lakes, that unionism has its principal strength. In all industries its influence is partial, and the great majority of the workers are outside its ranks. If their standards of living are to improve under the protecting shield of the tariff, the improvement must come through the aid of legislation.

We need scarcely stop to maintain the futility of state legislation in protecting labor in the tariff-protected industries. If the industry is competitive, the more advanced states like Massachusetts cannot afford to handicap too greatly their own manufacturers. If the industry is " trustified," the trust can shut down its factories in an advanced state and throw its orders to its factories in a backward state, like Pennsylvania. The tactics that defeat unionism are those that defeat state legislation.

As regards federal legislation there are serious questions of constitutionality and interference with state prerogatives. These have come to the front in the discussion that followed the Beveridge child labor bill and in the decision of the National Child Labor Committee to withdraw from that line of attack. It is doubtful whether such legislation can be brought in under the subterfuge of interstate commerce, or even under the " general welfare " clause. But more to the point is the fact that it is not based on the real consideration which the federal government offers to employers of labor as compensation for the expense which labor legislation imposes. This is the protective tariff. In this field questions of constitutionality have already been settled.

Congress may impose a tariff for protection as well as revenue. It may select the industries and articles to be taxed and determine the rate of import duty. Congress is also supreme in the matter of internal revenue taxes. It may impose such taxes for regulation as well as revenue. It coupled the National Bank act with a prohibitive tax of 10 per cent on state bank-notes. It has placed a heavy tax on colored oleomargarine in competition with dairy butter. In the field of customs and internal revenue taxation Congress " is supreme in its action. No power of supervision or control is lodged in either of the other departments of the government." [1] With this unquestioned control of the taxing power, the tariff can be made to pass over a share of its benefits to the wage-earners for whom it is intended. The method is merely a question of the technical drafting of the law, and not any innovation on the principles of legislation nor infringement on constitutional boundaries.

A feasible method has been suggested by the new Commonwealth of Australia in the taxation of agricultural machinery. The so-called " excise tariff " of 1906 was adopted on the same day as the " customs tariff." The customs tariff act imposes a schedule of duties on imported goods, and the excise law (*i.e.* internal revenue) imposes a schedule of one-half those rates on the same goods when manufactured at home. But it is provided that in certain cases the excise duty shall not apply. These are establishments where the " conditions as to the remuneration of labor " in the manufacture of the home product (*a*) " are declared by resolution by both Houses of Parliament to be fair and reasonable "; (*b*) are in accordance with an arbitration award ;

[1] 7 Wall. 433; 195 U. S. 57.

or (c) a trade agreement of employers and trade union
as provided in the conciliation and arbitration act of
1904; or (d) are declared fair and reasonable after a
hearing by a judge of the supreme court of a state or his
referee. The administrative details are of course unessential. The essential feature of the Australian arrangement is an internal revenue duty at a lower rate than the
customs duty on the competing article, and the remis-
sion of that duty if the home manufacturer, on whom is
the burden of proof, can show that his employees actually receive the benefits intended by the protective
tariff.

I do not overlook the fact that a policy of this kind
requires administrative machinery and scientific investigation. But this should be required under any kind of
tariff revision. The tariff should not be revised or reduced except on the basis of cost of production in this
country and foreign countries. This should include,
first of all, the comparative cost of labor. I believe all
tariff revisionists, as distinguished from free traders,
agree to this, in order that the tariff may be retained
ample enough to cover the higher costs of labor in this
country. But there is a menace imminent even in such
an investigation at the present time, because it assumes
that revision will be made on the basis of the existing
long hours, low wages and child and woman labor of
many protected industries. The actual cost of labor
is lower than it would be if the hours, wages and conditions were fair and reasonable. The people of this
country will gladly support a tariff high enough to pay,
not merely the existing wages, but better and even ideal
wages. They do not ask that the tariff be reduced to
the present labor cost. In some cases, like pig iron, that

cost is probably less than it is in England, but in England the blast furnace workers are on the eight-hour day, while here their day is twelve hours, seven days a week. The people willingly protect labor, but they would like to see the tariff actually passed along to the wage-earner. If, therefore, a tariff commission investigates the comparative cost of labor in this and competing countries, it should inquire whether the wages and hours are actually reasonable, and what would be the cost if they were made reasonable. It is on this ideal basis and not the actual basis that the tariff should be revised. If this is done, then the only serious difficulty of the plan, that of investigation, is already provided for. Such a tariff commission would necessarily be a permanent one.

A permanent bureau of this kind would receive general instructions from Congress as to what, from the standpoint of a reasonable American standard of life, should be the condition of labor. This might provide for all workers at least fifty-two full days of rest each year. It might provide that all continuous operations should be divided into three shifts of eight hours instead of two shifts of twelve hours. It might provide the eight-hour day in non-continuous operations for women workers and possibly for men. It might set the minimum age of child labor at fourteen. Other provisions, such as minimum rate of pay, might be more general and be left to the commission under general instructions to ascertain what is reasonable under the conditions. If upon investigation and inspection the bureau or commission finds that a given manufacturer is granting to his employees these reasonable conditions, a certificate to that effect would be the warrant of the internal revenue commissioner to remit the internal revenue

tax. All the machinery for imposing such a discriminating tax is already in existence in the administration of the oleomargarine tax which imposes a tax
of ten cents per pound on artificially colored oleomargarine and one-fourth of one cent per pound on uncolored
oleomargarine. This tax and its administrative machinery have been sustained by the Supreme Court of
the United States as being not in contravention of the
Constitution,[1] although the similar tax in Australia was
held unconstitutional. The only additional machinery
required is that which is already widely proposed in the
form of a permanent tariff commission. Such a commission, I believe, is favored by the National Association of Manufacturers, and their bill only needs the addition of a clause giving the commission power to issue
and revoke these certificates of character, in order to
make it an effective instrument of labor protection. This
would, of course, require a force of inspectors or agents
and considerable expense, but the expense would be met
by the added revenue.

[The discriminatory anti-phosphorus-match law, in effect July 1,
1913, is the first application of the foregoing principle. Its significance
is the use of the internal revenue taxing power to do for labor what the
same power had previously done for banking and farmers. The law is a
singular token to the constructive research of my former pupil, John B.
Andrews, now secretary of the American Association for Labor Legislation.]

[1] McCray v. U. S., 195 U. S. 27.

CHAPTER XIX

THE SCHOOLHOUSE IN A STATE SYSTEM OF EMPLOYMENT OFFICES [1]

WHAT is an employment office and what are its functions?

A place where buyer and seller of labor may meet with least difficulty and least loss of time.

This function is now performed by private agencies and newspapers. They fail of their complete purpose because there are many of them and each is small. The more places to look for work the more likely that man and job will miss each other. " Don't fly around looking for a job," says a newspaper. " Advertise." But without one central agency, workmen must do this.

The function of an employment office is best expressed by the British term " Labor Exchange." Exchange implies a market. It is an organization of the labor market, just as the stock market, the cotton market, the wheat market, are organized.

Manless Job and Jobless Man

Why is an employment office needed? Employers are constantly discharging and hiring laborers. Workmen are constantly looking for jobs. One firm in Milwaukee hires from 60 to 240 men a week. About 10

---

[1] *La Follette's Magazine*, Aug., 1912. This plan has been worked out by my former pupil, William M. Leiserson, now State Supervisor of Employment Offices for the Industrial Commission of Wisconsin.

per cent of all those employed change places because of seasonal work. Four out of every ten workmen have to look for work at least once a year. There is need of an organized market, because without such an exchange each factory and each district of a city tends to become a market. Each has its reserve labor force ready to work when needed. Many markets tend to increase the number of unemployed. Lack of organization causes maladjustment. "Manless job and jobless man" don't meet, and maladjustment of two kinds occurs. First, is an oversupply of labor in one place and lack of labor in another. Second, some occupations, particularly those of unskilled laborers, are greatly oversupplied, while many skilled occupations have not enough men.

The Ideal Exchange

What is the ideal organization of the labor market? Ideal organization would be national. One unified national labor exchange would reduce idleness by having a single market so that oversupply anywhere could be shifted to meet demand anywhere else. At present, each manufacturer and each district is interested in having idle workmen in the immediate neighborhood ready to go to work when they are needed. But it is impossible to get national action at once; we must begin with state action.

What is the ideal labor market of a state?

(*a*) Free employment offices maintained by the state.

(*b*) Free employment offices maintained by local committees.

(*c*) Private agencies regulated by state.

(*d*) Correspondents in various cities and industries.

(*e*) Reports from all to a central clearing-house.

(*f*) Periodical bulletin of the labor market.

What is the ideal for a city?

(*a*) Central office in the business centre.

(*b*) Branches in various residence districts.

The School as a Branch of the Employment Bureau

If each schoolhouse has a director of its social centre service, he could be supplied with blanks from the main employment office. A workman, by going to the school nearest his house to register, could be immediately connected with the whole organized labor market of the state. The fact that he is out of a job and the kind of work he can do will be immediately known at the city exchange, and in a day the central clearing-house will know. If a man of his trade qualifications is wanted anywhere in the city, the director of the social centre will be able to inform him after a talk with the central office in the city. If there is a place for him anywhere in the state, it will be known to him in the course of a few days. No discouraging tramping of city streets, no spending of precious pennies for car fare, newspapers or as fees to private agents.

This will tend to remove maladjustment of place. It is of use particularly to the immigrant and the ignorant. It would tend to distribute population by removing congestion in certain places.

The Vital Problem

Maladjustment of occupation belongs to the vocational bureau. The school, as a branch of the children's department of the employment office, will tend to remove this kind of maladjustment. British figures show that while about 75 per cent of applications for work cannot be filled, 40 per cent of the jobs could not be filled. How to direct some of the 75 per cent excess so as to reduce the 40 per cent lack is the problem of the school. Records of children's aptitudes should be kept in school. Teachers can best tell what the child is good for. The children's department of a free employment office has special blanks for children. These can be filled out in the schools with the aid and advice of teachers. The employment office has the best records of desirable trades, those which are growing. Children are thus directed into the most promising occupations. Vocational training in public schools and trade schools needs employment offices to connect children with the business world. The schoolhouse as a branch of the organized state labor market meets this need. Thus the free employment office connects up with the vocational bureau and its special juvenile advisory committee of employers, employees and educators to encourage apprenticeship, to visit parents and child and to encourage the boy to stick to trades and not to jump into " blind alley " employments.

How to induce school-teachers and principals to coöperate in this great agency, is a matter that can be worked out when once its importance is understood. The Wisconsin Industrial Commission is meeting with success in enlisting municipal authorities and local associations of manufacturers in supporting financially and supervising the employment offices. It has arranged with a few country bankers to act as agents for their localities. With a broadening idea of the school as a social centre and the employment of principals who are wide awake and alive to their social opportunities, the commission could enlist them as a part in a comprehensive scheme for the state. Such men should, of course, receive extra compensation, not only for this, but also for other work outside the usual pedagogical lines. The policy of the industrial commission, and the one that will make local coöperation most effective, indicates that these local expenses should be met by the local authorities, while the state meets the general expenses and the salaries of those in the larger offices who are required to give their entire time to the work.

CHAPTER XX

WHAT is the part that industrial education should perform in preventing vagrancy, irregular employment and pauperism?

Before we can answer the question we need to know what kind of industrial education we mean, and what kind of industry it is that needs this education.

If we want to see the industries of Wisconsin, let us begin, not at the factory or shop or farm, but at the Free Employment office in Milwaukee. Stand for an hour in that office and see the hundreds of men and boys waiting for jobs to turn up. There is the spot in the state where you can see passing before you, in miniature, the panorama of modern industry. For, industry is not merely the machines and shops, nor even the commodities turned out in amazing quantities, but it is mainly the boys and girls entering the shops and the men and women coming out. These are the commodities that the state is interested in. These are the machines that the state must depend upon for its future food, clothing and shelter, for its politics, its prosperity and its power of endurance.

We are accustomed to measure prosperity by the millions of dollars' worth of cheese and butter and machinery and leather put out and placed on the market.

[1] Address at the Social Service Institute, Milwaukee, April, 1913, on the subject of Industrial Education and Dependency.

Let us measure it by the thousands of men and women turned out and placed upon the labor market. What shall we say of a factory that hires and discharges a thousand men and boys in one year in order to keep up a steady force of three hundred? Modern industry must employ a hundred and fifty to five hundred men every year in order to keep a hundred positions steadily filled. Here is a kind of raw material taken in every day and a kind of half-finished product poured out, that means more for the state of Wisconsin than its inflow of pig iron and its outflow of machinery. As you look at the panorama passing through the employment office you see the human products of Wisconsin's prosperity.

You are astonished at seeing the crowds of boys and young men — the army of the semi-skilled. You offer them a position at a dollar or a dollar and a quarter a day, where they can learn a trade or get promotion, and they laugh at you. They have been spoiled. They could earn that much before they were sixteen years old! At the age of seventeen or eighteen they have been earning eighteen to twenty cents an hour — twice as much as you offer them. To the boy of sixteen, twenty cents an hour, at a two-months' job, looks bigger than the fifty cents or a dollar an hour and steady work at the end of a ten-year line of future promotion. He has suddenly found himself earning more than his immigrant father.

Why is it that these boys do not look ahead? Why do they not know that twenty cents is the highest they will ever earn? That they will scarcely hold such a job more than four or five months? That ten years from now they will be loafing in the back part of the employment office with the flotsam and jetsam that they already see behind them, vainly waiting for a twenty-cent job of two or three days, or else hopelessly accepting, for the rest of their lives, an old man's job at a dollar or so a day, long hours and Sundays thrown in?

Let us see where they got their notions of work and wages. At sixteen or seventeen they are put to work feeding a semi-automatic machine. In two months they have learned the job and got the speed. Their wages go up to eighteen or twenty cents an hour. But the work is monotonous — just one or two operations, hour after hour, ten hours a day, sixty hours a week. The monotony grows — gets unendurable. The older man at the machine is afraid to quit. He keeps on — his mind shrinks — he never thinks of his work unless something goes wrong — he thinks of other things — his childhood, his former playmates — his days and nights of fun and wild oats — anything to keep his mind off from the deadly monotony.

But the boy rebels. He must get a move. His foreman will not change him to a different machine or a different foreman. Other boys have got the speed there. The foreman must have output — he puts up with beginners and learners only because he must. The boy quarrels and quits in a huff; gets impudent and is "fired." He hunts another shop — gets on another machine or a similar machine under different surroundings. After a while he has learned several machines by a wandering apprenticeship through several shops.

The employer storms. Here he is paying eighteen to twenty cents an hour for work that takes little intelligence. Yet he cannot keep his hands. They quit on the least provocation. They are conducting a continuous, unorganized strike. When they get too speedy and earn too much, the employer cuts their piece-rate prices as much as he dares. Their high wages are not due to their skill or speed, but to their disgust. The employer ascribes their instability and impudence to their laziness, intemperance, vice. He compares them with himself and others who, by hard work, low pay and thrift, have climbed to eminence. He disregards the fact that, with his specialized machinery, he does not want intelligence, except in his foremen and master mechanics; that if the machine hand stops to think about his work, he promptly abhors it; that he sees nothing in it for him but the twenty cents he gets for it, and the cut in piece-rates if he gets more.

Large employers have begun to feel the pinch. It comes to them in the scarcity of all-round mechanics and intelligent foremen. They need a certain amount of brains, distributed through the shop, to supervise the machines and to " boss " the machine hands. If they can build up a skeleton framework of, say, a hundred foremen, superintendents, skilled mechanics and efficiency experts, who stay with the establishment permanently, then they are independent of the five hundred machine hands and common laborers that pass through their shops like subconscious machines. Their factories are not built to produce intelligence. So in the past ten or fifteen years they have begun to create positions for apprentices.

The old apprenticeship system went to pieces with the incoming of specialized machines and machine hands. The former apprentice worked with hand tools and learned all parts of the trade by imitating the journeymen. He became a skilled man working with his hands, rather than an intelligent one, working with his brains.

But the modern apprentice works with machines. The

machine is the accumulated intelligence of the past, harnessed up to belts and motors. The apprentice now needs *intelligence* more than manual skill. How shall he get it?

In the first place, he must learn to operate the machine. But he must not be kept on one machine. He must pass around the shop and learn to operate all the machines.

So far, the apprentice is merely a machine hand. His apprenticeship differs only from that of the other machine hands, in that he learns the different machines in the same shop, while they learn them by travelling from shop to shop.

But there is a difference. You can measure it by the rate of pay. The machine hand gets eighteen to twenty cents an hour on piece-work — the apprentice gets ten or twelve cents an hour on time-work. He is virtually paying the employer eight or ten cents an hour for the opportunity of leaving one machine as soon as he has learned to operate it, and learning to operate the next machine. A boy of eighteen years of age at ten or twelve cents an hour is *prima facie* an apprentice, although he may have no apprenticeship contract.

But this is not enough for modern apprenticeship. The machine is an iron brain. It is built on theories of mathematics and mechanics that have accumulated since the time of Archimedes. It moves by the generation of power that began with the brain of Isaac Watt, Michael Faraday, or the inventor of the gas engine. It is made up of metals, and it transforms raw material that can be understood only by a glimpse into chemistry or biology. The modern factory is indeed the forces of nature obeying the stored-up thought of man.

Consequently, the modern apprentice, if he becomes more than a multiplied machine-hand or an imitative journeyman, must understand the machines and the forces of nature that he is charged with directing. This does not mean that he must be a scientist, engineer, chemist or biologist. It merely means that he must think over again and understand the principles that philosophers, scientists, engineers and inventors of the past have embodied in the workshop of the present. If he is rightly instructed in shop mathematics and mechanical drawing, he is really thinking out for himself, the thoughts that go back to Newton, Watt or Faraday, and applying them to the machines and forces that he is pretending to manage. If he studies the raw material he is using, and compares it with other material, he is getting into such sciences as chemistry, biology or commercial geography.

But the modern factory is just as wonderful in its system of organization, division of labor, specialization and management as it is in its mathematics and engineering. Consequently, in the third place, if the apprentice studies different plans of shop organization, book-keeping, cost-keeping, efficiency, labor problems and so on, he is thinking out the elements of accounting, government, political economy and even psychology, as applied to the business of which he is a part. These studies open up to him the line of promotion to foreman, superintendent, manager.

It is this kind of training in intelligence and in learning to study and think, that the shop itself does not give. Hence, large employers, who can afford it, have set up apprenticeship schools in their establishments, where the apprentice puts in part time along with his shop work.

These schools, with their mathematics, designing, business organization and other studies, are the brain-factories of modern industry which produce intelligence, while the shop itself, like the older kind of apprenticeship, turns out only manual dexterity.

But this modern apprenticeship cannot go very far. It is expensive. Only large companies can afford it. Even the large companies keep it down to narrow limits. A shop of 5000 men will have only a hundred or two hundred apprentices. Worst of all, other employers " steal " the apprentices, and the company finds itself educating mechanics for the use of its competitors. Further, the employer's apprenticeship system really enlarges the evil which it should reduce. It develops the intelligence of a few, and makes it less necessary to develop the intelligence of the great mass of machine hands and common laborers. Instead of thousands of intelligent boys and young men in their shops from whom to select, the employers are compelled to resort to engineering colleges, and then to start their young engineers on a course of shop-apprenticeship. The separation of brains from hands is a business necessity. We must look elsewhere for the system that will unite intelligence and labor.

The common schools in America started off some sixty or seventy years ago with the idea of making the common laborer and the workingman an intelligent worker. There had been plenty of private schools for the education of boys to become doctors, lawyers, preachers and teachers, but there was little or nothing for the workingman except charity schools or pauper schools.

What happened to the common schools, however, was not the education of labor as such, but the instruction of labor toward the learned professions. This was inevitable, because there were as yet no teachers except those who had been taught in the learning that led to the professions. Numbers of " mechanics' colleges," " mechanics' institutes," " agricultural colleges," and so-called colleges of " learning and labor " were started and were expected to teach the boys to become intelligent farmers and mechanics; but they gradually slipped off into experiment stations, engineering colleges, the higher colleges of agriculture or the usual academic colleges of letters and arts. Instead of turning out teachers for the common schools, they turned out scientists, engineers and experts. Instead of making labor intelligent they added a number of scientific professions to the former number of learned professions. This, also, was inevitable and, indeed, advantageous, for such professions are needed. But it did not solve the problem of how to teach the millions of boys who must work with their hands for a living also to work with their brains at the same time.

This problem of industry and education, therefore, again forced itself to the front. Some twenty or thirty years ago the states began to enforce compulsory attendance at school and to prohibit child labor in factories. But compulsory attendance is not compulsory education. Boys and girls are eager to get to work. To meet this, a wave of manual training passed over the schools. But manual training starts from the standpoint of the professions. It is a good thing for the professional man to have done some work with his hands. A system of education that leads to the learned and scientific professions, conducted by teachers trained to that system, makes of manual training a branch of *liberal* education — *not industrial* education. No wonder that manual training has found its place in the high schools that lead to colleges and universities, and not much in the grade schools that stop where industry begins.

I might mention other efforts that have been made to connect up industry with education. A half century ago John Ruskin and William Morris revolted against the deadening effects of modern industry on the worker. Theirs was the artistic and romantic point of view. They went back to the time of small industries, when each worker made a complete article and had an interest and an ambition in his work. From Morris has come the so-called " arts and crafts " movement. This movement really accomplishes the object intended. It makes the worker see and understand both the beauty and the money to be obtained from his work. But it reaches such a small number of people, and is so remote from the great current of factory industry, that it needs only to be mentioned to show its inadequacy. It has inspired a few maiden ladies of Massachusetts, or a few mountaineers of North Carolina, to restore the quaint weaving and needle-work of colonial times. But, as soon as they secure a nation-wide market for their artistic product, then it pays to make it on a large scale, and the factory system comes in, with its designers and artists on the one hand, separated from its machine hands on the other. Just as modern industry has no need of intelligent workers to operate its machines, so it has no need of artistic workers. If the boy and the girl are to learn how to design and appreciate a beautiful product, they must learn it outside the factory.

So it is. No matter from what standpoint we start, we find the same result. If we start from the industrial side we find the overwhelming pressure of modern industry toward specialization. This separates out a few with the intelligent and artistic work, and leaves the thousands with only the manual and monotonous work. If we start from the educational side we find that the teachers, also, have been specialized in the learned, scientific or artistic professions. This limits their instruction to the benefit of the few whose work is to be intellectual or artistic, and neglects the thousands who must earn their living by manual work.

There is evidently needed something that will unite the factory and the school, that will bring together the employer and the school-master. Neither is competent to handle the problem by himself. When the employer starts off in the schooling business, he gets no further than the trade school. He thinks first of all of the dearth of skilled mechanics for his shop, or of the short supply of skilful cooks and domestic servants for his household. His idea of industrial education is the training of carpenters, plumbers, steam-fitters and the other unionized trades that have not yet been broken up by the factory system, or else the training of hired girls for the kitchen.

On the other hand, when the schoolmaster starts off in the industrial business, his idea is the training of the hand to supplement the training of the brain. He gets no further than manual training. He makes each boy take a course in carpentering, or drawing, even though the boy wants to be a grocery boy, a book-keeper, or a salesman.

The state of Wisconsin, at last, has adopted a system of continuation schools that is planned to remedy these things; *first*, to make the intellectual and artistic side of industry reach every boy and girl, instead of a few apprentices; and, *second*, to make the employer and the schoolmaster coöperate with and supplement each other, instead of duplicating and controverting each other.

The great danger that threatens this forward attempt is the same as that which has side-tracked similar attempts in the past; namely, the lack of teachers who have had a thorough acquaintance in the shop with some industry or trade, and at the same time are capable of using that knowledge to teach the intellectual and artistic principles that the boy does not get in the shop. This is the one great and pressing problem ahead of the continuation schools in this state — how to get and keep the right kind of teachers. Back of this is the bigger question — *how to know* the kind of teachers that are needed. If boards of industrial education do not know the kind of teachers required for this work, they are likely to get teachers who know only how to lead their boys and girls along the lines of manual training, where they simply try to teach what the boys can learn just as well or better in the shops; or else they get teachers who only know how to teach a trade, just as the old-style journeymen taught the apprentice to imitate himself.

Let us imagine these two kinds of teachers. Picture to yourself a school-teacher who starts her thirteen-year-old children off with what she calls the "principles of design." They are, first, she says, "Rhythm," which she defines as "joint movement or action"; second, "Harmony," or "the consistency of likeness," and third, "Balance," or "that repose which results from the opposition of attractions." It would not be strange if the children did not understand. Such a teacher is what we call "academic."

On the other hand, picture a teacher in a continuation

school who comes to his superintendent after the third day, and says: " I have shown the boys all I know about wiping joints, fitting pipes and using tools — what shall I teach them next?" This teacher is what would be called " practical."

In our revolt against academic teaching, which is merely brains without experience, we are in danger of going to the other " practical " extreme, which is experience without brains. One is half-baked philosophy — the other is rule-of-thumb. One extreme is the academic or normal school graduate who knows only the intellectual forms of education, and does not know by experience the shop practice that those forms are to be applied to. The other extreme is the mere shop-man or mechanic, who knows how to do a thing with his hands, but does not know anything of the science, philosophy or mathematics that are necessary to make the thing an intelligent process, and are necessary to set the worker to thinking out the reasons for the job that he is merely imitating.

The one is the type that leads to manual training, in order to supplement academic philosophy; the other that leads to trade schools, in order to supply manual dexterity. Neither leads to that combination of the shop and the school that should distinguish the method of the continuation school. A continuation school does not always need machinery and tools, like a manual training school — indeed, the great continuation schools of Magdeburg and Berlin in Germany have no machine equipment whatever. It is the mind, not the hand, that they are teaching. The hand is taught in the factory — the mind in the continuation school.

Far more important than the machinery and tools is the supply of teachers. The danger in Wisconsin grows out of our sudden and comprehensive plan of stimulating industrial education without securing in advance the quality of teachers required. Every town that starts a school and gets full attendance gets thereby a share of the state fund, and the effort in some of the towns is directed more to forcing large numbers of children into the schools from the homes as well as the factories, in order to qualify for the state fund, than it is to making sure that they will get the right kind of instruction after they are forced in. This may give an appearance of success, but, if it is success based on the police power of the state rather than the useful education secured, the success will only be temporary. The first thing is to go slow on numbers and, above all else, *get teachers*. Then the numbers will come. We are, in fact, calling for a new profession in teaching — the profession of the practical man who can teach the theory and science that underlie his practice. We are, indeed, already well prepared to train these teachers, provided they have had the shop experience that is first in order. The Stout Institute at Menomonie is recognized the country over as a normal school without a superior in the training of industrial teachers. Every local industrial board could well afford, at its own expense, to give to its teachers who have had shop experience a summer course every year in that school.

In fact, the continuation school in Wisconsin[1] is the

---

[1] It is sometimes stated that the Wisconsin system is a "dual system," that is, that it separates industrial education from the common schools and places it under the commercializing direction of employers of labor. Such is not the case. The industrial boards which control these schools are composed of two manufacturers, two wage-earners, and the superintendent of schools, all appointed by the board of education. This system is necessary as an effort to get the industrial schools away from

first step in recognizing the most important need of both modern industry and modern education — the need of making *apprenticeship universal*.

The law of 1911 requires boys and girls under sixteen, and apprentices over sixteen, to attend five hours a week in the day-time. But employers can evade the apprenticeship part of the law by refusing to make apprenticeship contracts, or by cancelling contracts already made. The excuse which some employers have offered for thus evading it, is that they do not purpose to pay their boys for something they do not earn — they will not pay apprentices for going to school. This excuse is plausible for the individual employer who looks only at his own personal profits. It is not reasonable from the standpoint of the state that takes into account the interest of *all* employers, as well as the future working population that all industries must depend upon.

A more rational excuse would be that the kind of teaching secured does not help the boys to become more intelligent workmen. If this is true, then the blame is on the teachers in the continuation schools. In some places, with the right kind of teachers, employers are gladly making apprenticeship contracts, where formerly they refused them or had cancelled them. We may expect that when teachers of continuation schools have learned to teach the theory and science which modern apprenticeship requires, then all boys and girls up to eighteen, and perhaps even to twenty-one years of age, shall be

the academic control of the teaching profession that knows too little of the shop and factory conditions to be met. As a matter of fact, the industrial schools are actually controlled by the teaching profession, for that is the only one that can teach. The manufacturers and mechanics on the boards do not control, but they are an industrial counterweight to what would otherwise be academic control.

declared by law to be apprentices; and all shall be required to attend the school on their employers' time, regardless of any apprenticeship contract. With such a system of industrial education, beginning at fourteen, extending to eighteen or twenty-one and supplementing the training of the shop, we may expect considerably to erase that blot on our modern industry — the boy of seventeen to twenty, vainly wandering from shop to shop in search for higher wages and an illicit apprenticeship, and finally sinking into the class of stupid, low-paid workers, or the class of dependent paupers.

Even for the boys and girls between fourteen and sixteen years of age the true object of the continuation school is not so much to teach them a trade different from that of the industry in which they are employed. It is rather to teach them the essentials which lead to promotion in that or any other industry. Most of them, indeed, are engaged in what is known as " blind-alley " jobs, that lead nowhere. They think they want to take up something else, such as machinery, carpentry or stenography. But they are not yet ready to take up a trade. They lack those essentials of shop arithmetic, elementary book-keeping, shop organization, business correspondence and so on. In many cases they lack even the essentials of common school education which parochial or common schools should have given them before they attempt to qualify for the industrial essentials. All of these are necessary to advancement in the industry in which they are employed, and will also be found necessary to any other industry that they may afterwards fall into.

In the case of girls there is an additional problem. The employer who hires a girl must be looked upon as making a present profit at the expense of the future homes of the state, as well as a profit at the expense of the girl's own future promotion in industry. It is but just that the employer should give up a few hours of his girl's time that she may get instruction in home-keeping, cooking, sewing and the like, as well as industrial and business essentials. This applies to both boys and girls in all of those subjects which the Wisconsin law includes under instruction in health, safety, citizenship and business. These are essentials that every workingman and workingwoman should know, for upon them depend their future ability to take care of themselves, and thus to become steady and successful workers instead of casual workers, paupers and dependents.

Of course, not all can get promotion to the higher positions. Machine industry compels the majority to stay with the machine and to remain common laborers. But the amazing stupidity of these workers, as it shows itself at the employment office, disqualifies them even for finding jobs at machinery or common labor. The one great handicap of this mass of laborers is their lack of intelligence. They do not know even how to hunt a job, still less to keep it. If the continuation schools can furnish them just simple ordinary intelligence, it will raise their level much above their present stage.

The law does not as yet apply, in its compulsory attendance requirements, to children who work at home, nor to girls in domestic service, nor to children on the farm. These have not, of course, been drawn into the stream that runs through the modern factory. But for them, industrial education should have a place as well as for the factory worker. Here the problem widens out and reaches into nearly every home. In some towns the continuation schools are beginning to provide for them. Outside the towns it is the problem of the rural schools in agricultural education. As fast as teachers are equipped, in town or country, for the kind of instruction that their children require, so fast may we expect the people and the lawmakers to require their children to attend.

Thus gradually shall we approach the new apprenticeship that modern business, in industry and agriculture, imperatively demands. It must be *universal;* in that every boy and girl must become a *business man,* if he would hold his own in the increasing competition of buying and selling; he must become an *intelligent worker,* if he would advance beyond the dead-line of dependency on others; he must become a *citizen,* in fact as well as law, if he would take his part in the complicated government that determines his opportunities and his burdens; he must protect his *health,* if he would stand the strain of study and exertion that are the first condition of promotion. All of these requirements are common to all occupations, yet no occupation of modern industry teaches them. The gap must be filled by the state, the school, the teacher. This is not trade education, nor even vocational education — it is that universal apprenticeship that is common to all trades and vocations.

I have been able to sketch only an outline of the relations between industrial education and dependency. Industrial education is one of the essential things needed to offset the monotony and specialization of modern industry, and to enable workmen to find and keep their jobs. Monotony and specialization terminate in mental degradation, irregular work, underpaid work or pauperism, for the grown-up workingmen of the state, although it is seemingly offset by fallacious high wages for boys. The boys make more money than their fathers who have gone through the same machine, and so their fathers get the pauper's idea of living on the wages of their children. Thus the evils create each other in a vicious circle. It would be far better for the boys to get lower wages, if thereby they get industrial education. This would be the case if all boys under eighteen, or perhaps twenty-one, were by law treated as apprentices. Not until such a policy is adopted can we predict that industrial education will do much toward reducing the amount of dependency that modern industry produces. Even then, there are many other things that are also necessary — a state-wide system of employment offices to reduce the time lost between jobs — to bring employees to the jobs they are fitted for — to equalize employment in dull seasons and busy seasons — to shorten hours of labor for monotonous and specialized work. Other policies that are necessary might also be mentioned. But this, at least, can be said for the state that takes the lead in industrial education, — if it adopts a comprehensive system for all boys and girls; if it exerts itself above all else to bring out and train teachers who combine practical shop work with an understanding of the theories and sciences that underlie intelligent shop work, and with ability to teach, then such a state will take the lead in the industrial development of the country. It will afford a wider range of selection for the mechanics, foremen and intelligent leaders in its industries. It will produce a larger proportion of steady and intelligent workers. It will produce a smaller proportion of helpless and ill-fitted workers — an expensive charge on the growing and changing industries of the state, or on the taxpayers who must provide their useless support.

Of course, it takes time. Social progress does not spring suddenly, like a full-grown talking-machine from the forehead of Edison. Three million people cannot figure out together in advance just what they will want. They can only pass upon the results after they have happened. It is the business of those who do the planning to know in advance what the results will be. Otherwise reaction occurs, and the programme goes further backward than it was at the beginning. This is especially true of such a profound and far-reaching reform as industrial education through the continuation school. It reaches into almost every workshop and every home in the state. It goes to the very sources of prosperity and poverty. No greater undertaking could be espoused by a democratic people. No other possesses greater promise of usefulness. Failures here and there will occur, but successes here and there will confute them. So important and vital is the movement that the failures must be promptly corrected and the successes be made universal. Then we may expect that industrial education will be accepted and enlarged ; that it will contribute a decisive share toward the reduction of dependency and the elevation of independence.

CHAPTER XXI

THE INDUSTRIAL COMMISSION OF WISCONSIN [1]

THE power to adopt measures for the protection of employees is a legislative power. The legislature must specify the things to be protected, and the courts construe their specifications strictly. If the law says that tumbling rods, set screws, shafting and all dangerous machinery must be safeguarded, an inspector has no authority to order a buzz saw to be safeguarded, because it is not like a tumbling rod, set screw or shafting. The inspector has no discretion in extending the law beyond the kind of things specified.

But, while the inspector's discretion is limited in extent, it has considerable range in another direction. He has authority to determine how much or how little the things specified shall be protected. The legislature gives authority to each inspector to go into an establishment and to order changes to be made such as will, in his judgment, make the machinery safe. The degree of safety, in the last analysis, turns upon the discretion of the inspector who makes the examination. Power is practically delegated to him in carrying out a legislative act.

In foreign countries, especially on the continent of Europe, the method is different. There the legislature

[1] Address delivered at Chicago Conference of American Association for Labor Legislation, Sept., 1911. *American Labor Legislation Review*, Vol. I, No. 4. This article is a foreword, prepared when the Commission was just beginning. The next article followed a year and a half of experience.

enacts a general rule or order requiring that all machinery and working places shall be kept safe and hygienic, and then leaves it to the administration officials to work out the details and to issue orders which shall determine how that law shall apply to different industries. So when, in France, parliament adopted a law requiring one day's rest in seven, it enacted a general law in a few words, and since that time the president of the republic through the Minister of Commerce and Labor, has been issuing orders prescribing the specific hours and days of labor in different industries.

But in America the legislature is supreme. The administration can issue only such orders as the legislature definitely lays down. Otherwise legislative power would be delegated, and, under our constitutions, with their dread of tyranny, this cannot be done. In order to get away from this restriction we have been compelled to create commissions, giving them power to issue orders similar in effect, but different in theory and procedure, to those issued in Europe. This came about first in the health department, and the Board of Health has power, within limits, to issue orders having the effect of law, as though issued by the legislature.

Following this has come the regulation of railroads and public utilities. Instead of enacting a law prescribing rates and services, the legislature merely enacts a general law requiring rates and services to be reasonable. A railroad commission is then created and authorized to investigate the facts and to discover and establish what is reasonable in each case. When the commission has published the rate, all parties interested can have a hearing. Everybody has an opportunity to protest and to present other facts, and then the order is finally issued and is binding. But any one dissatisfied can go into court and plead that it is unreasonable. If the court sustains him, it will issue an injunction against the enforcement of that order.

It is the theory of this procedure that the commission has no discretion. It merely investigates and announces a fact. That fact is the reasonable thing the legislature had in mind, but did not have the time and means to discover.

The procedure conforms to the theory. Everybody affected by the order must have had a chance to tell the facts he knew, and the commission must give them due weight. Finally, the court protects him against any unlawful act of the commission.

In the state of Wisconsin one very important device has been introduced to protect the Railroad Commission before the state courts. This is the provision that when an order of the commission is contested in court and an injunction is asked for, the railroad company is prohibited from bringing in any evidence which it has not already presented to the commission. If it presents any new evidence in court which it did not give to the commission, then the court is required immediately to send the whole case back to the commission and to give to it the opportunity to consider the new evidence and to modify its decision. This has taken away from the state courts the arbitrary feature of the injunction, because the commission is in better position than the court to get the facts. The court is restricted to technical rules of evidence. The commission takes any evidence which is presented; it can send out its own investigators to get facts openly or in secret. It forms its own conclusions and issues its orders on the basis of more facts than the court admits. Then when the case comes into court, the facts as stated by the commission are *prima facie* true. The court, of course, cannot be restrained from going behind these facts, but the law makes the commission in effect the standing referee of the court in matters of investigation. The commission can make investigations along economic and sociological lines, a procedure not practicable for the courts. If they could have made these investigations, and were not tied down by technical rules, the injunction would not have been a menace to reasonable regulation. For we certainly can trust the integrity of the courts as much as the integrity of a commission. But here we have not merely a matter of integrity — we have a problem of expert investigation.

If, then, the facts thus acquired bring the case within the police power of the state, the court sustains the commission. This has been the attitude of the Supreme Court of Wisconsin toward the Railroad Commission. The industrial commission law applies the same theory and procedure to the relations of capital and labor that the railroad commission law applies to the relations of public corporations and consumers.

One reason why labor questions in American states have not been acted upon according to the theory of a commission is the fact that the labor department is composed of a single chief and several deputies acting individually. The chief and each deputy have equal authority, and there are as many standards as there are deputies. The theory of the law is that the legislature has set the standard, and all the deputies are acting alike. But this theory is impracticable. There must be some leeway. It is the method of reaching a decision within this leeway that the constitution protects. " Due process of law " requires that decisions should be reached through public hearings after due notice so that all parties can have a voice. Then, after such thorough investigation, orders can be issued based on the findings.

But, properly, the investigation and decision should be made by more than one person. A single commissioner might be given the power to issue these orders, but our dread of tyranny revolts at this suggestion in matters affecting property interests. Consequently, the thing has worked itself out in public utility matters, so that we have adopted a commission usually of three members in the states, while the Interstate Commerce Commission is composed of seven. The industrial commission law of Wisconsin provides for a commission of three. It lifts the matter up from the level of decisions based on the opinions of a number of factory inspectors and concentrates it in the hands of three men, giving them power to get all the facts. At the same time the legislature lays down the general rule that every employer shall furnish to his employees the necessary protection to life, health, safety and welfare. This places the obligation upon the employer. He must maintain his place of employment and its premises so that the employee shall not incur the risk of accident. He must furnish safety devices and safeguards. He must adopt methods and processes which shall be safe for the employees.

But it is not left to the employer to tell what are those safe methods and processes, nor is it left to the factory inspectors. To the Industrial Commission is assigned the duty of investigating and ascertaining what safety devices and safeguards, what means, methods and processes, are best adapted to render the factory safe. Having ascertained what they are, the commission issues an order prescribing that they shall be installed for each factory or each class of factories. This, then, is the lawful order which all are required to observe.

The situation regarding prosecutions now takes on a different aspect. Hitherto, if a factory inspector went into a factory and found a machine not protected, he gave orders to the manufacturer to put on a protective device, and allowed, say, thirty days. If after thirty days the manufacturer had not complied, the inspector brought the matter to the justice's court. The justice had before him the factory inspector as prosecuting witness and the manufacturer as defendant. The justice perhaps immediately asked the inspector how he knew whether or not the machine was safe, or whether the device would make it safe, and went on to say that the manufacturer perhaps knew as much about it as the inspector. The case might not even go to the jury to decide the facts. The judge might say " case dismissed " on the ground of insufficient reason.

The great difficulty of factory inspection laws has been the prosecutions. Under the new Wisconsin law the question of reasonableness or necessity cannot be raised in the justice's court. The only question that can come up in the lower court is: What was the standard set by the commission for that machine? and the question for justice or jury then becomes: Did the manufacturer put on the safety device or not? One cannot raise the question in that court as to whether that is the right kind of a device. If he wants to raise that question, he can do it in two ways: (1) Appeal to the commission on the ground that the order is not adapted to his factory.

The commission must then hold a hearing and decide upon it. (2) Then if he is not satisfied, he cannot go back to the justice's court, but must prosecute the commission itself. There is but one court in the state where this can be done, the court of Dane County at the capital of the state. This action is given precedence over other actions of a different nature. It is carried thence to the Supreme Court. So the question of prosecution takes on a different aspect. Justices' courts now cannot take up the question of the validity of the order. They are restricted to the question of facts.

Furthermore, the factory inspector does not issue any orders. He merely notifies the commission, which in turn notifies the employer and issues an order, if necessary. Thus the inspector is both supported by standards well known throughout the trade, and shorn of that petty authority that sometimes irritates. The manufacturers also are in a better position, because they have a voice in making the standard through public hearings, and they have themselves taken part in deciding on what is to be adapted to their individual circumstances. The procedure is the same as when the Railroad Commission established the measure for 1000 cubic feet of gas. The engineer of the commission drew up his proposed orders as to what 1000 feet of gas should be, how rapidly it should flow, how the instruments should be constructed to measure it, what candle power it should yield and so on. This tentative measure was then sent over the state, and to outside experts, and the gas manufacturers came to Madison for their hearing. As a result of this hearing two standards were established: one for large cities and one for small cities. So it would be in standardization of safety and sanitation. Some qualified person, acting under the commission, would send out his tentative specifications, providing for what he thought was necessary to make the industry safe, and, after manufacturers, employees and others interested had examined the schedule, they would come together and discuss the matter with the commission. When the proper thing was decided upon, it would be adopted as a rule and be put into effect.

In the public utilities law, the legislature simply adopts the rule that rates shall be " reasonable." In labor legislation we have a different situation. The legislature may enact a rule that factories or places of employment shall be " reasonably safe," but reasonably safe, according to law, means just ordinary safety that any employer would exercise without taking extra care. That would not be a high standard for legislation. It would not make it possible for the commission to get the same kind of reasonable regulation as they get in railroad rates. Here it is not an ordinary railroad rate; it is something more. The definition for safety which appears in this law is as follows : " *The term ' safe ' or ' safety' as applied to an employment or a place of employment shall mean such freedom from danger to the life, health or safety of employees or frequenters as the nature of the employment will reasonably permit.*" We are required to have the word " reasonable," which in law means due consideration of all the facts in the case. Otherwise, the law is unconstitutional. But we need something more than ordinary safety. If any new methods of safety have been devised and are practicable, and therefore reasonable, the commission can require all employers to put them in, for they are as reasonable as the nature of the employment will permit. In other words, it is possible by this definition of safety to improve the standards and to secure more than ordinary safety.

Both employer and employee are required to observe these orders of the commission. The requirement upon employees is a new feature arising from the fact that the employer under the new compensation law must pay damages to the employee who injures himself, as well as to the employee who is injured through the negligence of a fellow-employee. The old doctrine held that, if a person injured himself (and everybody could do as he pleased with himself) the employer need not pay for the injury. The question which now arises is, can the employee be compelled to make use of the safety devices which are furnished? Under the old liability law, if a moulder let melted iron fall on his feet, that was not the fault of the employer. He could not bring suit against the employer and get damages for his burned feet, but under the compensation law he can. The employer will be required to pay him 65 per cent of the loss of wages for injury which he has suffered. Now, the employer would naturally want that man to wear Congress shoes that could be quickly snatched off, and he might even furnish them to him at cost. The question arises, can that man be compelled to wear those protective shoes? This is an open question and is not decided. It is attempted, however, in this law to come as near to it as possible. There are two points: (1) Employees can be required to refrain from destroying devices which the employer puts in. (2) Employees can be punished for preventing another employee from using safety devices. The other question, whether he can be punished for refusing to use them himself, is an open one. The law reads: " No employee shall remove, displace, damage, destroy or carry off any safety device or safeguard furnished and provided for use in any employment or place of employment, nor interfere in any way with the use thereof by any other person, nor shall any such employee interfere with the use of any method or process adopted for the protection of any employee in such employment or place of employment or frequenter of such place of employment, nor fail or neglect to do every other thing reasonably necessary to protect the life, health, safety or welfare of such employees or frequenters." The commission would be called upon to issue a rule requiring the moulder to wear boots, and then the question would arise, would the courts sustain this order? It certainly is reasonable, from the standpoint of workmen's compensation, that employees shall take care of themselves and thus protect the employer in his new duties of protecting them.

Another feature is the control which the commission has over the construction of new factories. New buildings must be cared for as to safety and sanitation, the same as old ones. The law says that " no employer or other person shall hereafter construct or occupy or maintain any place of employment that is not safe."

There are three kinds of orders dealt with in the law: (1) general orders applying to all manufacturers or all persons of the same class throughout the state; (2) special orders applying only to one factory, one establishment or one person; (3) local orders, or orders of similar and conflicting nature issued by municipal councils, boards of aldermen or local boards of health. It is provided that if the commission standardizes an industry and issues its orders, any rule of a local board in conflict therewith shall be void. Meanwhile the local

board can go ahead and issue their orders, the employer
being protected by the right of appeal to the state commission to determine whether there is a conflict or
whether the local order is unreasonable.   This is necessary in order to have uniformity of standards throughout
the state.   It has been criticised as a violation of home
rule, but it is really a protection for local boards of health
and municipal councils, because their orders are subject
to court review and injunction.   The law simply provides
that if an employer objects to any prohibition in a local
rule, he is not allowed to go first into court, but must first
go to the commission.   Then if not satisfied with the
commission's orders, he can go into the Dane County
Court, and then to the Supreme Court.   Consequently,
uniformity of all orders is approximated and the local
boards are protected.

The practical outcome of this new procedure should be
a progressive and accurate adjustment of factory inspection to the changes in industry and the new risks
that accompany modern industry.   Hitherto, when it
was discovered that the buzz saw or the set screw had
been omitted from the law, it was necessary to get together the Federation of Labor, the Women's Trade
Union League, and all the friends of labor, to organize
them into a lobby and to go down to the legislature in
order to get the words " buzz saw " and " set screw "
inserted in the law.   Now it is only necessary for the
Industrial Commission to show that these things are
dangerous and the protection practicable.   The difference is obvious.   It now is practicable in Wisconsin,
without further legislation, for the Industrial Commission to adopt and enforce the admirable rules of the
Massachusetts Board of Boiler Rules, if they are found to

be adapted to Wisconsin conditions. So also, the commission may learn from the novel work of " medical " inspection of the Massachusetts Board of Health and the New York Department of Labor, and may adapt to Wisconsin, so far as practical, the best that other states and countries have been able to work out for safety and sanitation of work places.

This law goes further, with the object of centring in one body all the relations of employer and employees, just as the Railroad Commission centres in one body all of the relations of the public utility corporations and the consumers. Everything that comes up between the two interests is under the jurisdiction of one commission. This includes, for example, everything relating to bargains between employer and employee. The law abolishes the Board of Mediation and Arbitration and turns over that work to the commission with the aid of temporary local boards.

The same is true of unemployment. The commission has power to establish and conduct free employment agencies, and to supervise private agencies. It goes further with reference to directing apprentices and minors into promising employments. It takes up matters of industrial and agricultural training, and ·may establish offices in the state.

The legislature has not, however, given to the Industrial Commission any authority in the execution of the child labor, woman labor, and other labor laws similar to its authority in the factory inspection laws. The new ten-hour law for women, with its requirement of a full hour for dinner, has already pointed plainly to the need of such authority. Many cases have come up, especially in restaurants, where it seems that a public hearing would establish the fact that a different schedule of hours within the ten-hour limit would be more " reasonable " than the rigid schedule of the legislature. Perhaps, if the new law works well in safety and sanitation, its principles and procedure may be extended by a future legislature to additional subjects.[1]

[1] This has been done by the legislature of 1913. See next chapter.

CHAPTER XXII

INVESTIGATION AND ADMINISTRATION [1]

EMPLOYERS of Wisconsin paid $1,025,000 to liability insurance companies in 1911; scarcely $300,000 of it reached the pockets of the employees or their dependents. Ten thousand industrial accidents occur in Wisconsin each year; 100 of these are fatal; the others cause disability of seven days or more. But scarcely 10 per cent of the injured received any share of the $300,000.

This is the big problem of the Industrial Commission of Wisconsin —to reduce the $1,025,000 paid by employers, to raise the $300,000 received by employees, and to distribute it among 10,000 instead of 1000 employees. The commission has a margin of $725,000 to work upon, and a great margin of public welfare to promote. It can reduce the $1,025,000 by reducing accidents and improving the health of employees. It can increase the $300,000 and distribute it better by fixing definitely the compensation for all employees.

Instead of creating a commission to administer the compensation law, and then leaving the factory inspector to enforce the safety laws, as other states have done, the Wisconsin legislature of 1911 consolidated the two departments in a single commission. And instead of specifying the many details of factory inspection, the legislature boiled them down into one paragraph, re-

[1] *Survey*, Jan. 4, 1913, under the title, "Constructive Investigation and the Wisconsin Industrial Commission."

quiring the employer to protect the life, safety, health and welfare of employees, and authorizing the commission to draw up rules and orders specifying the details as to how it should be done.

The commission is a fourth branch of government combining, but not usurping, the work of the three other branches. It is a legislature continually in session, yet the power of legislation is not delegated. It is an executive sharing with the governor the enforcement of laws, but also enforcing its own orders. It is a court deciding cases that the judiciary formerly decided, but not assuming the authority of the courts.

This fourth function of government is sometimes designated as the administrative function. But administration, as usually understood, is merely the details of execution. Administration and execution are synonymous. The real distinction which entitles the commission to its position as a fourth branch of government is not administration, but investigation and research. But its investigations are not the academic research of the laboratory and study, nor the journalistic investigation of the agitator, but the constructive investigation of the administrator. It is this constructive investigation that gives to the commission its lawful position in government and its effective position in the enforcement of law.

Constructive investigation should tell us whether the damage to the employee is public in its nature, requiring legislation, or only private, requiring exhortation. It should reveal the nature and cause of the injury, its cure and the practicability of its prevention. It should lead to such administration of the law that those enjoined to obey it would respect and support it.

We concede that in legislation and administration for the protection of health and safety of employees, we are behind the nations of Europe. This is due partly to ignorance through lack of investigation, partly to piece-meal legislation that hits one evil at a time when it gets sufficiently exposed, partly to the veto of our courts. To those who, perhaps, look upon Americans as materialistic, we might protest that we have put into practice Plato's ideal of government by philosophers, for we have set apart a faculty of sociological philosophers in each state and the nation, who have the last word on our laws and their administration. Their vetoes often expound the philosophy that preceded the French Revolution, num-bering such sages as Grotius, Rousseau and Montesquieu, and such doctrines as the law of nature, natural rights and the general will. In harmony with the latter, and in conformity with constitutions framed during the vogue of that philosophy, they separate the body politic into three departments — the legislative, representing the general will; the executive, physically enforcing it; and the judiciary, the intellect over all.

Recently some dissatisfaction has arisen over this division of functions. It has shown itself in threats to " recall " the judges or to " recall their decisions." For some time, too, the executive departments, from president down to policeman, have not been content blindly to follow the legislature as the sole custodian of the general will, and have taken to themselves consider-able discretion in enforcing the laws. Citizens, also, take liberties with the general will, trusting to slip through somewhere between the three branches of gov-ernment.

But the courts have begun to recognize another branch

of government. This branch has come forth especially to provide for that extension of the police power required to meet the rapidly changing and widely varying conditions of modern life and business. It, therefore, combines to a certain degree, the activities of legislation, execution and judgment; but its peculiar activity, which gives it a separate place as the custodian of the police power in the body politic, is that of investigation. It is upon the validity of its investigations that it is allowed to execute the general will and to survive the scrutiny of the courts.

The doctrine which the court applies to this function of investigation is both the noblest and the most practical of legal doctrines — "reasonableness." By this doctrine the court applies its philosophy to the particular facts, but requires that all of the facts be taken into account. The drastic programme of disciplining the courts by the recall on the ground that they are removed from acquaintance with the common life and are living in an eighteenth century philosophy, might be somewhat modified if advantage were taken of this exalted doctrine. It may be that the critics of the judiciary have not performed their part in bringing before the court all of the facts of the modern development of industry and society which the doctrine of reasonableness requires. Counsel often leaves the court in the predicament of falling back on its own knowledge of what is " common knowledge." Often this kind of knowledge is several years behind the times, because a serious injury to the common good usually arises and spreads extensively before the scientific experts and the journalistic agitators are able to make it a matter of common knowledge. The investigative branch of government should be the one that furnishes the court with judicial knowledge of injury to the public in advance of common knowledge. Being also an administrative branch, it should carry over promptly the results of scientific investigation into their practical application. Its function of the police power is the power of reasonable regulation through constructive investigation.

The legal doctrine of reasonableness provides ample opportunity for protective legislation if once its principles and procedure are complied with. It requires that all of the facts must be considered and weighed " as may be just and right in each case." It prohibits class legislation, but permits classification. The one is based on merely private or class benefit, the other on public benefit ascertained by investigation. While permitting reasonable classification it requires equal treatment of all in the same class. Its conclusions must be practical under existing conditions.

The procedure for securing these standards is well known to the law. It centres on the main requirement that all parties affected shall have opportunity to be heard, and when this is complied with, the findings of the properly constituted board or commission become *prima facie* the facts of the case and the reasonable regulation to be enforced. Its findings are the conclusive results of constructive investigation.

Thus, in addition to the legislature expressing the general will, the judiciary testing it by its political philosophy of the constitution, and the executive enforcing it, we have the administrative branch of government investigating its application to existing conditions in the light of existing science and practice, for the information of all branches of government.

The several states and the federal Congress have recently sought in various fields to elevate this work of investigation to the high position in our frame of government that the courts had assigned to it in the procedure of government. The legislatures had previously from time to time broken up the executive department by creating separate departments to execute specific commands of the legislature. Usually a single officer was placed at the head of each of these departments, until a great variety of minor executives had arisen, such as the health officer, the factory inspector, the railroad commissioner and so on.

At the same time the legislature attempted to enumerate in detail the things that each officer should do and each citizen obey. Two difficulties appeared. The courts often declared these elaborate laws unconstitutional, as being unreasonable, and the executives were restrained from dealing with any specific evil that the legislature had failed to enumerate. These difficulties first appeared in the health department, and the legislatures proceeded to change the character of that department by creating a board of physicians, with power to issue orders based on their expert knowledge and having the force of law, though not enumerated in the law. Next, in the regulation of railroads, instead of the detailed schedules of rates that characterized the early granger laws, the legislatures advanced to the position which culminated in the railroad and public utility laws of Wisconsin, — of merely declaring (what the courts had already declared) that rates and services should be "reasonable," but creating a commission with powers of investigation equal to those of the courts, to discover and announce in each case as it arose what was the reasonable rate or service. Where the investigations of the courts are limited by the technical rules of testimony, the commission can investigate, on its own initiative and in its own way, all the circumstances that it considers relevant. In fact, the commission is made a kind of standing referee of the court, directed by the legislature to report all of the facts that go to determine what is reasonable. Instead of a referee appointed by the court, usually a lawyer with the lawyer's limitations as to the relative value of different facts, the commission is a body of men compelled by their duties to give weight to social and economic facts that otherwise do not get before the court.

Wisconsin now has ventured to adopt this same principle in matters of labor legislation. The occasion grew out of the adoption of a workmen's compensation law, wherein it was deemed necessary to create a state Industrial Accident Board with power to decide all disputed claims for compensation. These claims, in the Wisconsin law, are not specific amounts for enumerated injuries, but are a certain proportion of the loss in wages. The accident board was made the investigating body to ascertain the actual loss in each case where appeal was made, and to make an award on that basis.

At the same time it was realized that compensation should not be merely a new kind of employer's liability, but should be an additional means of preventing accidents. Consequently, the legislature proceeded to abolish the old bureau of factory inspection, as well as the Industrial Accident Board, which it had just created, and to merge the two into a new administrative and investigating board, to be known as the Industrial Commission. Instead of the long list of dangerous points, such as set screws, belts, fire escapes, dust, etc., which successive legislatures had accumulated during the past thirty years, the new law expresses the general will in the most general way, as the duty of the employer to safeguard the life, health, safety and welfare of employees and frequenters, and the duty of employees to coöperate with their employers.

The law applies as broadly as possible, not to enumerated factories, shops, etc., but to all "places of employment," except agricultural and domestic employments not using mechanical power. In effect, all physical property used to furnish employment to labor is declared to be " affected by a public use," and must be so managed as to promote the public welfare in the persons of those who come within its zone of danger.

The definition of safety is not that of the " ordinary " safety of the common law, but " such freedom from danger to the life, health or safety or welfare of employees or frequenters, as the nature of the employment will reasonably permit." The definition of welfare is " comfort, decency and moral well-being."

Here, then, is the field of investigation assigned to the commission. It must call to its aid scientific experts in engineering and hygiene. It must ascertain where danger lies and where life, health, safety and welfare are menaced. It must discover the devices, processes and management that will avoid these dangers, and must ascertain whether they are practicable. This is the constructive investigation that conforms to reasonableness. Once ascertained and published as an " order " of the commission, the conclusions of its investigations have the force of law, the will of the legislature is executed, the philosophy of the court is observed.

As a matter of economy to the state and convenience to employers, as well as recognition of the wide scope of administrative investigation, all of the departments dealing with employees and employment were consolidated under the same commission. These include the state employment offices, the board of arbitration, child labor, street trades, truancy, women's hours of labor, apprenticeship, etc. In the matter of employment the commission is authorized to use all of its power to eliminate unemployment, by the establishment of free offices, supervision of private agencies, coöperation with agencies for vocational and industrial education, etc. In the matter of arbitration it is limited to voluntary conciliation, with powers of compulsory investigation. The legislature did not go so far as to authorize the commission to investigate and determine reasonable hours of labor for women and children, apart from the rigid limits laid down in the law, so that the procedure described in this article applies mainly to life, health, safety, welfare and compensation, with limited application to unemployment, conciliation and street trades.[1]

In the matter of organization such combination of duties as deliberation, investigation, hearings, findings of fact and execution of laws suggests a board or commission of more than one member, acting jointly, instead of the single head of an executive department. Although each matter is determined jointly, yet each requires to be handled from the three standpoints of legality, investigation and execution. The members cannot be experts in all the technical fields of engineering, hygiene,

[1] The legislature of 1913 extended the same principle to the regulation of women's hours of labor, prohibited employments for minors, private employment offices and public buildings.

sanitation and so on, but they certainly must be capable of conducting investigations and determining their scope and the legality of their action, as well as organizing and handling a field force of inspectors and deputies. The Industrial Commission law leaves to the governor and senate a wide range of selection, in that the specific qualifications of commissioners are not prescribed, but the selections actually made at the inauguration of the present commission have been made with this threefold division of law, investigation and execution in mind.

It goes without saying that the selection of commissioners, and the selection of subordinates are the two decisive factors that determine the success or failure of administration. Wisconsin has had for seven years a Civil Service Commission, and nearly all of the employees of the Industrial Commission were placed under the provisions of the civil service law. This has worked to advantage, although the Industrial Commission law has required a reversal of the original theory of civil service examinations. Instead of classified positions and salaries fixed by the legislature, the Industrial Commission fixes the compensation of its employees, makes its own classification and transfers employees from one class to another. The legislature creates but two positions, that of " deputies " and that of clerks. The intention is to substitute for the competition of candidates for a job fixed by the legislature, the opposite process of competing against other employers for the services of employees fitted for positions which the commission creates. The civil service law is indispensable, in that it offers a permanent tenure similar to that of private employment. It obstructs, if conducted in such a way that those who are doing the best work for private employers are unwilling to become candidates in a formal examination for a public office. The Civil Service Commission of Wisconsin adapts its examinations to these conditions, so that through coöperation of the two commissions, the deputies of the Industrial Commission are coming to have the full confidence of employers and employees as practical men.

This, it will be seen, is essential in the conduct of investigations and the administration of orders that shall comply with the doctrine of reasonableness. When the commission began its work of selecting its staff, it had entertained the idea that it should place at the head of its safety and sanitation work engineering and medical experts. But after interviewing a number of these experts it was discovered that they considered their problem to be that of drawing up ideal or standard specifications, which the commission, going out then with a " big stick," should compel employers to adopt.

For two reasons, this was decided to be impossible. A monarchical country, like Germany, with its executive independent of political changes, might call in its experts and be governed by them, but a democratic country would not consent to be ruled by those whose ideal standards might be removed from the everyday conditions of business. This decision of the commission also conforms to the doctrine of reasonableness, which requires practicability adapted to existing conditions. It was found that most of the successful work in safety and sanitation during the past ten years had not been in charge of technical engineers, but had been in charge of shopmen or even claim agents of the corporation; and their success had come about, not mainly through their knowledge as mechanical experts, but through their ability to get the services of engineers and medical men when needed, and especially their ability to get the co-operation of superintendents, foremen and workmen in a united effort to stop accidents and preserve health. In other words, they were experts in arousing the spirit of " safety first " and in organizing the shop so as to keep that spirit on top. For, scarcely a third of the accidents can be prevented merely by mechanical safe-guards — at least two-thirds must be prevented by attention, instruction and discipline.[1]

It is also this spirit of safety among the shopmen that brings out the most effective safeguards — effective in the sense of full protection without interfering with output. The engineer can devise safeguards — he needs the shopman to safeguard the output. The " safety expert " is the one who can bring these two elements together, and thus work out the practical rules for the commission to adopt. He guides the investigators, who determine what is " reasonable " both in the shop and in court. It is for this reason that the Wisconsin Commission has not been able to follow the remarkable and extensive safeguards devised and enforced in Germany. They seem to lack that element of practicability, which the shopman, as distinguished from the technical expert, insists upon.

But in the arrangement finally decided upon, the scientist, the engineer, the physician, the sanitarian, who are the technical experts, are called in and utilized, just as they are in private employment, when their services are needed and when the practical men have problems beyond their technical knowledge. If, however, the

[1] The commission has begun a promising campaign among employers and workmen to secure "shop organization for safety."

scientists dominated the investigations, their results, however brilliant and conclusive, might not be reasonable. Their investigations are indispensable and fundamental, and must be taken into account and should be liberally provided for. But, unless they lead to practicability, which only can be supplied by the practical man, they run the risk of unconstitutionality. It is for this reason that the representative of the Wisconsin Commission, at the meeting of the section on hygiene of occupations of the recent International Congress on Hygiene and Demography, resisted the proposed resolution of turning over all investigations of industrial hygiene to medical men. A similar resolution had been adopted, naturally enough, at a previous session held in Europe. The American delegates were willing to accept the substitute that investigations in physiology and pathology should be entrusted to medical men, but this substitute was not approved by the permanent commission. Constructive investigation differs from scientific investigation in that it must be guided towards practical ends under existing conditions. The distinction is vital in America, if not in Europe, for that which is scientific may be unconstitutional, because not reasonably practical.

But the selection of a proper staff is not enough to insure practicability. The Wisconsin law authorizes the commission to appoint " advisors " without compensation, to assist the commission in any of its duties. Acting on this authority, the commission invites the Wisconsin Manufacturers' Association and the Merchants' and Manufacturers' Association of Milwaukee, as well as other associations of special trades, such as the master bakers, the woodworkers, etc., to name representatives;

also the Wisconsin State Federation of Labor, the employers' liability insurance companies and the Wisconsin Employers' Mutual Liability Company organized in Wisconsin after the German model under the compensation law; and in addition the commission invited certain corporations which had done the best safety work in the state to permit their safety experts to meet with the committees. The commission also secured the assistance of physicians on special subjects, of the chief sanitary officers of the cities of Milwaukee and Chicago, of the State Board of Health, the State Hygienic Laboratory and representatives of the Consumers' League and the State Federation of Women's Clubs. These various representatives were grouped into a main Committee on Safety and Sanitation, with sub-committees on boilers, elevators, bakeries, sanitation and so on, and deputies of the commission were assigned to work with them. In this way the commission has had the assistance of scientific experts, of representatives of the interests affected by the orders to be issued, representatives of the public as consumers, representatives of overlapping agencies such as insurance companies and boards of health, and its own experts.

This has brought to the commission the assistance of some of the leading men of the state in their several lines of work. These men have given an astonishing amount of time, at their own expense, which, if paid for at commercial rates, would have required an expenditure far beyond the appropriation which the legislature allowed to the commission. Such men have looked upon their work not merely as a public service, but mainly as a vital matter in the future conduct of manufacturing in the state. The following partial list of these advisory committees indicates the wide range of representative expert and practical men to whom the commission and the state are indebted for this fundamental part of its work :

Committee on Safety and Sanitation: Representing Wisconsin State Federation of Labor: Joseph Gressler, machinist, Milwaukee; George Krogstad, patternmaker, Milwaukee.

Representing Milwaukee Merchants' & Manufacturers' Association: Charles P. Bossert, Pfister & Vogel Leather Company; Edward J. Kearney, Kearney & Trecker Company (machinery), chairman of committee.

Representing Milwaukee Health Department: Joseph Derfus, chief sanitary inspector.

Representing Wisconsin Manufacturers' Association: Thomas McNeill, Sheboygan Chair Company, Sheboygan; H. W. Bolens, Gilson Manufacturing Company (engines), Port Washington.

Representing Employers' Mutual Liability Company, Wausau: W. C. Landon (lumber), Wausau.

Representing Industrial Commission of Wisconsin: John W. Mapel, Pfister & Vogel Leather Company; Fred W. McKee, Fairbanks-Morse Company (engines), Beloit; Ira L. Lockney, deputy to the Industrial Commission; C. W. Price, assistant to the Industrial Commission and secretary of the committee.

Sub-committee on Elevators: C. F. Ringer, inspector of buildings, City of Milwaukee; Otto Fischer, inspector of elevators, City of Milwaukee; P. Jermain, Otis Elevator Company; F. A. Barker, inspector of safety, Ætna Life Insurance Company; G. N. Chapman, inspector of safety, Travellers' Insurance Company; John Humphrey, deputy to Industrial Commission; C. W. Price, assistant to Industrial Commission.

Sub-committee on Boilers: Theodore Vilter, superintendent Vilter Manufacturing Company (boilers); W. D. Johnson, secretary, Milwaukee Boiler Company; H. F. Bowie, boiler inspector, Hartford Steam Boiler Insurance & Inspection Company; J. Humphrey, deputy to Industrial Commission; R. Kunz, chief examiner and inspector of stationary engines, Board of Examiners of Milwaukee.

Sub-committee on Electricity: Walter Nield, chief electrician

Illinois Steel Company, Milwaukee; Charles Dietz, chief electrician, Commonwealth Power Company, Milwaukee; Thomas E. Barnum, chief electrician of a company making controlling apparatus, and chairman of the Electric Engineers' Society of Milwaukee; P. A. Schroeder and W. S. Gute, State Federation of Labor.

Sub-committee on Sanitation: Fred Swartz, Pfister & Vogel Leather Company, Milwaukee; H. W. Page, Sturtevant Company; A. W. Ruttan, Metal Polishers' Union, Milwaukee; C. B. Ball, chief sanitary inspector, Board of Health, Chicago.

Committee on Safety Exhibit: Walter Goll, factory manager, Fort Wayne Electric Works, Madison; Hobart S. Johnson, vice-president, Gisholt Machine Company, Madison; Frank C. Niebuhr, Carpenters' Union, Madison.

Committee on Bakeries: Frank Schieffer, Association of Master Bakers, Milwaukee; August Schmitt, Association of Master Bakers, Milwaukee; M. H. Carpenter, Wisconsin Association of Master Bakers, Milwaukee; R. Colvin, Wisconsin Wholesale Bakers' Association, Janesville; C. B. Ball, chief sanitary inspector, Board of Health, Chicago; C. J. Kremer, bakery inspector, Industrial Commission.

These committees proceed to make their investigations, to draw up tentative rules and to submit them to the commission for public hearings. After the hearings, the rules are referred back to the committee for further investigation, and finally, as rapidly as completed, are issued by the commission as " General Orders " applying to the entire state, and are published in the official paper and in the bulletins of the commission.

The commission has also been greatly aided by the United States Bureau of Labor, which made investigations of laundries and pea canning establishments in the state, availing itself of contemporaneous investigations made by the commission. The bureau's investigation of course had reference to the adoption of rules that would be applicable to all the states. These investigations suggest an invaluable arrangement that might be made by which the federal bureau could furnish scientific experts and investigators whose work would be at the disposal of the states. The latter are not always in position to carry on systematically this line of investigation, and if they should do so the great object of uniformity throughout all the states would not be sufficiently cared for. Besides, the federal bureau, not being encumbered with administrative duties, is in a position to carry on scientific investigations, which would be all the more valuable when directed towards the constructive needs of the state departments.

The fact that both the law and the commission contemplated the coöperation of employers and employees, has resulted in a code of rules which are not only reasonable in law but reasonable in the minds of employers. It is an application of the well-recognized principle of political economy that the competition of the worst employers tends to drag down the best employers to their level. In this case, however, the corollary law is brought into play. The most progressive employers in the line of safety and sanitation draw up the law, and the business of the commission is to go out and bring the backward ones up to their level. As a matter of fact, it has been found that the employers on the committees have been more exacting in their search for the highest practicable standards than the representatives of labor on the committees. As a consequence, the work of the commission in bringing other employers up to their level has been almost entirely transformed from what they consider an irritating and arbitrary interference in their business, into a work of instruction and education. The employer who resists the adoption of safeguards and processes approved by his fellow-employers is not only unreasonable in the opinion of his peers, but *prima facie* unreasonable in court.

The work of education which the commission has naturally resorted to has been that of bringing to the attention of employers not only the rules but the devices and methods which will comply with them. A safety exhibit, or rather a triplicate exhibit, after being passed upon by an advisory committee, has been inaugurated. It consists of photographs and blue prints, and is transported with the inspectors on their rounds over the state. This exhibit is installed in a public place during the period of local inspection, and one of the exhibits is kept permanently in the rooms of the Merchants' and Manufacturers' Association of Milwaukee. It is found that these photographic exhibits have a certain advantage over the " museums of safety " of European countries, where the actual machines with safeguards are installed permanently in a building, because, not only is the expense reduced, but the exhibit can be carried almost to the doors of the employer and his superintendents, foremen and mechanics. The commissioners and their deputies usually arrange for an evening of lectures in connection with the exhibit, when the various laws are explained and questions answered. These are attended by representatives of practically all the employing establishments in the town and surrounding country. The exhibit itself is built up and improved by photographs which the deputies take on their rounds, and the main object is to arouse the " safety spirit " and to show how practicable it is for establishments to devise and install their own safeguards without depending too much on patented articles.

The way in which this conversion of an executive department into a department of investigation and education appeals to the employers of the state, may be judged by the following extract from a speech made by William George Bruce, secretary of the Merchants' and Manufacturers' Association of Milwaukee, before the National Congress on Safety and Sanitation, October 1, 1912:

The success which has been attained in Wisconsin on the subject of safety and sanitation is due not only to a good law, but also to a wise administration of the same. The authorities approached their difficult task in a spirit of absolute fairness. But, they did more. They drew the manufacturers into their confidence and secured their loyal coöperation in the administration of the law.

They assumed that the manufacturer is a law-abiding citizen and that if he were asked to give meaning and force to the new law he would respond. The attitude which the Industrial Commission maintained through the introductory period of their exacting and herculean task was bound to be followed by success.

But the commission practised wisdom also in bringing to its work experts of character and efficiency. Favoritism was cast to the winds. The men best fitted for the task were selected.

Men like Mr. Crownhart and Mr. Beck of the commission realized that an antagonistic or arbitrary spirit would be resented and cause difficulty. They were tactful and discreet, but made it absolutely plain that both the spirit and the letter of the law must be carried out. Would the manufacturer lend his coöperation? And he did.

Men like Mr. Price, capable and judicious, formerly at the head of similar work with the International Harvester Company, were chosen to perform the delicate and difficult task of working out, together with the manufacturer, a reasonable and workable programme.

They not only succeeded in creating a coöperatve attitude on the part of the manufacturers, but they also secured much valuable time and effort at the hands of some of the most important manufacturers in the state.

Thus I am safe in saying the work of industrial safety and sanitation in Wisconsin which is progressing in a most successful manner, has the good will and support of the manufacturing interests of the state.

The legal effect of the commission's orders turns upon the constitutional position which belongs to constructive investigation. These orders are not a delegation of legislative power, but an investigation and publication of facts. The courts have long held that the legislature may determine that a given law shall go into effect at a future date on the occurrence of a specified event. The law in this case is the obligation placed on employers to protect the life, health, safety and welfare of employees. The future occurrence when it takes effect is thirty days after official publication of the findings of the commission.

Neither are the commission's investigations and findings a usurpation of the authority of the courts. This is cared for by the procedure. Formerly a factory inspector issued orders on the spot, and prosecuted for disobedience in the trial courts. The court was at liberty to raise the question whether the order was necessary, or whether too expensive or confiscatory, or whether the manufacturer was not as competent as the inspector to determine the effectiveness of his safeguards. Now these questions of reasonableness cannot be raised in the trial court. Only the fact of compliance or non-compliance can be raised. If the question of reasonableness is raised it must come up in an action against the commission in the county court at the state capital, and thence in the supreme court of the state. Furthermore, if the petitioner introduces evidence which was not before the commission, the case must be remanded back to the commission with the new evidence, and the commission must be given opportunity to change its order if it so determines. The case can then go back to the court.

In this way, the commission's complete power of investigation is protected, its orders are made *prima facie* reasonable, and the burden is on the petitioner to break them down in court. The court retains all of its powers of investigation and philosophy, as far as it chooses to use them. But the commission's investigations are not limited by the strict rules of evidence prevailing in court. It can consider all of the facts without objection. It can initiate investigations. It is, in fact, a body of social and economic investigators, rather than a tribunal restricted to technical rules of evidence. The supreme court of the state has sustained the commission so far as it affects procedure under the compensation law. The procedure respecting safety and health is similar, but has not as yet been passed upon, although in the case of the Railroad Commission, with similar procedure respecting reasonable rates and services, its findings of fact have been held to be conclusive.

The Industrial Commission is also made an appellate administrative court in all cases of local boards of health, common councils or other local bodies that issue orders on places of employment. Their authority to issue such orders has not been infringed upon, but they are protected against court injunctions by the requirement that appeal shall first be made to the Industrial Commission. The latter, on investigation, may affirm the local order, or may substitute a " reasonable one," and the petitioner must then proceed against the commission as above explained, in place of the local authority. The commission has endeavored to bring about agreement with local boards by securing their representatives on the advisory committees and it is expected in this way that state and local inspectors will not issue conflicting orders on employers.

Advisory committees of employers and employees have also been enlisted in the administration of the free employment offices. The Milwaukee committee consists of representatives of the Manufacturers' Association and representatives of the trade unions. They assist the Civil Service Commission in the examination of applicants, and have thus overcome the two greatest obstacles in the way of successful operation of such offices by the state — politics and trade unions. The superintendents and assistants of these offices are not only removed from political influence, but are removed from all suspicion of using their position for or against employer or employee in the case of strikes. The growth of business transacted by the Milwaukee office has been phenomenal during the first year of this method of management, and its transformation from a mere charitable agency to find work for unemployables, into a labor exchange bringing employer and employee together, is evidenced by the following statement made by the chairman of the committee and representative of the employers, A. T. Van Scoy of the International Harvester Company.

I was not particularly enthusiastic at first over this movement, but have changed my views in regard to it, and believe it has been of great benefit to the working people in that it has, through what might be called a clearing-house, enabled them to obtain employment quickly and without expense, and it has also been equally valuable to the employer, in that it has enabled him through this employment bureau or clearing-house to obtain, usually without effort on his part other than telephoning his wants, the help desired.

Its work is broadening all the time, employers learning that an effort is made, and generally successfully, to furnish them with the kind of help desired, instead of sending men promiscuously, and employees learning that the quickest and most expeditious way for them to obtain employment is through the bureau.

The opinion of the trade unions is represented by the following statement of the representative of the Federated Trades Council:

Without blare of trumpets the free state employment office in Milwaukee is doing one of the best works at present going on in the city. It is supplying a head centre where men needing work may go and where work seeking men may also apply. Its offices on Fourth Street, just north of Grand Avenue, always present a busy scene. . . . While the work of such offices seems local, the unemployed problem is a state-wide problem and even more, and can best be met and handled as it is now being handled under the Industrial Commission with coöperating offices in the principal cities of the state. One praiseworthy thing that the free employment office has done must not be overlooked. It has cut down the crowds of hundreds of work-hungry men at the factory gates mornings. This sort of a scramble, often by men almost despairing, with families waiting to learn of the success or failure of the quest, is not only a pathetic sight, but often downright tragedy. The free employment office provides the better way, and the manufacturers themselves have come to realize it. It is certainly more humane for the men, saves them a lot of tramping and is a great convenience in the securing of workmen. Nay, more, it saves his feelings, for it is found that the rebuffs that he gets at factory gates have a souring effect on a man in spite of himself.

A peculiar use of advisory committees has been undertaken in the administration of the street trades law in Milwaukee. The law is supplementary to the child labor law in that the children concerned are mainly not employees but are merchants, and therefore without employers who can be held liable for violation of the child labor and truancy laws. The newsboys, numbering about 4000, have been organized in the "Newsboys' Republic" for the purpose of enforcing the law. The Republic itself, including certain adults chosen jointly by the boys and the commission, constitute a lively advisory committee to the commission. The plan is only now in process of installation, after careful investigation had been made of the administration of similar laws, and especially of the similar organization in Boston.

In the administration of the new apprenticeship law, supplementing the industrial education law, the commission is aided by a committee of the Manufacturers' Association and the labor unions.

Wherever practicable, the commission has found that these advisory committees are invaluable in the enforcement of laws under its charge. They are being extended wherever it is found that the commission needs the coöperation of the classes affected by the administration of the law or their judgment upon the reasonableness of its orders. It will be seen, too, that this practice meets the political objection against the multiplication of commissions and "government by commissions." The Industrial Commission consolidates what otherwise might be three or four commissions and executives, thus reducing the expense. It does not remove government "from the people" and place it in the hands of "experts," for it necessarily and actually, both in full compliance with the doctrine of reasonableness and in securing full coöperation of the public in understanding and enforcing the laws, brings the government directly into the hands of the people. It is certain that the state must have executives in order to enforce the labor laws, as well as other laws. To object to them is like urging your son to learn to swim but forbidding him to go near the water. The real question is not how to avoid commissions, but how to organize them, how to do away with overlapping commissions, how to make them efficient and economical, how to keep them near to the actual life of the people; in short, how to make them the branch that fills the gap of constructive investigation in our scheme of government.

It has been suggested by inquirers from other states, and it might be inferred from the emphasis here laid on investigation, that the executive part of the commission's work should be kept separate with a single head, as it has been in the past, in order to centre responsibility for the enforcement of laws. In that case a board of experts might be created for the purpose of investigating and drafting the rules, which the independent executive would be required to enforce. For several reasons, this separation of departments would probably be impracticable. The most valuable agents for the kind of investigation required are the inspectors, whose duty it is to enforce the rules. By associating them with the advisory committees, they enter into the spirit of co-operation, they learn the principle of reasonableness and they acquire the virtue of tact. If they have no knowledge of the reasons for the rules, and therefore no reason for patient instruction of employers and superintendents, their attitude is likely to be that of the typical factory inspector who says to the employer, " Well, I didn't make the law — there it is, and you've got to obey it." Instead of inspiring the " safety spirit " throughout the state, they stir up needless opposition and friction between the factory inspector and the board of experts.

Furthermore, no system of general rules laid down in

advance can anticipate all of the special conditions or
obstacles in the way of enforcement. The Wisconsin
law cares for this by means of " special orders " in addition to " general orders." But these special orders can
only be issued on investigation and public hearing, precisely the same as the general orders. The inspector,
therefore, instead of insisting upon something impracticable, can join with the employer in asking for a special
order before proceeding to prosecution. These " special
orders " are, indeed, one of the most important features
in the enforcement of the law. An employer, for example, is convinced that a general order, say the order
requiring all elevators to be covered by screens, is not
necessary in a certain case. The inspector agrees with
him. Instead, however, of leaving it to the inspector
to pass over that case, he is required to report the violation, and the employer can then request the commission,
on a special blank prepared for the purpose, to order a
special hearing by one of its deputies and to make a different order. In this way the inspector is deprived of that
discretion which may be abused and which might come
very near to corruption, and both the commission and
the employer are protected against suspicion or abuse
of power, because the special order is a matter of publicity and public record, the same as the general order.
The law is thus made elastic so as to fit actual conditions,
but the elasticity is open and aboveboard, and not a
matter of secret favor. If, now, the inspector is subject
to an independent executive, desirous of making a
reputation for the enforcement of law, not only is he
tempted to discredit the work of the expert commission,
but he is under no obligation to join with the commission
in perfecting its orders so as to conform to the rule of

reasonableness. The deputies of the Industrial Commission are continually reporting omitted points or impracticable applications, and the execution of the law becomes a continuous investigation and progress towards reasonableness. With separate departments for investigation and execution, the investigations would doubtless fall into the hands of experts not familiar with the great variety of conditions to be met, and the execution would be that perfunctory and blind enforcement which has already brought discredit on much of the American factory inspection.

Finally, the commissioners themselves cannot divide their work into the separate fields of law, investigation and execution, especially where, as with the Wisconsin commission, such a wide range as fourteen departments are brought together under one head. Each commissioner must take his share in the executive work of different departments, and each must carry on continually the constructive investigation that the law implies. It is only by this means of administration and investigation combined in a single commission that friction and antagonism between overlapping officials can be avoided, coöperation with employers and employees secured, and obedience to the authority of the judiciary observed.

This suggestion that the " expert " work of the commission should be separated from the executive work, is really based on a misapprehension of the peculiar position occupied by the commissioners. They are not " experts " in the ordinary, scientific and technical meaning of that term. They are not engineers, physicians, sanitarians or statisticians. Such technical experts must necessarily be employed by the commission or persuaded to serve on its advisory committees. The commissioners occupy a middle position between their experts, their inspectors and the employing and employed public on the one hand, and the legislature, the court and the chief executive on the other. Their time is occupied in supervising the work, directing investigations, explaining the laws and orders, listening to appeals, holding public hearings, conducting prosecutions and so on. In so far as they are experts, their field is that of determining what is the lawful or " reasonable " thing to be done under all the circumstances, rather than the scientific, technical, idealistic or popular thing to be done.

It is for this reason that they cannot be selected through civil service examinations, nor elected by popular vote. The one method might secure a technical expert, the other a political favorite or accident. Neither method would secure that confidence in their " reasonableness " which is essential to the position. At the same time, appointment and removal by the governor, an officer whose position is essentially political, cannot always be depended upon to select and maintain a commission that meets these requirements. A governor, elected as in Wisconsin, through the direct primary system, may be expected to rely for popular support upon the high character of his appointments rather than upon the aid of a political machine. But the growing demand for popular control, the impending adoption of the initiative, referendum and recall, give indications that confidence in commissions will require a more direct power over them on the part of the voters. Appointment by the governor offers that wide range of selection which neither civil service rules nor popular election provides. But recall by the people is needed, both to protect against political influences, and to insure closer responsibility to the people. This is really the same as that responsibility to " prevailing morality or strong and preponderant opinion " of what is " greatly and immediately necessary to the public welfare," which Justice Holmes describes as the basis and purpose of the police power.

While the Industrial Commission is modelled after the law creating the Railroad Commission, its field is widely different. The Railroad Commission regulates monopoly ; the Industrial Commission regulates competition. It endeavors to enforce " reasonable " competition in so far as dealings with employers are concerned, by raising the level of labor competition. The distinction offers a practicable suggestion for the creation of a commission by the federal government for the regulation of " trusts." Such a commission need not have the power to regulate prices, as the Railroad Commission does, on the theory that monopoly is inevitable, nor to give special privileges to so-called " good " trusts that accept federal incorporation or federal license, and agree to abide by the commission's orders. Rather should a federal commission be a " fair trade " commission, controlling all interstate trade so far as necessary, for the purpose of investigating and prohibiting all kinds of " unfair competition." It would take the place which the federal courts now assume, of dissolving and regulating corporations. But instead of committing this power to lawyers it would be committed to a body of men representing the everyday life of all the people, equipped to conduct constructive investigations, to prosecute for violations of the anti-trust laws, to prescribe and enforce rules of

reasonable competition and so to raise the level of
business competition.[1]

[1] A bill creating a "market commission" was introduced at the instance of Governor McGovern at the session of the Wisconsin legislature
of 1913, carrying with it, among other things, the rule of fair competition
in price-making.

INDEX